ASSESSING AND RESPONDING TO THE Growth of Computer Science Undergraduate Enrollments

Committee on the Growth of
Computer Science Undergraduate Enrollments

Board on Higher Education and Workforce
Policy and Global Affairs

Computer Science and Telecommunications Board
Division on Engineering and Physical Sciences

A Consensus Study Report of

The National Academies of
SCIENCES · ENGINEERING · MEDICINE

THE NATIONAL ACADEMIES PRESS
Washington, DC
www.nap.edu

THE NATIONAL ACADEMIES PRESS 500 Fifth Street, NW Washington, DC 20001

This activity was supported by the National Science Foundation, Grant Number 1551227. Any opinions, findings, conclusions, or recommendations expressed in this publication do not necessarily reflect the views of any organization or agency that provided support for the project.

International Standard Book Number-13: 978-0-309-46702-5
International Standard Book Number-10: 0-309-46702-0
Library of Congress Control Number 2018930771
Digital Object Identifier: https://doi.org/10.17226/24926

Additional copies of this publication are available for sale from the National Academies Press, 500 Fifth Street, NW, Keck 360, Washington, DC 20001; (800) 624-6242 or (202) 334-3313; http://www.nap.edu.

Printed in the United States of America

Suggested citation: National Academies of Sciences, Engineering, and Medicine. 2018. *Assessing and Responding to the Growth of Computer Science Undergraduate Enrollments*. The National Academies Press, Washington, DC. https://doi.org/10.17226/24926.

The National Academies of
SCIENCES · ENGINEERING · MEDICINE

The **National Academy of Sciences** was established in 1863 by an Act of Congress, signed by President Lincoln, as a private, nongovernmental institution to advise the nation on issues related to science and technology. Members are elected by their peers for outstanding contributions to research. Dr. Marcia McNutt is president.

The **National Academy of Engineering** was established in 1964 under the charter of the National Academy of Sciences to bring the practices of engineering to advising the nation. Members are elected by their peers for extraordinary contributions to engineering. Dr. C. D. Mote, Jr., is president.

The **National Academy of Medicine** (formerly the Institute of Medicine) was established in 1970 under the charter of the National Academy of Sciences to advise the nation on medical and health issues. Members are elected by their peers for distinguished contributions to medicine and health. Dr. Victor J. Dzau is president.

The three Academies work together as the **National Academies of Sciences, Engineering, and Medicine** to provide independent, objective analysis and advice to the nation and conduct other activities to solve complex problems and inform public policy decisions. The National Academies also encourage education and research, recognize outstanding contributions to knowledge, and increase public understanding in matters of science, engineering, and medicine.

Learn more about the National Academies of Sciences, Engineering, and Medicine at **www.nationalacademies.org**.

COMMITTEE ON THE GROWTH OF COMPUTER SCIENCE UNDERGRADUATE ENROLLMENTS

JARED COHON, NAE,[1] Carnegie Mellon University, *Co-Chair*
SUSANNE HAMBRUSCH, Purdue University, *Co-Chair*
M. BRIAN BLAKE, Drexel University
TRACY CAMP, Colorado School of Mines
DAVID E. CULLER, NAE, University of California, Berkeley
SUSAN B. DAVIDSON, University of Pennsylvania
BRIAN K. FITZGERALD, Business-Higher Education Forum
ANN Q. GATES, University of Texas, El Paso
CHARLES ISBELL, Georgia Institute of Technology
CLAS A. JACOBSON, United Technologies Corporation
MICHAEL McPHERSON, Spencer Foundation
ERIC ROBERTS, Stanford University
VALERIE TAYLOR, Argonne National Laboratory
JODI TIMS, Baldwin Wallace University
SARAH E. TURNER, University of Virginia

Staff

EMILY GRUMBLING, Program Officer, Computer Science and Telecommunications Board (CSTB)
ADRIANA COUREMBIS, Financial Manager, Board on Higher Education and Workforce (BHEW)
JANEL DEAR, Administrative Assistant, CSTB
JON EISENBERG, Director, CSTB
KATIRIA ORTIZ, Research Associate, CSTB
TOM RUDIN, Director, BHEW

[1] Member, National Academy of Engineering.

BOARD ON HIGHER EDUCATION AND WORKFORCE

RICHARD K. MILLER, NAE,[1] Olin College of Engineering, *Chair*
LAWRENCE D. BOBO, NAS,[2] Harvard University
ANGELA BYARS-WINSTON, University of Wisconsin, Madison
JAIME CURTIS-FISK, The Dow Chemical Company
APRILLE ERICSSON, NASA Goddard Space Flight Center
RICHARD FREEMAN, Harvard University
PAUL J. LeBLANC, Southern New Hampshire University
SALLY F. MASON, University of Iowa
FRANCISCO RODRIGUEZ, Los Angeles Community College District
SUBHASH SINGHAL, NAE, Pacific Northwest National Laboratory
KUMBLE R. SUBBASWAMY, University of Massachusetts Amherst
SHELLEY WESTMAN, Protegrity
MARY WOOLLEY, NAM,[3] Research!America

Staff

TOM RUDIN, Director
AUSTEN APPLEGATE, Senior Program Assistant
ASHLEY BEAR, Program Officer
LIDA BENINSON, Program Officer
FRAZIER BENYA, Program Officer
JAIME COLMAN, Senior Program Assistant
MARIA LUND DAHLBERG, Associate Program Officer
LEIGH MILES JACKSON, Senior Program Officer
IRENE NGUN, Research Associate
LAYNE SCHERER, Program Officer

[1] Member, National Academy of Engineering.
[2] Member, National Academy of Sciences.
[3] Member, National Academy of Medicine.

COMPUTER SCIENCE AND TELECOMMUNICATIONS BOARD

FARNAM JAHANIAN, Carnegie Mellon University, *Chair*
LUIZ ANDRÉ BARRASO, Google, Inc.
STEVEN M. BELLOVIN, NAE,[1] Columbia University
ROBERT F. BRAMMER, Brammer Technology, LLC
DAVID CULLER, NAE, University of California, Berkeley
EDWARD FRANK, Cloud Parity, Inc.
LAURA HAAS, NAE, University of Massachusetts, Amherst
MARK HOROWITZ, NAE, Stanford University
ERIC HORVITZ, NAE, Microsoft Research
VIJAY KUMAR, NAE, University of Pennsylvania
BETH MYNATT, Georgia Institute of Technology
CRAIG PARTRIDGE, Raytheon BBN Technologies
DANIELA RUS, NAE, Massachusetts Institute of Technology
FRED B. SCHNEIDER, NAE, Cornell University
MARGO SELTZER, Harvard University
JOHN STANKOVIC, University of Virginia
MOSHE VARDI, NAS[2]/NAE, Rice University
KATHERINE YELICK, NAE, University of California, Berkeley

Staff

JON EISENBERG, Director
LYNETTE I. MILLETT, Associate Director
VIRGINIA BACON TALATI, Program Officer
SHENAE BRADLEY, Administrative Assistant
JANEL DEAR, Senior Program Assistant
EMILY GRUMBLING, Program Officer
RENEE HAWKINS, Financial and Administrative Manager
KATIRIA ORTIZ, Research Associate

For more information on the CSTB, see its website at http://www.cstb.org, write to CSTB, National Research Council, 500 Fifth Street, NW, Washington, DC 20001, call (202) 334-2605, or e-mail the CSTB at cstb@nas.edu.

[1] Member, National Academy of Engineering.
[2] Member, National Academy of Sciences.

Acknowledgment of Reviewers

This Consensus Study Report was reviewed in draft form by individuals chosen for their diverse perspectives and technical expertise. The purpose of this independent review is to provide candid and critical comments that will assist the National Academies of Sciences, Engineering, and Medicine in making each published report as sound as possible and to ensure that it meets the institutional standards for quality, objectivity, evidence, and responsiveness to the study charge. The review comments and draft manuscript remain confidential to protect the integrity of the deliberative process.

We wish to thank the following individuals for their review of this report: W. Richards Adrion, University of Massachusetts, Amherst; Fiona Doyle, University of California, Berkeley; Michael Franklin, University of Chicago; Mary Hall, University of Utah; Jennifer Hunt, Rutgers University; Louise Kirkbride, Broad Daylight, Inc.; Edward Lazowska, University of Washington; Greg Morrisett, Cornell University; Linda Sax, University of California, Los Angeles; Chris Stephenson, Google, Inc.; and Telle Whitney, Anita Borg Institute for Women and Technology.

Although the reviewers listed here provided many constructive comments and suggestions, they were not asked to endorse the conclusions or recommendations of this report nor did they see the final draft before its release. The review of this report was overseen by Susan Curry, University of Iowa, and Philip Neches, Teradata Corporation. They were responsible for making certain that an independent examination of this report was carried out in accordance with the standards of the National Academies and that all review comments were carefully considered. Responsibility for the final content rests entirely with the authoring committee and the National Academies.

Preface

Computer science (CS) and information technologies have transformed all sectors of society, businesses, and government. Today, the transformation continues and much is driven by artificial intelligence, robotics, the Internet of Things, information security, and data science. A wide range of jobs in virtually all sectors demand computing skills to an unprecedented extent. And every academic discipline finds itself incorporating computing into its research and educational mission.

The centrality of computing has manifested itself in dramatic increases in enrollment in undergraduate computer science courses in colleges and universities. Institutions have to make decisions ranging from allocating resources to accommodate demand to imposing limits on course enrollments and course offerings, and managing increasing enrollment of non-majors. In addition, with industry hiring the majority of new Ph.D.s, growing the number of faculty is a challenge for many departments. Strains on educational institutions are significant; there is a growing sense of an impending crisis in many universities.

This committee was created at the request of the National Science Foundation to explore this enrollment crisis and to make recommendations to address it. The charge to the committee prompted the committee to address three sets of questions:

1. Computer science enrollments are at an all-time high and non-majors are increasingly seeking to enroll in not only introductory but also more advanced CS courses. How can institutions best manage high enrollments? What are drivers of the increased interest in CS courses? What predictions can we make about future enrollments?

2. The pressures and demands felt in computer science departments and their universities are real, severe, and current. What strategies and tactics can institutions adopt to respond in the short as well as the long term?
3. Computer science is among the least diverse disciplines in terms of both gender and minority representation. Most institutions have adopted strategies to increase diversity, but what will the increase in enrollments mean for diversity? How can the surge of interest enhance or provide new opportunities for increasing diversity?

The committee, with input from several participants in a workshop convened for that purpose and the support of Academies staff, worked diligently to respond to these questions. We hope this report and our findings and recommendations will assist the academic community, the National Science Foundation, and others to formulate and implement effective actions for what is a pressing and important problem.

PLAN OF ATTACK

The committee, which comprised experts with a wide range of perspectives and experiences, tapped data sets and reports from many different sources. A public workshop was held in August 2016 to bring before the committee additional experts from government, industry, and academia.[1] The committee sought to marshal evidence to determine the extent of the enrollment crisis, to form a view of future enrollment trends, and to understand the effects of enrollment growth on diversity. Not surprisingly, the data sets were not as complete or extensive as the committee would have liked. Nevertheless, the committee believes its conclusions and recommendations are well supported. The limitations of the evidence are identified and discussed in the relevant chapters.

ACKNOWLEDGMENTS

This report is the result of a group effort by the Committee on the Growth of Computer Science Undergraduate Enrollments. The committee recognizes that its analyses, deliberations, and results would not have been possible without the insights and contributions from a number of briefers and agents of the Academies. First, the committee thanks staff and members of the Computing Research Association, especially Betsy Bizot and Jane Stout for their assistance in interpreting the results of their recent CS enrollments surveys, and for stimulating discussion of this topic more broadly, and to Yan Timanovsky for assisting with data from the Association for Computing Machinery's NDC survey (a survey of "Non-Doctoral-Granting Departments in Computing"). The committee also thanks all

[1] See Appendix B for the workshop agenda and list of panelists.

of the speakers at the August 2016 workshop for their insights—they stimulated important discussions among members of the committee, and provided helpful data and perspectives.

Special thanks go to Professor John Bound and Nicolas Morales from the University of Michigan for their thoughtful analysis on the computing labor market in the Academies-commissioned paper appended to this report. Professor Lynne Molter and Allan Moser with the Consortium for Undergraduate STEM Success also contributed a commissioned summary analysis of undergraduate participation in computing at the sample of institutions in the consortium. Professor Linda Sax and Dr. Ellen Stolzenberg each helpfully provided information from the Higher Education Research Institute's Freshman survey about student intent to major in computer science. Last, Professor Jennifer Hunt of Rutgers University also provided a helpful assessment on the economics of enrollment in computing in the form of a white paper, which has also been appended to this report.

Jared Cohon and Susanne Hambrusch, *Co-Chairs*
Committee on the Growth of Computer Science Undergraduate Enrollments

Contents

Boxes, Figures, and Tables

BOXES

FIGURES

TABLES

Summary

The field of computer science (CS) is currently experiencing a surge in undergraduate degree production and course enrollments, which is straining program resources at many institutions and causing concern among faculty and administrators about how best to respond to the rapidly growing demand. There is also significant interest about what this growth will mean for the future of CS programs, the role of computer science in academic institutions, the field as a whole, and U.S. society more broadly.

This study was convened to provide a better understanding of the current trends in computing enrollments in the context of past trends. It examines drivers of the current enrollment surge, relationships between the surge and current and potential gains in diversity in the field, and the potential impacts of responses to the increased demand for computing in higher education, and it considers the likely effects of those responses on students, faculty, and institutions. The committee provides recommendations for what institutions of higher education, government agencies, and the private sector can do to respond to the surge and plan for a strong and sustainable future for the field of CS in general, the health of the institutions of higher education, and the prosperity of the nation.

THE CHANGING COMPUTER SCIENCE ENROLLMENT LANDSCAPE

A primary task for the committee was to address the question of whether the current enrollment increases "are similar to other cyclic fluctuations that have occurred in the past or whether they are more likely to be sustained." A review of past degree, enrollment, and employment trends informed our projections for the future, which indicate that strong demand for CS and related courses will likely continue for many years to come.

The past four decades have seen the rise of computer science as a creative and evolving field, with striking growth in undergraduate degree production in computer science and related fields. That growth, however, has not been uniform over time. Both core CS[1] and the broader category of "computer and information science and support services" (CIS)[2] saw two major fluctuations in degree production in the form of pronounced peaks and valleys in the 1980s and in the early 2000s. These past booms in CIS degree production coincided with the appearance of personal computers in the 1980s and the dot-com explosion in the late 1990s.

The growth has also not been uniform across institutions. On average, institutions with very high research activity have experienced the greatest growth in CIS degree production among not-for-profit institutions between 2009 and 2015 (by 113 percent). However, it is important to note that average trends by institution type do not adequately reflect the unique conditions at institutions experiencing the largest enrollment increases.

Although authoritative degree production data provide a helpful historical picture, degree production does not equal enrollment, which includes non-majors. Furthermore, degree production obviously lags current major enrollments by 1 to 4 years. Thus, one must look at course and program enrollment data to understand better the current conditions at institutions of higher education. Unfortunately, data on course or program enrollments are not tracked in the national statistics.

For this, the committee turned to the results of surveys conducted by the Computing Research Association (CRA), the Higher Education Research Institute (HERI), the Consortium for Undergraduate STEM Success, the Computing Alliance of Hispanic-Serving Institutions, and the American Society for Engineering Education. While these data sets have inherent limitations, they provide the best information available about current conditions in academia.

Enrollment growth varies by course level and institution. Historical data from the CRA Taulbee survey show that the number of CS majors in U.S. computer science departments responding (a subset of all institutions with CS Ph.D. programs) has been on the rise since 2006, and rose at a steeper rate beginning in 2012. From 2006 to 2015, the average number of CS majors increased for large departments (25 or more tenure-track faculty) from 341 to 970 and for small departments from 158 to 499 majors.[3] These data likely underestimate the

[1] Defined here as those programs categorized via the Classification of Instructional Program (CIP) as "computer and information sciences, general" (CIP 11.0101) or "computer science" (11.0701) in the national degree completion statistics available from the Integrated Postsecondary Education Data System (IPEDS); it is important to note that there were changes to the CIPs within the 11 series in 2000 and 2010 which could affect the accuracy of the time series trends for any of the six-digit CIPs.

[2] Defined by the CIP 11.x series in the IPEDS national degree completion.

[3] From the raw data plotted in Figure B.2 of CRA (2017a), "Generation CS: Computer Science Undergraduate Enrollments Surge Since 2006," http://cra.org/data/Generation-CS/, provided courtesy of CRA.

actual demand, because some of these institutions cap the number of students who may major in a program.

The CRA Enrollments Survey similarly illustrates that enrollments in all levels of CS courses have increased at the group of CS Ph.D.-granting and non-Ph.D.-granting units that responded to the poll. The average increases reported ranged from 75 percent in upper-level courses at non-doctoral CS institutions to 181 percent in upper-level courses at doctoral CS institutions, with similarly impressive increases in lower-level courses. While these data are not necessarily representative of national trends, they are the best data available; they make it clear that significant growth is under way at many institutions.

THE FUTURE OF COMPUTER SCIENCE ENROLLMENTS

What can we expect in the future for CS degrees and enrollment? It is easy to predict with confidence that degree production will increase sharply for at least the next few years, in light of the rapid and significant increases in enrollments in the major, in the absence of enrollment limits. Beyond that time the picture is necessarily less clear.

A student's decision to enroll in a major or course is influenced by many factors, and one of those is job and economic prospects. The demand for employees with computer science and computing expertise is high and has grown steadily over time. According to data from the Bureau of Labor Statistics (BLS), employment in computer occupations grew by nearly a factor of 20 between 1975 and 2015, nearly twice as fast as production of CIS bachelor's degrees. BLS has projected that demand for computer science workers will continue to grow over the next decade at a rate higher than that of overall job growth, particularly as computing becomes more central to a wider range of industrial sectors. Employment demand is particularly intense in some specialty areas, including cybersecurity, data science, and machine learning.

Job prospects likely also contribute to the demand for CS courses from non-majors, but this portion of the enrollment increase is also driven by the impact of CS and computing in other fields. Computer science and its related endeavors such as data science have produced powerful tools and software systems that are used by and affect every discipline, giving rise to exciting subfields, such as computational biology, computational economics, computational chemistry, and digital humanities, with more emerging. These subfields require expertise in the traditional domain and a general fluency in tools and methods from computer science. The advantages of a deeper knowledge of computer science in many domains has also led to the recent emergence of new degree programs at several institutions that fuse curricula and formal requirements of CS with those for one of a range of disciplines (referred to as "X+CS").

The conditions exist for continued growth in the demand for CS and related jobs, degrees, and courses. Every economic sector depends on computing, and the way we interact with each other and with social institutions has been fundamentally changed by information technology. This dependence will surely grow, and our increasing the demand for mobility, security, privacy, and connectivity will drive further innovation and demand for CS expertise.

Finally, there have been numerous recent efforts to enhance interest and participation in CS at the K-12 levels, including to broaden participation among women and underrepresented minorities in the field. It is likely that some of the recent interest in undergraduate CS has been driven by these initiatives, and that they may continue to drive interest in the future.

While it is impossible to say with certainty whether the current enrollment boom will be followed by a significant decline in degree production as it was in both the 1980s and early 2000s, the committee believes that computing's deep and growing penetration in virtually all sectors of the economy, all academic disciplines, and all aspects of modern life, and the broad opportunities in computing in both the labor market and for enabling a host of intellectual pursuits, will continue to be drivers of increasing enrollments in undergraduate computer science, from both majors and non-majors. There will probably be fluctuations in the demand for CS and related courses, but the longer-term trend is likely to be high or growing numbers of enrollments for many years to come.

Nonetheless, it is important to note that the way institutions respond (or not) can itself have a significant impact on future enrollments and the health of the field. Indeed, there is anecdotal evidence that the historical fluctuations in CS enrollment may have been, at least in part, a result of institutional actions to limit student numbers.

DIVERSITY IN A TIME OF BOOMING ENROLLMENTS

Computer science is one of the least diverse disciplines in terms of the representation of women and underrepresented minorities, both in higher education and in the workforce. Many ongoing efforts are under way to improve diversity in the field, and it is of acute interest to understand the potential implications of increasing enrollments on these efforts.

Women and underrepresented minorities make up a larger fraction of CIS bachelor's degree recipients at for-profit institutions than at not-for-profit institutions, and they are less well represented in core CS than in CIS more broadly.[4] Between 2009 and 2015 the average percentage of CIS degrees conferred to Hispanic students increased somewhat, as has representation of this group among college graduates in general, from 7.1 to 9.4 percent for CIS (and 6.5 to 8.6 percent for core CS) at not-for-profit institutions. The percentage of degrees going to black or African American students at not-for-profit institutions decreased from 9.4 to

[4] Here, "CIS" refers to the IPEDS CIP 11, "Computer and Information Science and Support Services;" "core CS" refers to the subset of this category including 11.0101, "computer and information sciences, general," and 11.0701, "computer science."

7.9 percent for IS (and from 8.7 to 6.1 percent for core CS) during this time. The percentage of CIS degrees going to women has changed little since 2009, remaining around 18 percent across all race/ethnic groups; the share of core CS degrees going to women is lower, but increased slightly, from 13.6 to 15.9 percent from 2011 to 2015. Although relative representation is not generally increasing, the increasing numbers of both majors and non-majors interested in CS could be a source for engaging more women and underrepresented minorities.

According to the HERI Cooperative Institutional Research Program national survey of freshmen, the relative growth in the percentage of freshmen intending to major in CS was higher for female freshmen than for males, and intent to major in CS is also rising among underrepresented minorities. The CRA Enrollments Survey results also indicate, along with increasing enrollments overall, a larger percentage of CS course and program enrollments comprising female and underrepresented minority students among responding institutions. This increase in participation is likely due to many factors, including a host of broadening participation efforts for women and underrepresented minorities in computing at the K-12 and undergraduate levels.

While prospects for diversity look positive, it is important to recall that increasing participation among women and underrepresented groups may not translate to an increased share of all CS degrees or enrollments, because the absolute number of participants is increasing among all groups. Furthermore, retention upon entering a CS program is not guaranteed, and women and underrepresented minorities have higher rates of attrition.

In the face of increasing enrollments institutions would do well to take lessons from the past. The share of CIS and CS bachelor's degrees going to women decreased precipitously beginning in the mid-1980s, and again during the dot-com bust. These drops coincided with past peaks in CS degree production, suggesting that high-enrollment conditions or the actions taken by institutions in response to these surges may have contributed to the decrease in representation of women in undergraduate CS during these times. Enrollment management actions taken by institutions in times of high enrollment can be implemented to avoid long-term detrimental effects on diversity in their programs, and to support a culture of inclusivity.

INSTITUTIONAL CHALLENGES AND STRATEGIES

Departments facing sharp increases in demand for computing courses have experienced significant strain on a wide range of resources. Failure to respond thoughtfully to the demand and the resource deficits will result in negative conditions for students, faculty, the programs, and/or the institution as a whole in the near or long term.

The most common resource challenges that surveyed departments face include increased faculty workload; too few faculty, instructors, or teaching assistants; increased need for academic undergraduate advisers and administrative support; and increased need for classroom, lab, and office space. Finding enough faculty is a particular problem. Data from the CRA Enrollments Survey and CRA's Taulbee Survey indicate that from 2006 to 2015, a period of significant growth in CS majors, the relative increase in tenure-track CS faculty at research institutions surveyed was about one-tenth of the increase in the number of CS majors. Ph.D.s represent a relatively small fraction of degrees in CS, and in recent years most Ph.D.s have taken jobs in industry. This has major implications for the ability of institutions to fill faculty positions and hire short-term or contract lecturers.

U.S. institutions of higher education have differing missions, priorities, and business models, and serve different populations with different needs. There is no one-size-fits-all solution for responding to enrollment increases. Decisions about how to deal with high demand for courses must be made based on each institution's needs and priorities. Although approaches and best practices will differ by the type and mission of institutions, there is a common need to assess the role of computer science and computing and make strategic plans. These plans must address realistically and effectively the demand for courses, student interests and needs, faculty and staff workloads, research and teaching allocations, and physical resources. At all institutions, there is an opportunity to reassess the role of computer science and to consider changes that go beyond the current challenges and position the institution for future success.

In light of the diversity among institutions, the committee did not attempt to recommend universal courses of action. Instead, the committee identified a range of potential strategies that could be pursued alone or in combination, and the advantages and risks of each, along with key areas for self-assessment to inform institutional action. The reader is referred to the full discussion in Chapter 6 as a guide to support planning and decision making at institutions of all types. The nature and availability of instructional resources (faculty and teaching staff, teaching assistants, support staff, facilities and associated equipment, and other local or regional resources) will affect an institution's ability to respond to demand for CS courses via any of the particular strategies.

FINDINGS AND RECOMMENDATIONS

FINDING 1: National bachelor's degree production in computer and information science and support services at not-for-profit institutions increased significantly between 2009 and 2015 (by 74 percent), above and beyond the general rate of increase of bachelor's degree production overall (16 percent) during this period. Over the longer term, the rate of growth has varied, with two notable large declines but with a positive long-term trend, and it has differed by institution type and among individual institutions.

FINDING 2: Enrollments in CS courses and the number of CS majors have risen markedly since 2005 at many institutions, and there is no indication that enrollments will fall in the near term. Both CS majors and non-majors have contributed significantly to the recent growth in enrollment in undergraduate CS courses. Information about current program enrollment trends suggests that the boom in enrollments has only begun to register in the national data on CS degree production, and that CS bachelor's degree completions will rise sharply for at least the next few years in the absence of institutional actions to limit or discourage participation in the major.

FINDING 3: With more than half of new CS Ph.D.s drawn to opportunities in industry, hiring and retaining CS faculty is currently an acute challenge that limits institutions' abilities to respond to increasing CS enrollments.

FINDING 4: Employment in computing fields has grown steadily since 1975, and the number of jobs in computing occupations far exceeds bachelor's degree production in CS. The BLS projects that employment in computer occupations will rise more quickly than overall job growth for at least the next several years.

FINDING 5: Computing is pervasive, and its penetration is deep and growing in virtually all sectors of the economy, all academic disciplines, and all aspects of modern life. The broad opportunities in computing, both in the labor market and for enabling a host of intellectual pursuits, will continue to be drivers of increasing enrollments in undergraduate computer science, from both majors and non-majors. While there will probably be fluctuations in the demand for CS courses, demand is likely to continue to grow or remain high over the long term.

FINDING 6: CS and CIS have historically had low representation of women and underrepresented minorities. This trend of underrepresentation in bachelor's degree completions had not improved significantly as of 2015, but there is some evidence that representation may be improving among students currently majoring or interested in majoring in CS.

FINDING 7: There is no guarantee that the representation of women and underrepresented minorities in CS will improve without a focused effort. Retention is always a challenge, and adverse conditions associated with high demand for courses—as well as actions taken by institutions in order to manage enrollments—could negatively impact the inclusiveness of undergraduate computing programs.

FINDING 8: Departments facing sharp increases in demand for computing courses have experienced significant strain on a wide range of resources. Failure to respond thoughtfully to the demand and the resource deficits will result in adverse conditions for students, faculty, the programs, and the institution as a whole in the near or long term. Conditions such as an unwelcoming academic climate and loss of faculty members can be especially harmful in the long term.

FINDING 9: U.S. institutions of higher education have differing missions, priorities, and business models, and serve different populations with different needs. There is no one-size-fits-all solution for responding to enrollment increases. However, all institutions need to assess the role of computer science and related fields and make strategic plans to address realistically and effectively the high demand for courses, student interests and needs, faculty and staff workloads, research and teaching allocations, and physical resources. At all institutions there is an opportunity to reassess the role of CS and computing and to consider changes that go beyond the current challenges and position the institution for future success.

In light of the preceding findings, the committee sees both an urgent need and an opportunity to evaluate strategically the role of computer science and related fields at academic institutions and plan for a compelling future where student, departmental, institutional, and national needs can be met.

RECOMMENDATION 1: The leaders of the institutions of higher education that have experienced rapid increases in computer science course enrollments should take deliberate actions to address this trend with a sense of urgency.

RECOMMENDATION 2: A range of actions should be considered as part of a comprehensive institutional strategy, from targeted controls on enrollments or resource additions to meet demand, to more extensive institutional changes that extend beyond the computer science department.

RECOMMENDATION 2.1: Institutions experiencing a computer science enrollment surge should seriously consider an increase in resources to address the rising workload on faculty and staff in computer science and related departments, and the limitations arising from inadequate facilities.

RECOMMENDATION 2.2: Some institutions may view the imposition of limits on enrollment in computer science and related courses as desirable or unavoidable. However, before imposing limits on

course or major enrollments, the consequences of doing so should be considered comprehensively, and the benefits and costs weighed for the entire university community.

RECOMMENDATION 2.3: Institutional leadership should engage directly with computer science departments or programs to develop appropriate faculty hiring and faculty size targets, and develop strategies to improve faculty retention. Increasing the number and enhancing the role of academic-rank teaching faculty should be given serious consideration.

RECOMMENDATION 2.4: Larger institutions—in particular, research universities—should reevaluate the organizational placement of the computer science department and other departmental units with a computational mission.

RECOMMENDATION 2.5: Institutions should pursue innovative strategies for using technology to deliver high-quality instruction at scale to large numbers of students, and pursue additional, creative strategies for meeting demand for quality computer science courses and skills development among the entire student body.

RECOMMENDATION 3: Institutions should take deliberate actions to support diversity in their computer science and related programs. In particular:

RECOMMENDATION 3.1: Institutions should assess how computer science enrollment growth—and any actions or strategies for responding to it—affects the diversity of their student bodies, and deliberately align their actions and the culture of their programs with best practices for diversity and retention.

RECOMMENDATION 3.2: Institutions should leverage the increasing interest in computer science and related fields, among both non-majors and intended majors, to engage, recruit, and retain more women and underrepresented minorities into the field to help address the diversity problem proactively.

RECOMMENDATION 4: The National Science Foundation (NSF) can be especially helpful in advancing undergraduate computer science education in the context of increasing enrollments, for both majors and non-majors. The following actions should receive serious consideration:

RECOMMENDATION 4.1: Use NSF's convening power to bring computer science faculty and institutional leaders together to identify best practices and innovation in computer science education in times of limited departmental resources. This should include assessment of the computer science skills and knowledge needed in non–computer science academic disciplines.

RECOMMENDATION 4.2: Support research on how best to use technology in teaching large classes. Such research should be multidisciplinary, spanning learning sciences, educational pedagogy for computer science, development and deployment of assessment instruments, and technology design.

RECOMMENDATION 4.3: Support research to advance the understanding of best practices for diversity in computing, including rigorous and longitudinal assessment of the efficacy of specific institutional practices, especially those taken or considered in times of high enrollments. This research should be multidisciplinary, with experts in both micro- and macro-level social science research, statistics, computer science education, and diversity in STEM (science, technology, engineering, and mathematics) and computing.

RECOMMENDATION 4.4: Create an initiative to expand instructional resources in computer science, informed by an understanding of the constraints and dynamics of the supply and demand for computer science Ph.D.s. This might include research support and doctoral fellowships for domestic computer science undergraduates, and support for incorporating teaching into computer science doctoral programs and junior faculty research.

RECOMMENDATION 5: Computer science departments and the computing industry should develop new partnerships to help higher education meet workforce needs, continue to graduate well-prepared students, encourage industry to provide increased support for research funding, and allow a better exchange of Ph.D.-level researchers between academia and industry.

RECOMMENDATION 6: Public institutions produce a significant fraction of each state's workforce and the nation's computer science undergraduate degrees. States should provide sufficient support to their public institutions to enable them to support fully their academic missions, including with respect to computer science education.

RECOMMENDATION 7: To prepare students better for the expanding role of computing in academia, industry, and daily life underlying the increase in interest in computer science, government agencies and states should support local, state, and national programs for computing education for the purpose of increasing exposure to computing, computational principles, information security, and data analytics throughout the K-12 pipeline.

RECOMMENDATION 8: Actions should be taken to facilitate an improved understanding of national undergraduate enrollment trends by improving the primary data available about them, and facilitating the availability of those data in a timely fashion. In particular, the following actions should be considered:

RECOMMENDATION 8.1: Improved data sources about undergraduate enrollment should be pursued by federal and state governments in collaboration with academic institutions. To the extent possible, data should be made available in a time frame where the information can be useful for academic and government planning purposes.

RECOMMENDATION 8.2: The taxonomies and classifications for undergraduate computing degrees and jobs should be reexamined and updated, so that those used in national statistics are more easily brought into alignment, and map more directly to the current organization of computer science and related fields in higher education.

RECOMMENDATION 8.3: In the absence of comprehensive national statistics, the computer science community, in collaboration with education, social sciences, and statistics researchers, should continue to pursue or refine effective strategies for tracking enrollment, retention, and graduation rates and measuring student diversity.

1

Introduction

BACKGROUND AND CONTEXT

The field of computer science (CS) is currently experiencing a surge in undergraduate degree and course enrollments. This surge is straining program resources at many institutions, and causing concern among faculty and administrators about how best to respond to the rapidly growing demand. There is also concern about what this will mean for the future of these CS programs, the field as a whole, and U.S. society more broadly. The computing community has recently begun calling attention to and seeking solutions to this challenge.[1]

The Committee on the Growth of Computer Science Undergraduate Enrollments was asked to examine the recent phenomenon of increasing enrollments in undergraduate computing courses and to assess the scope of this trend and the underlying drivers, likely future enrollment trends, and the impact of recent enrollment growth on diversity in the computing disciplines. The committee's full Statement of Task is contained in Box 1.1 (and in Appendix A).

The following report is the output of the committee's work. It explores existing data and evidence about historical and recent trends in computing, distills key findings, identifies actions that can be taken in response to increasing demand for computing courses and programs, and recommends strategies for institutions to consider in order to prepare for success in meeting their priorities in the middle and long term. Understanding this phenomenon and formulation of an effective response are crucial for the success of institutions, their students and faculty, and the nation.

---

[1] In particular, the Computing Research Association (CRA) has led significant efforts to gather data, track enrollment trends, and stimulate awareness and consideration of this topic.

BOX 1.1
Statement of Task

An ad hoc committee will examine potential responses to the current large influx of undergraduate students enrolling in computing and computer science (CS) courses in 4-year institutions. This study will investigate the following:

- Current and projected patterns of enrollment in undergraduate courses in computer science, computer engineering (CE), and information (within undergraduate information schools), including an analysis of the factors that have driven recent growth and may drive future growth. Data will be disaggregated by type of 4-year institution (e.g., top 50, R-1). The study will include an analysis of enrollment patterns among CS/CE/information majors and minors and science, technology, engineering, and mathematics (STEM) and non-STEM majors taking service courses offered by CS/CE/information departments or enrolling in CS/CE/information courses on an elective basis. A primary goal of this effort is to determine whether the recent increases in enrollment are similar to other cyclic fluctuations that have occurred in the past or whether they are more likely to be sustained.
- Strategies that various institutions are using to respond most effectively to enrollment growth while maintaining or enhancing course access as well as the quality of instruction, considered by type of college or university. The study will examine the impacts those strategies are having on CS/CE/information departments in terms of, for example, faculty and graduate student hiring and workload (including non-CS faculty), student retention, and support for the needs of different categories of students (such as non-CS majors, CS minors, STEM majors, and non-STEM majors).
- The impact of enrollment growth on efforts to increase the enrollment of women and underrepresented minorities in CS/CE/information courses and degree programs, as well as on strategies for retaining those students in the CS/CE/information field and encouraging their pathways toward graduate degrees and careers in related fields.

The committee will produce a report with findings and recommendations, as well as questions for additional research.

CONTEXT ON THE COMPUTING DISCIPLINES

Since the emergence of the personal computer in the 1980s and the Internet in the 1990s, the field of computer science has seen an expansion of research areas and has been the driver of incredible economic growth, creating new industries and changing how society and businesses operate. Computation, from simulation and modeling to data mining, drives progress in many research areas, and has helped create new fields, such as computational biology, digital health, digital humanities, and more. Several key areas are generally viewed as having direct impact on most other aspects of contemporary society and businesses: data science and machine learning, which enable gleaning of new knowledge from the vast quantities of digital information produced today, and cybersecurity, vital for keeping computing systems operational and protected from unwanted intrusion in the face of growing cyber threats.

Historically, computer science programs were formed as departments within some larger unit. Over time universities and other institutions of higher education have increasingly been creating colleges of computing, information schools, schools of information and computer science, schools of informatics, or other larger organizational structures. Today the nature and locations within an organization of computer science and related departments are varied, and depend on the size, history, and priorities of a given institution. Small colleges typically have computer science departments but no engineering programs, and some may combine computer science and mathematics, with courses for undergraduates only. Large universities may have both computer science and computer engineering programs, housed in colleges of arts and sciences or engineering, or in one of the newer, separate, computing-centric schools or colleges.[2] Clarification of the terms related to the scope of computer science and related disciplines is provided in Box 1.2.

It is important to acknowledge that computing fields are grouped differently at different academic institutions, and that their boundaries have changed—and continue to change—over time. Tracking the temporal trends within a given field is thus a challenge, and the limited data available may be grouped in such a way as to impede such analysis.[3] The discussions in this report aim to be inclusive, but in some cases are limited by availability and specificity of data. The committee explicitly states throughout which groups are included in any given analysis.

This study is concerned with undergraduate enrollments in computer science and related fields, both in the context of majors (students who declare as majors, and whose course of study leads to a degree in the field) and non-majors (students who take one or more computing courses but do not go on to receive a degree in the field). At a practical level, these categories cover enrollment in both computer science courses and degree programs. Information about the number of minors in computer science and related fields is also of interest; this is discussed where possible in the report, but this discussion is highly limited due to a lack of data.

DATA USED IN THE DEVELOPMENT OF THIS REPORT

Consistent with their charge, the committee sought out evidence from a range of sources. In addition to expert testimony and publications, several data sets were a source of significant input to the committee's assessment; evidence

---

[2] For a more detailed history of the computing disciplines, see The Joint Task Force for Computing Curricula (2005).

[3] The limitations of available data sets are discussed in more detail in Chapters 2 and 3.

BOX 1.2
The Scope of Computer Science and Related Disciplines

While the committee's charge calls out the fields of computer science, computer engineering, and information science, the scope of computer science–related disciplines is broad, and not limited to these fields. In some cases, these and related fields can be discussed separately. However, at a practical level, the boundaries between fields are not always well or consistently defined, even by those in the computer science community. To assist the reader in the context of this report, key terms relating to computer science enrollments are highlighted here; deeper discussions of computer science and related disciplines are available from the Association for Computing Machinery (ACM), the Accreditation Board for Engineering and Technology and the Computing Sciences Accreditation Board, who have done significant work on curricula and accreditation.[a]

Computer science—"[T]he study of computers and algorithmic processes, including their principles, their hardware and software designs, their applications, and their impact on society."[b] "Unlike ... computer engineers, computer scientists deal mostly with software and software systems; this includes their theory, design, development, and application."[c]

Computer engineering—The study of "the design of digital hardware and software systems, including communications systems, computers, and devices that contain computers."[d]

Information science—"[Has] no uniformly accepted definition. It is commonly defined as the study of the representation, storage, analysis, collection, classification, manipulation, retrieval, dissemination, and protection of information."[e] In academic units containing computer science it has also been defined as "the combination of computer science with the social sciences to study how people and societies interact with information."[f]

Information technology—The study of computing infrastructures to meet the "needs of business, government, healthcare, schools, and other kinds of organizations."[g]

drawn from these sources is presented and discussed throughout the report. In the following, the source, content, and limitations of each data set are described as context for their discussion in subsequent chapters.

Integrated Postsecondary Education Data System (IPEDS)

Degree production at U.S. academic institutions is tracked over time by the U.S. Department of Education via the Integrated Postsecondary Education Data System (IPEDS), including those institutions in all U.S. states and territories and the District of Columbia. Degree completions and other information are reported by all institutions that receive funding under Title IV of the Higher Education

Software engineering—The study and practice of "developing and maintaining software systems that behave reliably and efficiently, are affordable to develop and maintain, and satisfy the requirements that customers have defined."[g]

Data science—An interdisciplinary field spanning computer science, statistics, and specific knowledge domains that uses models, processes, and systems to extract insights from data.

Computing—This term is used broadly to refer to all areas of computer science, all interdisciplinary areas computer scientists work in, and all fields using computer science or computational methods and principles to advance the field. This includes both academic and occupational fields, such as bioinformatics, medical informatics, library sciences, digital archives, computational sciences, and more.

---

[a] The Joint Task Force for Computing Curricula. 2005. Computing Curricula 2005: The Overview Report. ACM and IEEE. Online. Available at http://www.acm.org/education/education/curric_vols/CC2005-March06Final.pdf.

[b] K-12 Computer Science. 2017. Defining Computer Science. Online. Available at https://k12cs.org/defining-computer-science/.

[c] University of Maryland. 2017. What Is Computer Science? Online. Available at https://undergrad.cs.umd.edu/what-computer-science.

[d] Association for Computing Machinery. Computing Degrees and Careers. Online. Available at http://computingcareers.acm.org/?page_id=11.

[e] Stock, W.G., and M. Stock. 2013. *Handbook of Information Science*. Walter de Gruyter, Berlin.

[f] Cornell University. 2017. Information Science Major. Online. Available at https://admissions.cals.cornell.edu/academics/majors/information-science.

[g] Shackelford, R., A. McGettrick, R. Sloan, H. Topi, G. Davies, R. Kamali, J. Cross, J. Impagliazzo, R. LeBlanc, and B. Lunt. 2006. Computing Curricular 2005: The Overview Report. In *Proceedings of the 37th SIGCSE Technical Symposium on Computer Science Education (SIGCSE '06)*. ACM. New York, NY. 456-457. http://dx.doi.org/10.1145/1121341.1121482.

Act of 1965, as amended, with institutions self-reporting information that they classify according to the IPEDS taxonomy via the IPEDS Completions Survey (years available: 1966-2015) in general, and the IPEDS Completions Survey by Race (years available: 1977-2015) when considering race/ethnicity demographics of degree completions. This is the most comprehensive data set about U.S. post-secondary degree completion available, and it may be queried via the Web-based Computer-Assisted Science Policy Analysis and Research System (WebCASPAR) database maintained by the National Science Foundation's (NSF's) National Center for Science and Engineering Statistics.[4] Two distinct data sets are available

---

[4] See NSF (2017), https://ncsesdata.nsf.gov/webcaspar/.

for both surveys, one from NSF and one from the National Center for Education Statistics (NCES); the NCES data set is the source of data presented in this report.

The IPEDS tracks these data using a range of classifiers, such as institution type, and level and discipline of degree conferred. These classifiers have been periodically updated and adjusted to reflect changes in the IPEDS taxonomy as academic trends change. Academic disciplines are identified via its Classification of Instructional Program (CIP) codes, identified with varying specificity by six-digit (for the most specific classification of discipline) or four-digit decimal codes or discipline names, or a more general (termed "detailed") classifier (e.g., "Computer Science").

The detailed classifier of "Computer Science" includes all CIPs of the general form 11.XXXX, referred to as "Computer and Information Sciences and Support Services" (referred to in this report as CIS for short) in the "6-digit Classification of Instructional Program" categories (NCES, 2010a). This classifier spans computer science, information science/studies, and information technology, as well as other specific fields that may be more relevant to certificates or associate's degrees.

- 11) COMPUTER AND INFORMATION SCIENCES AND SUPPORT SERVICES.
  - 11.01) Computer and Information Sciences, General.
    - 11.0101) Computer and Information Sciences, General.
    - 11.0102) Artificial Intelligence.
    - 11.0103) Information Technology.
    - 11.0104) Informatics.
    - 11.0199) Computer and Information Sciences, Other.
  - 11.02) Computer Programming.
    - 11.0201) Computer Programming/Programmer, General.
    - 11.0202) Computer Programming, Specific Applications.
    - 11.0203) Computer Programming, Vendor/Product Certification.
    - 11.0299) Computer Programming, Other.
  - 11.03) Data Processing.
    - 11.0301) Data Processing and Data Processing Technology/Technician.
  - 11.04) Information Science/Studies.
    - 11.0401) Information Science/Studies.
  - 11.05) Computer Systems Analysis.
    - 11.0501) Computer Systems Analysis/Analyst.
  - 11.06) Data Entry/Microcomputer Applications.
    - 11.0601) Data Entry/Microcomputer Applications, General.
    - 11.0602) Word Processing.
    - 11.0699) Data Entry/Microcomputer Applications, Other.

11.07) Computer Science.
    11.0701) Computer Science.
11.08) Computer Software and Media Applications.
    11.0801) Web Page, Digital/Multimedia and Information Resources Design.
    11.0802) Data Modeling/Warehousing and Database Administration.
    11.0803) Computer Graphics.
    11.0804) Modeling, Virtual Environments and Simulation.
    11.0899) Computer Software and Media Applications, Other.
11.09) Computer Systems Networking and Telecommunications.
    11.0901) Computer Systems Networking and Telecommunications.
11.10) Computer/Information Technology Administration and Management.
    11.1001) Network and System Administration/Administrator.
    11.1002) System, Networking, and LAN/WAN Management/ Manager.
    11.1003) Computer and Information Systems Security/ Information Assurance.
    11.1004) Web/Multimedia Management and Webmaster.
    11.1005) Information Technology Project Management.
    11.1006) Computer Support Specialist.
    11.1099) Computer/Information Technology Services Administration and Management, Other.
11.99) Computer and Information Sciences and Support Services, Other.
    11.9999) Computer and Information Sciences and Support Services, Other.

It is important to note that the CIP 11.x series includes several fields that are not considered traditional CS programs but are more likely to be considered "information technology" or "computer or information support services." However, these fields comprise a relatively small fraction of the bachelor's degrees awarded at nonprofit institutions in the CIS category. For example, no bachelor's degrees have ever been reported for "11.0203) Computer Programming, Vendor/Product Certification," or any of the fields under "11.06) Data Entry/ Microcomputer Applications." However, the six-digit classifiers were introduced in 1987 and updated in 2000 and 2010; and there is no way to distinguish between all of the subfields over the whole time frame of 1966-2015.

It is also worth noting that, because a significant number of these degrees are classified as "11.0101) Computer and Information Sciences, General," it is also not practical to separate CS from information science completely—indeed, some institutions themselves may not treat them separately.

Given these factors, along with uncertainty in how institutions may self-identify the CIPs for their programs, the general variation in the nature of computing programs in the first place, discontinuities in the classification and reporting of subfields over time, and the difficulty in comparing cross sections of this category to national labor statistics data, the committee has chosen to present the whole 11.x series (CIS) in most of its analyses.

Other analyses of CS degree trends have examined a narrower set of classifiers; in particular, the Computing Research Association (CRA) has chosen to analyze only those degrees designated "11.0101) Computer and Information Sciences, General" and "11.0701) Computer Science," in order to focus on core or traditional CS degrees in recent years (Camp et al., 2017a). There are several instances in this report where analyses regarding recent trends would be affected by using this narrower set of CIPs; these are noted and commented upon as the committee found appropriate.

Prior to 1987 computer engineering (CE) degrees were counted under other categories. CE degree production is tracked beginning in 1987, when it emerged as a unique classifier, as the 14.09 series. While some CS degrees may be categorized as CE (and vice versa), and CE is an important area of computing, the committee chose to keep it separate from CS to enable examination of time series trends.

IPEDS data are central to the discussions in Chapters 2 and 5. The specific data presented therein may be reproduced by an interested reader via the WebCASPAR system by querying the database with the same classification parameters used by the committee, as indicated for each figure in Appendix E.

Computing Research Association Survey Data

CRA Taulbee Survey

The CRA Taulbee Survey is administered annually to all North American Ph.D.-granting institutions that subscribe to the CRA. This survey collects computing departments' self-reported bachelor's, master's, and Ph.D. degree trends. This annual survey has been a "principal source of information on the enrollment, production, and employment of Ph.D.s" in computing since it was first administered in 1974 (CRA, 2015). An adaptation of this survey has also been sent to institutions whose CS units do not grant Ph.D.s (known as non-doctoral colleges) since 2012 via the ACM, as a supplement to the Taulbee Survey.

Results from this survey are discussed in Chapters 3, 4, and 5.

CRA and NDC Enrollment Surveys

In the face of increasing CS bachelor's degree production and major enrollment, in 2016 the CRA sent out a supplemental Enrollment Survey to "units" (programs, departments, divisions, schools, or colleges) in the Taulbee and NDC groups responsible for serving bachelor's-level majors in computer science.[5] This survey collected supplemental information about undergraduate major enrollments and course enrollments. The results were recently published online by CRA in a report titled "Generation CS" (Camp et al., 2017a, 2017b; CRA, 2017).

The CRA Enrollment Survey asked responders for the numbers of students (separated by majors and non-majors) in four categories of courses representing different points in computer science education: an introductory course for non-majors, an introductory course for majors, a mid-level course, and an upper-level course. Results were obtained for three years: 2005, 2010, and 2015.[6] Overall, 134 of 190 doctoral-granting institutions surveyed responded, 45 of which reported course enrollment numbers (~24 percent response rate); 93 of the 706 non-doctoral institutions surveyed responded, 20 of which provided course enrollment numbers (~2.8 percent response rate). These are the best quantitative data available about current undergraduate computing course and major enrollments at U.S. institutions of higher education; nonetheless, they are not comprehensive, and, because responses were voluntary, they may reflect self-selection bias, so in general should be interpreted with caution.

The Freshman Survey of the Cooperative Institutional Research Program

The Freshman Survey of the Cooperative Institutional Research Program, (currently administered by the Higher Education Research Institute) has been administered to first-year, full-time students at a national sampling of 4-year colleges and universities since 1966, and covers a wide range of topics, including intended major. This survey is administered to freshmen "during registration, freshman orientation, or the first few weeks of classes." The data are extensive, and designed to reflect the profiles of all new full-time students at 4-year colleges and universities nationwide. The results for fall 2016 reflect the responses of 137,456 students at 184 colleges and universities, weighted to reflect profiles of all new full-time students nationwide (Eagan et al., 2016). Statistics on student intent to major in computer science obtained from this survey between 1971 and 2015 are presented and discussed in Chapters 3 and 5. However, we caution that the uncertainties in these data are not easily quantified.

---

[5] Units responsible for degrees in other areas of computing—that is, information science and computer engineering—were not included.

[6] The CRA Enrollment Survey surveyed only computer science units, rather than computer engineering or information science. "Non-majors" here refers to students not currently enrolled in computer science degree programs (though it is possible that they may later choose to do so, and become majors).

Student Academic Data from the Consortium for Undergraduate STEM Success (CUSTEMS)

The Consortium for Undergraduate STEM Success (CUSTEMS) is a growing coalition of institutions for which enrollment data have been collected on a voluntary basis beginning in 2008 in order to track retention of women and underrepresented minorities in STEM degree programs.[7] The CUSTEMS data set includes course enrollment, grades, and admissions records for students at participating institutions. Upon commission from the committee, the CUSTEMS team provided information about enrollment in CS courses at eight historically black colleges and universities, five liberal arts colleges, and one large public research university—all of the institutions for which the team had student-level data for the years of 2009 through 2014. The identities of the institutions remain confidential for privacy protection. Additional information about this data set is available in Appendix F.

The Current Population Survey (CPS)

The Current Population Survey (CPS) is administered jointly by the U.S. Census Bureau and the Bureau of Labor Statistics (BLS) on a monthly basis to a sample of 60,000 occupied U.S. households. The survey results are the basis for monthly (and annualized) statistics about the labor force, including occupational field, educational attainment level, and wages. The actual survey is conducted via in-person or over-the-phone interviews, with Census Bureau employees recording responses in a computerized system. Occupations are classified according to the BLS Standard Occupational Classifications (SOCs), which can be linked via a crosswalk to the taxonomies for the American Community Survey (ACS) and to the IPEDS CIPs.[8]

This report includes discussion of CPS data provided to the committee in a white paper written by economist Jennifer Hunt of Rutgers University, which is discussed in Chapter 4 of this report and included in Appendix D. Specifically, median wages and share of all U.S. employment are provided for computer and mathematical occupations (2010 SOCs 15-0000/2010 Census codes 1000-1240), engineering and architecture occupations (2010 SOCs 17-0000/2010 Census codes 1300-1560), and science occupations (2010 SOCs 19-0000/2010 Census codes 1600-1965). While the category of "Computer and Mathematical Occupations" is broader than those grounded in computer science skills, it does include most CS occupations, and is helpful for illustrating relevant trends.

---

[7] Consortium for Undergraduate STEM Success, http://www.custems.org/.

[8] More data on this survey, its methodologies, and coding taxonomies can be found via the Census website, https://www.census.gov/programs-surveys/cps.html.

The American Community Survey (ACS)

The American Community Survey (ACS) is administered by the U.S. Census Bureau to approximately one in 38 U.S. households each year.[9] The responses of this survey are the basis for national statistics on topics such as U.S. jobs, wages, occupations, and educational attainment of the population. Individuals write in information about their occupation, which is coded according to a predefined taxonomy (the Census code) that is periodically updated, and which maps to the Standard Occupational Classifications used in the CPS. In Chapter 4, ACS data about the field of bachelor's degree held by workers in computer occupations and the industries employing CS bachelor's degree holders are discussed.

ORGANIZATION OF THIS REPORT

The following report presents available evidence about computing degree production, CS course enrollment trends and impacts, drivers of course and program enrollments, and diversity in computing. It outlines key findings, a spectrum of possible strategies for institutions experiencing CS enrollment increases, and general recommendations. Specifically, the report is organized as follows:

- Chapter 2 discusses historical and recent trends in computing degree production, and past actions taken by computing departments in response to growing enrollments.
- Chapter 3 examines recent trends in enrollment in computer science programs and available data about the impact of increased enrollments at institutions experiencing growth, as well as actions institutions are taking or considering by way of response.
- Chapter 4 explores drivers of the recent increase in demand for computing, including the labor market for computing and the changing landscape of computing in academia and today's society.
- Chapter 5 assesses diversity in computing in recent years, and the relationship between enrollment growth and student diversity, including impacts of actions taken by faculty, departments, and institutions in response to increasing demand.
- Chapter 6 explores institutional needs and priorities, and possible actions to take in response to increasing enrollments.
- Chapter 7 presents recommendations for responding to the current enrollment boom and planning for the future.

[9] This and additional information is available via the Census website, https://www.census.gov/programs-surveys/acs/.

2

Historical Degree Production in Computing

Before assessing current undergraduate computing enrollment trends at U.S. institutions, it is imperative to consider the historical context. The most authoritative data on the historical production of computer science (CS) bachelor's degrees lie in the national statistics on degree completions tracked by the Department of Education's Integrated Postsecondary Education Data System (IPEDS).

This chapter presents and discusses time series trends in degree production to provide context for discussion of current enrollment trends. Specifically, it examines degree production trends in CS and related fields relative to net production of bachelor's degrees over time, distribution of postsecondary degrees produced in these fields, past economic and institutional factors that likely contributed to past CS bachelor's degree production trends, and variations by institution type from 2009 to 2015 to highlight the range of experiences at different institutions.

The IPEDS data discussed in this chapter come from three different cross sections of CS and related fields, labeled and defined as follows:[1]

1. *CIS*—Includes the entire 11.x series of IPEDS Classification of Instructional Programs (CIPs), referred to within IPEDS alternately as "computer science" and "computer and information science and support services." This broad category includes core computer science, information science/studies, information technology, and related fields, some of which are more vocational than traditional computer science programs.

[1] See the section "Data Used in the Development of This Report" in Chapter 1 for additional discussion of the IPEDS classification system for CS and related fields.

2. *Core CS*—Includes only "Computer and Information Sciences, General" (11.0101) and "Computer Science" (11.0701). These two CIPs have been considered to be closest to the core computer science degree programs currently offered at institutions of higher education offering bachelor's and higher-level degrees. However, this set of classifiers may not necessarily reflect temporal trends in degree production accurately, due to the changes in IPEDS CIP codes in 2000 and 2010.
3. *Computer engineering (CE)*—Includes degrees from the 14.09xx series, identified as "Computer Engineering, General" (14.0901), "Computer Hardware Engineering" (14.0902), "Computer Software Engineering" (14.0903), and "Computer Engineering, Other" (14.0999).

Details about the full set of classifiers of all plotted data from IPEDS are described in Appendix F.

HISTORICAL PRODUCTION OF CIS AND CE BACHELOR'S DEGREES

Since the emergence of CS programs in the 1960s, overall production of CS and related bachelor's degrees at U.S. institutions of higher education has grown significantly. CE was first uniquely identified as a subfield of engineering in federal education statistics in 1987, and generates about 10 percent of the number of graduates produced in CIS. The number and share of CIS and CE degrees produced over time are illustrated in Figure 2.1, with total bachelor's degree production in all fields indicated as a dashed line for context (vertical scale read from the right axis).[2] The plots for "All Institutions" include bachelor's degrees at all public, private not-for-profit, and private for-profit institutions; plots for "Not-for-Profits" exclude the bachelor's degrees conferred by for-profit institutions.

The significant growth in the 50 years since the emergence of computer science as a unique academic discipline is marked by two striking peaks, with subsequent valleys resetting at a higher absolute level than the presurge level. Specifically, the absolute number of CIS bachelor's degrees reported annually rose from 89 in 1966 to 60,309 in 2015, with peaks in 1986 (42,195 bachelor's degrees) and 2003 (57,926 bachelor's degrees) and valleys in between (24,553 in 1994 and 38,496 in 2009). CE also exhibits historical fluctuations.

CIS BACHELOR'S DEGREES GOING TO FOREIGN STUDENTS

The total number and fraction of all U.S. postsecondary degrees awarded in CIS to temporary residents (international students) are illustrated in Figure 2.2.

[2] See Chapter 1 for a more detailed description of the associated data source (IPEDS degree completions data) and associated limitations.

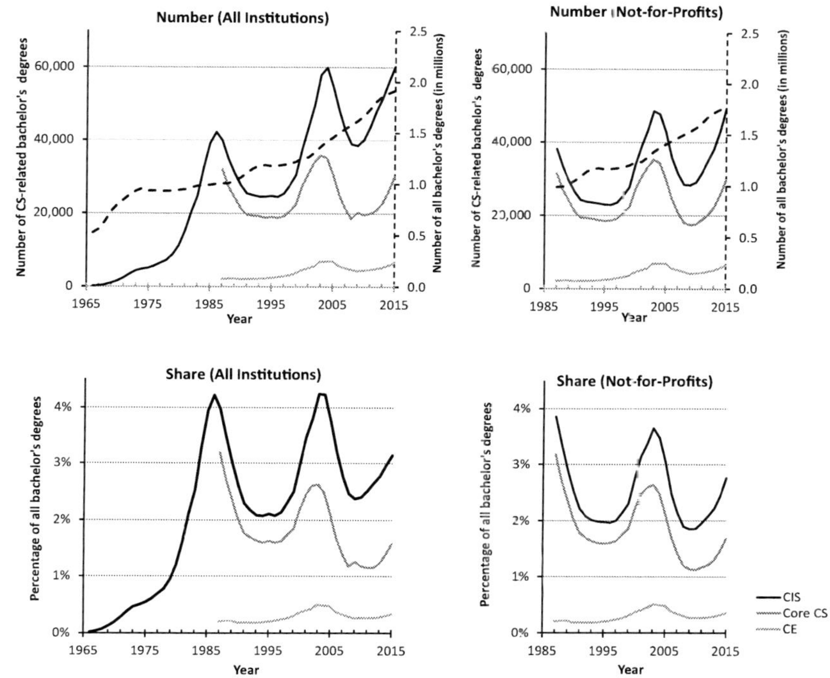

FIGURE 2.1 Historical year-to-year U.S. production of bachelor's degrees in computer and information science and support services (CIS, black line), core CS (dark gray line), and computer engineering (CE, light gray line), in absolute number (top row) and as a percentage (bottom row) of all bachelor's degrees at all institutions (left column) and at not-for-profit institutions (right column). The total number of bachelor's degrees produced in the United States each year in all fields is included in the top row for all institutions (left panel) and for not-for-profit institutions (right panel) as a dashed line for reference, with the vertical scale indicated on the right-hand axis. SOURCE: Data from IPEDS completions survey accessed via the WebCASPAR online database. See Appendix F for details.

Although a moderate increase in the share of CIS bachelor's degrees earned by international students occurred between 2008 and 2015 (from 4.6 to 5.6 percent overall), this constitutes only a small portion of U.S. bachelor's degree production, and suggests that little of the recent surge is due to increased participation among foreign students.[3] The fraction of CIS bachelor's degrees awarded to temporary residents in 2015 remained below past peak levels.

[3] Note that there is some uncertainty in these data given that a nontrivial fraction (around 10 percent in recent years) of these students declared neither a specific race/ethnicity nor status as a temporary resident (which are treated as mutually exclusive categories within the IPEDS classification system).

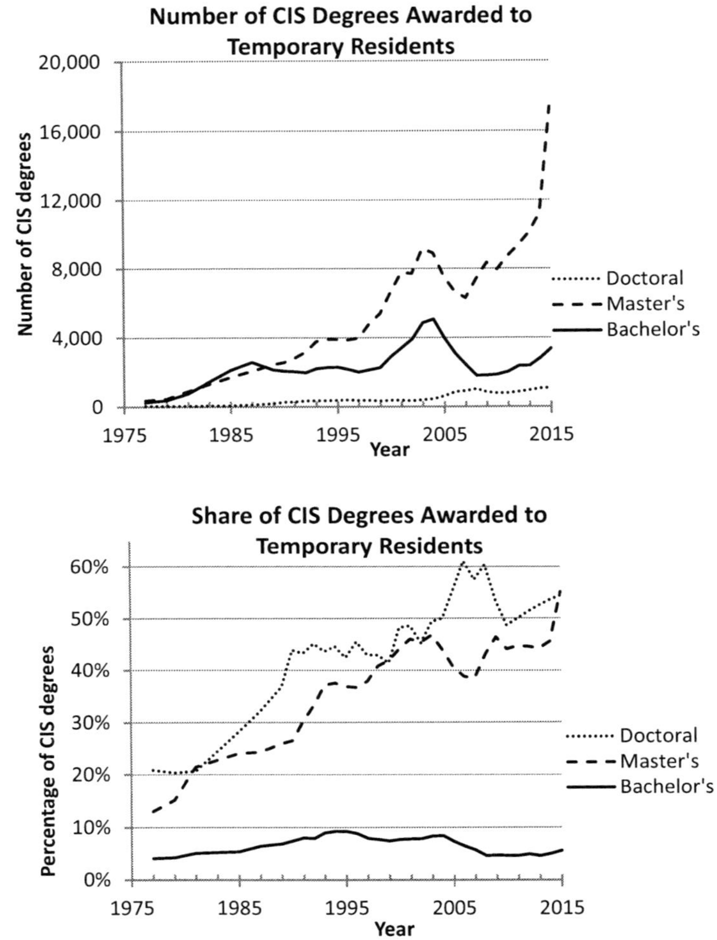

FIGURE 2.2 Number and share of U.S. degrees in CIS awarded to students designated as temporary residents of the United States (foreign students). SOURCE: Data from IPEDS completions survey accessed via the WebCASPAR online database. See Appendix F for details.

VARIATION IN CIS BACHELOR'S DEGREE PRODUCTION BY INSTITUTION TYPE

While the overall picture of computing degree production is helpful, it represents only aggregate trends and not the variation of experiences at different institutions. In the following these data are broken out in more detail using the IPEDS classifiers of "Institutional Control" (to identify trends at public, private, and for-profit institutions) and "Carnegie Classification" (to identify trends by institution type).

Public, Private, and For-Profit Institutions

The historical production of degrees (at all levels) in CIS and CE is broken out for the categories of public, private, and for-profit institutions in Figure 2.3, beginning with the earliest dates for which data with the corresponding classifiers are available.

Between 2000 and 2005, for-profit institutions emerged as a significant source of CIS degrees, roughly matching the number awarded at not-for-profit private institutions. It is noteworthy that CIS accounted for between 8 and 28 percent of bachelor's degrees awarded at for-profit institutions since 1987, but accounted for only between 2 and 4 percent of bachelor's degrees at public and private institutions. Again, this likely reflects both the breadth of the CIS classifier in IPEDS and the nature of the computing labor market. Since 2013 the number of CIS bachelor's degrees awarded at for-profit institutions has been falling, as has the relative fraction of bachelor's degrees conferred in CIS (compared to the number conferred in all disciplines) at for-profit institutions.

CIS degree production at public and private not-for-profit institutions has surged since 2009. The increases have been most pronounced at public institutions, which produced more degrees in 2015 (33,930) than during the dot-com era peak in 2003, representing an increase of 87 percent since the post-dot-com

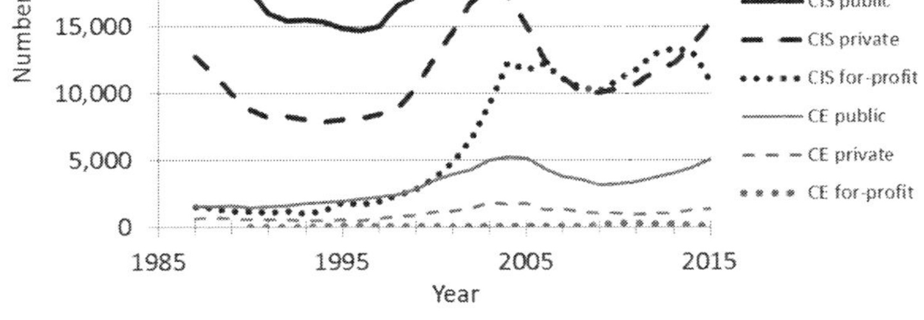

FIGURE 2.3 Bachelor's degree production from 1987 to 2015 in CIS and CE at public, private, and for-profit institutions reporting to IPEDS. SOURCE: Data from IPEDS completions survey accessed online via the WebCASPAR online database. See Appendix F for details.

low of 18,189 in 2009. At private institutions 15,361 degrees were produced in 2015 (compared to a peak of 17,846 in 2003), a 52 percent increase since 2009.

As previously noted overall bachelor's degree production has also been increasing, as illustrated in Figure 2.4. Nonetheless, CIS bachelor's degree production has been increasing at an even higher rate, as illustrated in Figure 2.1. The number of CIS bachelor's degrees produced annually at all not-for-profit institutions increased by 74 percent between 2009 and 2015, compared to an overall increase in bachelor's degree production of only 16 percent at not-for-profits during the same period.

Carnegie Classification

American institutions of higher education are very diverse, and it is important to consider how CS production has varied at the different institution types to get an accurate picture. To illustrate which institutions have experienced the most growth in recent years, these data are broken down further by survey-specific (2010) Carnegie Classification[4] and by for-profit status.[5] Degree production trends by institution type are illustrated in Figure 2.5 for the following categories of institution:

- *Research* includes institutions classified as not-for-profit doctoral-degree-granting institutions with "very high" or "high" research activity, both public and private.
- *Doctoral* includes all other not-for-profit doctoral degree granting institutions, both public and private.
- *For-profit doctoral* includes all for-profit doctoral institutions.
- *For-profit, other* includes all other for-profit institutions.
- *Master's* includes not-for-profit institutions whose highest degree offered (in any field) is at the master's level (many of these have a professional character).
- *Bachelor's* includes not-for-profit institutions at which a bachelor's is the terminal degree, including many liberal arts colleges.
- *Associate's* includes institutions that primarily offer associate's degrees, but also have some bachelor's degree programs.
- *Other/unknown* includes not-for-profit tribal colleges, special-focus institutions, and institutions that did not report a Carnegie Classification.

Combined, research and master's institutions have long produced the majority (67 percent in 2015) of all CIS bachelor's degrees. Research institutions reached a peak in CIS bachelor's production in 2003, then fell until 2008, after which the number climbed again, surpassing the 2003 peak in 2015. Doctoral, master's, and

[4] For the Carnegie Classification definitions and methodology, please see The Carnegie Classifications of Institutions of Higher Education (2017).

[5] Via the IPEDS "Institutional Control" classifier.

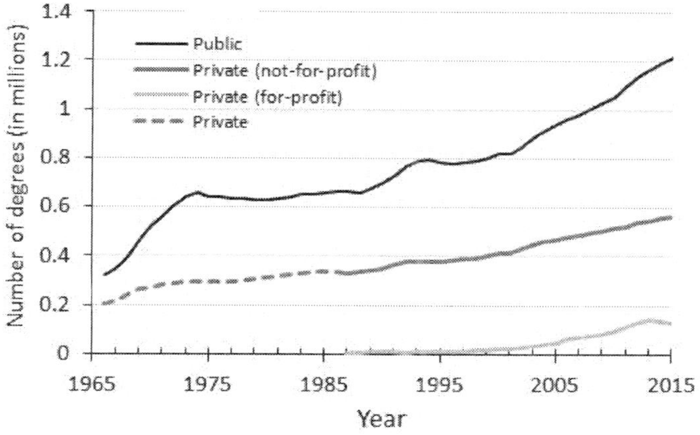

FIGURE 2.4 Total annual bachelor's degree production over time for public, private, and for-profit institutions (all academic fields). Private not-for-profit and private for-profit institutions were not distinguished prior to 1987. SOURCE: Data from IPEDS completions survey accessed via the WebCASPAR online database. See Appendix F for details.

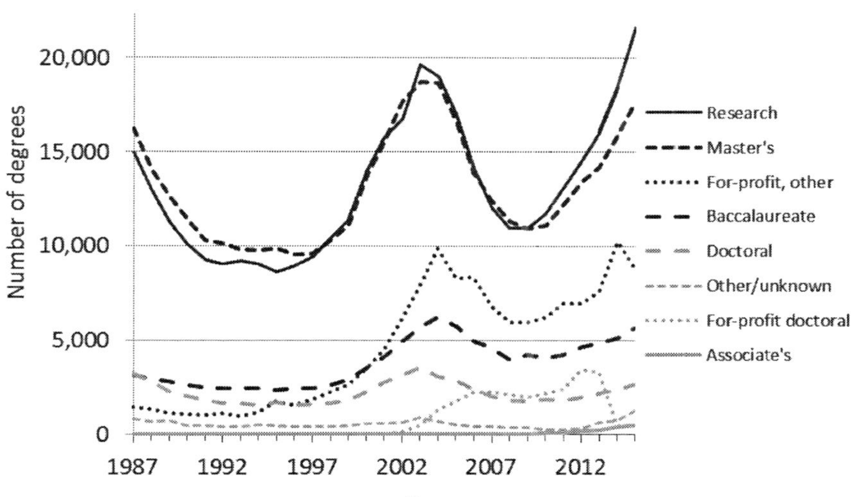

FIGURE 2.5 CIS bachelor's degree production by category of institution. Categories include only not-for-profit institutions, unless otherwise indicated. SOURCE: Data from IPEDS completions survey accessed via the WebCASPAR online database. See Appendix F for details.

bachelor's institutions follow a similar trend, but only nearly reaching their 2003 peaks in 2015. Production at for-profit institutions has exhibited a significant fall-off beginning in 2013 (for-profit doctoral institutions) and 2014 (other for-profits).

Since 2009, growth in CIS bachelor's degree production has occurred at research, master's, doctoral, and bachelor's institutions, though at different average rates. For-profit institutions experienced some growth, and then dropped precipitously. The recent (between 2009 and 2015) growth is having the largest impact on research institutions (97 percent increase), followed by master's institutions (69 percent increase), other doctoral institutions (50 percent increase), and bachelor's institutions (33 percent increase), on average.

For a closer look at relative trends in research institutions, this category was further separated by level of research activity. Figure 2.6 illustrates the total number of CIS degrees produced over time for those institutions with very high research activity (The Carnegie Classifications of Institutions of Higher Education, 2017). Active research institutions display much more pronounced growth than nonresearch doctoral institutions. Thus, production has shifted toward leading research institutions. As with the other categories, time will determine whether this reflects concentration at the top or a lag in growth.

To provide a sense of the nature of the recent onset of growth at not-for-profit institutions, the average number of degrees per institution in 2009 and 2015 is listed in Table 2.1 for all institution categories that have displayed increased

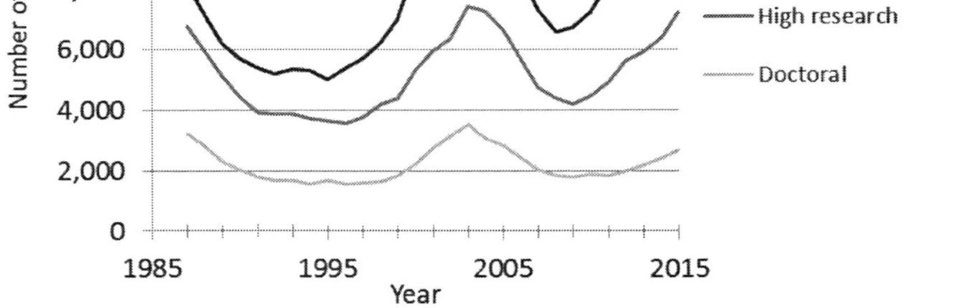

FIGURE 2.6 Historical CIS bachelor's degree production at not-for-profit doctoral (Ph.D.-granting) institutions, including very-high-research-activity institutions, high-research-activity institutions, and other doctoral institutions, 1987-2017. SOURCE: Data from IPEDS completions survey accessed via the WebCASPAR online database. See Appendix F for details.

TABLE 2.1 Change in Average Number and Institutional Share of CIS Bachelor's Degrees Produced per Institution by Not-for-Profit Institution Type, 2009-2015

Survey-Specific Carnegie Classification of Institution	CIS Average Number (and Share) of Bachelor's Degrees per Institution		Percent Increase in Average Number of Degrees per Institution
	2009	2015	
Very high research	65 (1.6%)	138 (3.0%)	113%
High research	44 (1.8%)	76 (2.6%)	74%
Doctoral	29 (1.9%)	42 (2.5%)	45%
Master's	21 (1.9%)	35 (2.7%)	69%
Bachelor's	10 (2.3%)	15 (2.8%)	42%
Associate's	15 (4.9%)	26 (5.0%)	72%

NOTE: Average number of degrees per institution rounded to nearest integer. Only institutions reporting CIS bachelor's degrees are included in each category. SOURCE: Data from IPEDS completions survey.

degree production since 2009. Average relative increases in program size are clearly higher for the more research-intensive institutions and for master's institutions as compared to bachelor's.

Some caution should be exercised when using these data to make assumptions about the nature of any particular CIS program, as program size does not follow a normal distribution. Overall, the top 10 percent of CIS degree producers are responsible for more than 50 percent of the degrees, and the smallest 50 percent of the institutions produce less than 10 percent. Less than 10 percent of the institutions experiencing growth are responsible for more than 50 percent of the growth. Furthermore, degree production is but one aspect of the experience in computing programs.

FINDING 1: National bachelor's degree production in computer and information science and support services at not-for-profit institutions increased significantly between 2009 and 2015 (by 74 percent), above and beyond the general rate of increase of bachelor's degree production (16 percent) overall during this period. Over the longer term, the rate of growth has varied, with two notable large declines but with a positive long-term trend, and it has differed by institution type and among individual institutions.

National degree production data do not provide any indication that the growth will soon abate. Given a finite population, it must level off eventually, or even peak, but there is no strong basis for predicting when that will occur.

Comprehensive national data are not available on growth of course enrollments, which reflect the increase in demand for courses both by majors and by the general student population, as well as the emergence of various blended majors.

This topic is explored further in Chapter 3. Nonetheless, these data provide illustrative analyses of historical CIS degree production trends—in particular, in the context of the recent boom.

OTHER LEVELS OF DEGREE

Surges also occurred in the number of CIS associate's degrees (peaking in 1984 with 12,913 degrees and in 2003 with 46,400 degrees). CIS certificates also exhibited a peak in 2003 (25,646 certificates), as did CE bachelor's and associate's and CIS master's. In this recent growth wave, associate's degrees in CIS from for-profit institutions have fallen substantially.

From Figure 2.7 it is apparent that a large number of CIS associate's degrees and CIS certificates have been awarded, similar in magnitude to the number of CIS bachelor's and master's degrees, respectively, since the mid-1990s. It is notable that CIS, as classified in IPEDS, produces relatively more associate's degrees and certificates than other science, technology, engineering, and mathematics fields.[6] Several factors may contribute to this pattern. First, the large number of CIS certificates may reflect interest among non-majors in obtaining computing skills. The types of degrees that are categorized as CIS in IPEDS may also be at play—the corresponding CIP is inclusive of disciplines such as "Information Technology," "Word Processing," and "Computer Support Specialist," which may be more vocational and thus more likely to offer these degrees. Finally, the nature of the market for computing skills may stimulate interest in these degrees.[7]

RESPONDING TO ENROLLMENT SURGES

In general, several categories of responses are available to institutions in the face of booming enrollments: (1) limit participation, (2) grow programs and the resources that feed them, (3) leverage resources in new ways, (4) restructure the nature of computing education within the institution, and (5) make no active changes, allowing higher burdens to be placed on existing resources. The categories range from maintaining current practices, to relatively inexpensive and nondisruptive actions, to significant changes in organization or resource commitments. They are not exclusive and typically are deployed in combination. A range of influences, including specific institutional actions and other influences, may apply over the course of a student's academic career, and may affect the character and culture of the program and institution.

In the rest of this report dimensions of the current CS enrollment surge are explored, including potential impacts of related institutional actions, which are discussed in more depth in Chapter 6. A discussion of anecdotes from past CS enrollments surge is provided in Box 2.1.

[6] This is discussed further in Chapter 4.

[7] See Chapter 4 for further discussion of the labor market.

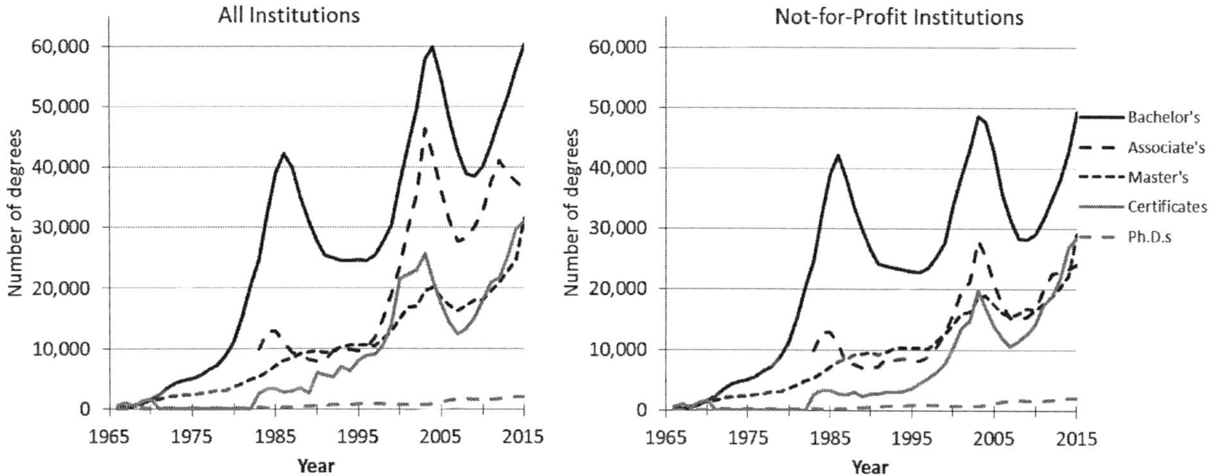

FIGURE 2.7 Historical annual degree production in CIS by level of degree. All institutions are illustrated in the left-hand panel, and not-for-profits only in the right-hand panel. Data are for all institutions that reported to IPEDS. SOURCE: Data from IPEDS completions survey accessed via the WebCASPAR online database. See Appendix F for details.

BOX 2.1
Learning from the Past

Today, many universities see increasing student demand for computer science courses, straining program resources. Low production of Ph.D.s in computer science and ample and lucrative opportunities in industry make it hard to fill open faculty and teaching positions. Many universities and colleges have instituted enrollments controls, including restricting the number of students allowed to declare a major and limiting access to computer science courses. Computer science faced similar challenges in the early 1980s, when students were attracted to CS by the development of widely available personal computers, and again in the late 1990s. During these times enrollments rose quickly, strain increased on existing faculty, and departments struggled to fill open faculty lines and teaching positions.

In each of these past cycles, universities tried several approaches to raise capacity: increasing class sizes and teaching loads, hiring adjunct faculty from industry, retraining faculty from other disciplines to teach courses in CS, and relying more on graduate students to teach. These strategies had mixed success. As student numbers continued to rise, many departments determined that they could not meet the needs of all students, and capped course enrollments and the number of majors, making it challenging for students to secure a place in the courses they needed to graduate on time in the context of a newly competitive environment.

Unfortunately, the passage of time has made it difficult to gather quantitative data about how institutions responded to the challenges of two or three decades ago. Only a handful of universities documented their strategies in detail or conducted comprehensive studies of how well those strategies worked. Even so, it is possible to get a general sense of the pressures universities faced from the historical reports we have and from the summary analyses prepared by government agencies and professional societies.

Useful histories may be found from Purdue University and the University of Maryland, both of which cover actions taken by those departments in response to the enrollment crisis of the 1980s.[a,b] These institutions should not be taken as representative of higher education as a whole or even of large public research universities; what is significant about these institutions is that they recorded their decision-making processes and tracked the effects those restrictions had on degree production and class sizes.

In the Purdue report, the authors state that computer science "growth was nationwide":

> This crisis should be placed in the context of the national situation. Enrollments were ballooning wherever they were not strictly limited.

Both Purdue and the University of Maryland instituted restrictions on the number of computer science majors in the mid-1980s. The changes in the number of majors over time at Purdue and Maryland are shown in the bar graphs in Figure 2.1.1, which come directly from the histories recorded by these institutions.

Although a complete understanding of these graphs requires knowing more details about the specific situation faced by each institution, the decrease in the

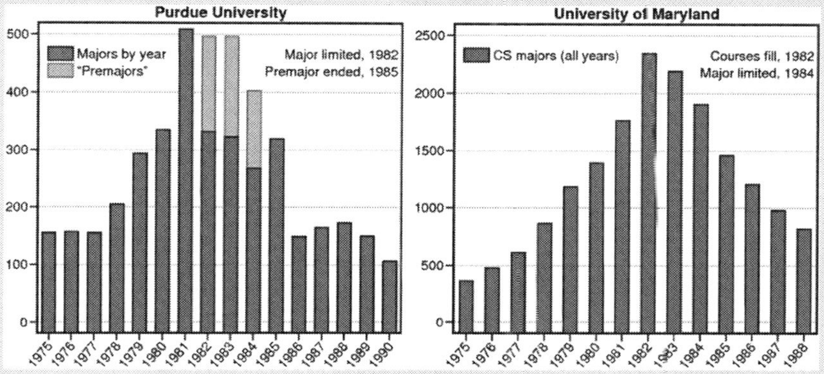

FIGURE 2.1.1 Number of CS majors before and after enrollment limitations at two universities in the 1980s. SOURCE: Adapted from Rice, J.R., and S. Rosen. 1990. History of the Computer Sciences Department at Purdue University. Purdue University Computer Science Technical Reports, Report Number 90-1003; Zelkowitz, M.V. 2007. Maturation of Computer Science Research and Education at the University of Maryland. University of Maryland Computer Science Department and Institute for Advanced Study of Computer Science. Technical Report CS-TR-4882 and UMIACS-TR-2007-40, September 2007.

number of majors is similar to those of CS bachelor's degree production nationwide. The number of undergraduate majors rose in the early 1980s and reached a peak around 1982, reflected in the degree-production numbers after a 2-year lag. The numbers continued to decline for several years, just as they did in the nation as a whole.

The pattern of degree production at Purdue and Maryland illustrates that explicit steps taken at each institution to limit enrollment directly precede the decline in student numbers. At Purdue, student interest remained high throughout the period covered by the graph, as evidenced by the fact that students tried to circumvent the restrictions by switching to the pre-major category until the university closed that path.

More broadly it was commonly believed among members of the computer science education community that the 1980s decline in degree production was caused not by a decline in student interest but by the inability of academic institutions to respond quickly to the increase in demand. Many believe that students at that time did not decide against majoring in computer science, but that they were instead prevented or discouraged from doing so by institutions that needed to manage an otherwise impossible load.

continued

BOX 2.1 Continued

The problem of insufficient teaching capacity was documented in multiple reports that appeared in the early 1980s, both from professional societies and from governmental agencies. In October 1980 the Department of Education and the National Science Foundation released a report titled "Science and Engineering Education for the 1980s and Beyond," which highlighted the faculty shortfall throughout engineering and computing fields, exacerbated by ramped up industry hiring to expand their R&D activities:

> There are, today, severe shortages of qualified faculty members in most fields of engineering, as well as in the computer professions. Industries have expanded their research and development efforts and have increased the rate at which new, sophisticated products are introduced. To effect this, they are luring faculty members away from the universities into challenging well-paid positions. At the same time, they are making such attractive job offers to bachelor's degree recipients that many who would once have gone to graduate school now opt for positions in industry. The net effect has been a reduction in the ability of universities to provide education in engineering and the computer professions, although undergraduate demand for these areas is more intense than ever. Unless the problem of faculty erosion is alleviated, it is possible that many engineering schools and departments that educate computer professionals may have to reduce their enrollments during this decade, thereby reducing the numbers of trained people in these fields that the Nation's future requires.

In the end universities in the 1980s were unable to expand their teaching capacity and were forced, as predicted, to reduce their enrollments.

SOURCE: Adapted in part from Roberts, E. 2016. A History of Capacity Challenges in Computer Science. Online. Available at http://cs.stanford.edu/people/eroberts/CSCapacity.pdf.

---

[a] Rice, J.R. and S. Rosen. 1990. History of the Computer Sciences Department at Purdue University. Purdue University Computer Science Technical Reports Report Number 90-1003.

[b] Zelkowitz, M.V. 2007. Maturation of Computer Science Research and Education at the University of Maryland. University of Maryland Computer Science Department and Institute for Advanced Study of Computer Science. Technical Report CS-TR-4882 and UMIACS-TR-2007-40, September 2007.

3

The Current Landscape of Computer Science Enrollments

INTRODUCTION

As discussed in the previous chapter, the number (both relative and absolute) of bachelor's degrees awarded in computing fields has been increasing significantly since 2008. However, data about computer science (CS) degree completions fails to tell the full story of current enrollment in computing majors and courses and the impact this demand is having on colleges and universities, their computing departments and programs, and their students.

For a deeper picture of the current undergraduate computing enrollment landscape, the committee turned to recent survey data, including the following:

1. The Computing Research Association's (CRA's) Taulbee and non-doctoral-granting departments in computing (NDC) survey results on recent enrollments in computing major programs at a sampling of computing Ph.D.-granting universities and non-doctoral colleges, respectively;
2. The Freshman Survey of the Cooperative Institutional Research Program (CIRP), provided by the Higher Education Research Institute (HERI);
3. The CRA Enrollment Survey results on recent enrollments in computing courses for subsets of Ph.D.-granting universities and non-doctoral colleges, respectively;
4. Aggregated student academic data from institutions participating in the Consortium for Undergraduate STEM Success (CUSTEMS), from an Academies-commissioned paper.

5. Recent undergraduate CS major enrollment trends within engineering schools, from a report of the American Society for Engineering Education.[1]

While the corresponding data do not provide a comprehensive record for all U.S. institutions, and in general are sampled from quite different universes of U.S. institutions of higher education, they represent the best data available to the committee at present for understanding the contemporary CS enrollment environment. National data on U.S. undergraduate enrollments would enable a more comprehensive analysis and a better understanding of U.S. undergraduate enrollment trends in CS and in general. However, such data are not available at a national level.

Nonetheless, the committee believes that the characterizations in these data are reasonably accurate, and can be taken as indicative of trends at the type of institution sampled.

This chapter explores recent trends in enrollment in the CS major, interest and participation of non-CS majors in computing courses, the impact of course enrollment by non-majors on CS departments, and the changing needs of non-CS majors with respect to computing education and skills. It then discusses the current landscape of hiring of new CS faculty and the responses that institutions have considered or begun taking in response to increasing enrollments.

BACHELOR'S DEGREE ENROLLMENT IN COMPUTER SCIENCE

The data presented in the previous chapter clearly illustrate the recent boom in CS degree production through 2015, but do not provide insight into the number of majors currently in the pipeline. The CRA and CIRP survey data help to shed light on these trends. It is worth noting throughout these discussions that different institutions may have slightly different definitions of CS and somewhat different major enrollment requirements, and may require students to select majors at different points in their undergraduate career.

Recent Computer Science Major Enrollment

The CRA Taulbee Survey is administered annually to all North American Ph.D.-granting institutions that belong to the CRA, incorporated in 1990. This survey collects computing units' (e.g., a CS department or a college of computing) self-reported bachelor's, master's, and Ph.D. degree trends. This annual survey has been a principal source of information about the enrollment, production, and employment of Ph.D.s in computing since it was first administered in 1974 by Professor Oren Taulbee at the University of Pittsburgh (CRA, 2015). An adaptation of this survey has also been sent to non-CS-Ph.D.-granting 4-year

[1] See ASEE (2015).

institutions' departments in computing (known as NDCs) since 2012 via the Association for Computing Machinery (ACM), as a supplement to the Taulbee Survey. According to these results, the average number of students majoring in computer science (freshmen through seniors) at Taulbee institutions more than tripled between 2006 (192.4 per unit) and 2015 (721.4 per department), as illustrated in Figure 3.1. Since 2013, the average number of majors has significantly exceeded that experienced at the dot-com peak in 2001 (398.1 per unit); in 2016, the number of majors was nearly double that experienced at the dot-com peak. In fact, 82 percent of the 119 institutions that responded to the CRA Taulbee Survey in both 2009 and 2014 experienced an increase of 50 percent or more in the number of CS majors between 2009 and 2014 during this time frame; 63 percent of responding institutions grew by 100 percent or more. The survey data also reveal that the number of computer science majors has been increasing at similar rates between 2006 and 2015 at both "large" (from 341 to 970 majors) and "small" (from 158 to 499 majors) Taulbee institutions (institutions that grant Ph.D.s in computing and have greater or fewer than 25 tenure-track faculty in computer science, respectively) (CRA, 2017a).

A recent report from the American Society for Engineering Education also provides time series data on CS major enrollments for those CS programs housed

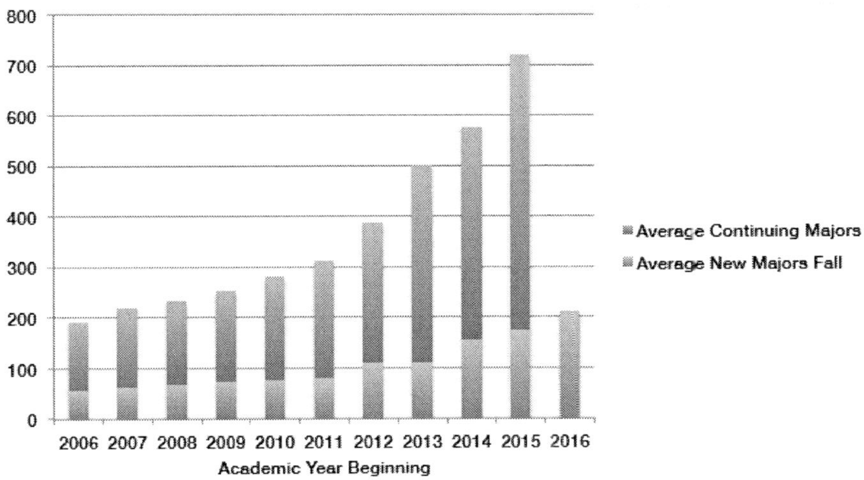

FIGURE 3.1 Average number of declared CS majors (freshman through seniors) per unit at U.S. Taulbee (computing Ph.D.-granting) institutions since 2006. Blue bars correspond to the fraction due to newly declared majors through the fall semester of 2016. SOURCE: CRA (Computing Research Association). 2015. The Taulbee Survey. Online. Available at http://cra.org/resources/taulbee-survey/.

within engineering units, reporting growth of 136 percent among full-time CS majors and 128 percent among part-time CS majors between 2006 and 2015.[2]

Freshman Interest in Majoring in Computer Science

Another indicator of student demand for CS is student interest in majoring in computer science. The Freshman Survey of the Cooperative Institutional Research Program (CIRP, currently administered by the Higher Education Research Institute, or HERI) has polled the intended majors (among other data) of freshmen at a national sampling[3] of institutions of higher education since 1975. This survey is administered to freshmen "during registration, freshman orientation, or the first few weeks of classes"; the results for fall 2016 reflect the responses of 137,456 students at 184 colleges and universities, weighted to reflect profiles of all new full-time students at 4-year colleges and universities nationwide (Eagan et al., 2016). Their results on the fraction of students intending to major in CS over time are plotted in Figure 3.2.

The results of this survey of student intent to major in CS display peaks and valleys quite similar to those seen in the Integrated Postsecondary Education Data System (IPEDS) degree completions data, but with peaks offset by 3 to 5 years, roughly the delay expected to correspond to completion of a bachelor's degree, suggesting that, qualitatively, the HERI data have been a good leading indicator of CS degrees in the pipeline overall. Given that interest in CS as a major has increased steeply from 2011 to 2015, the data suggest that in 2015 CS degree production as a fraction of all degrees had just begun to increase sharply, and will continue to increase through at least the spring of 2020 in the absence of any unforeseen disruption or widespread actions taken by institutions to limit the number of majors.

HYBRID MODELS OF COMPUTER SCIENCE MAJORS

While the preceding section provides evidence that enrollments in some CS degree programs is surging, other types of degrees with significant computational components are simultaneously emerging. In particular, much interest has been generated in pilot programs offering joint degrees (1) where the degree is based in some discipline X with a significant educational component in CS (referred to as X+CS); (2) where the degree is thought to be equally shared among two disciplines, one being CS; or (3) where the degree is based in CS but has significant substance and coursework based in some other discipline (referred to as CS+X). In this report, for simplicity, any such program will be referred to as X+CS. Box 3.1 highlights a case study of such a program.

[2] See ASEE (2015).

[3] This universe differs from that of the CRA Taulbee Survey. For more information on HERI's sampling methodology, see Eagan et al. (2016).

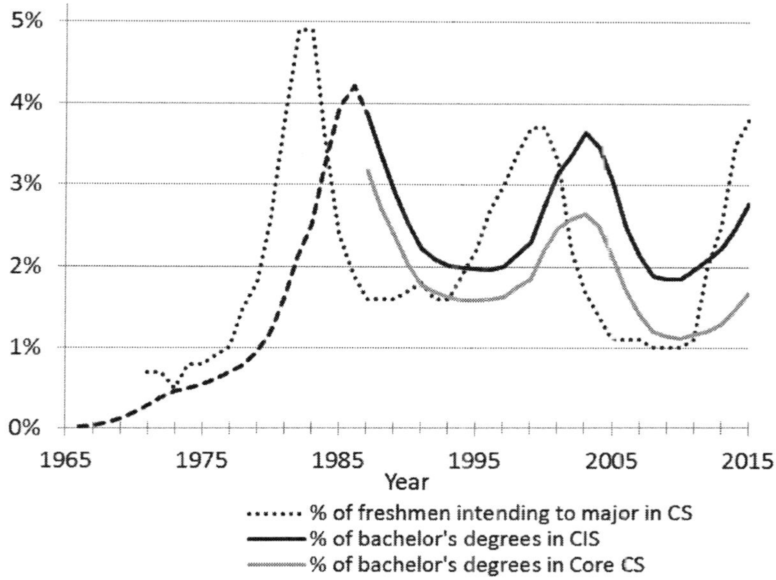

FIGURE 3.2 Share of undergraduates participating in CS bachelor's degree programs at the beginning and end of the undergraduate career. The dotted line indicates the fraction of freshmen at U.S. not-for-profit institutions intending to major in CS from 1971 to 2015, according to the HERI CIRP survey results. The fraction of bachelor's degree recipients from 1966 to 2015 whose degrees were in computer and information science and support services (CIS) and core CS, according to the IPEDS NCES completions data, is included for all institutions prior to 1987 (dashed line), and not-for-profit institutions from 1987 to 2015 (solid line). SOURCE: Data from IPEDS completions survey accessed via the WebCASPAR online database (see Appendix F for details) and HERI CIRP Freshman Survey.

BOX 3.1
UIUC: A Case Study of a Hybrid Program

The University of Illinois, Urbana-Champaign, is one institution offering an X+CS program. In 2014 the institution began accepting admissions for their new X+CS degree program in four fields: anthropology, astronomy, chemistry, and linguistics. Two years later, 11 percent of anthropology, 25 percent of astronomy, and 28 percent of linguistics students had entered into the X+CS version of these three programs. Furthermore, there is significant interest from other disciplines on UIUC's campus in modifying their curriculum to add significant computing education, such as advertising, music, philosophy, crop science, economics, art design, and English.

There is currently no apparent way to track such a hybrid major in the national IPEDS completion statistics; presumably, institutions must classify them as either degrees in X or degrees in CS, or as dual majors. Computer science and X+CS majors are only part of the story of growth in undergraduate computing enrollments—that is, computing departments have both a thriving major and a thriving service component.

NON-MAJORS

The needs of undergraduate students with respect to computing vary widely. It can be useful to think about all students' relationships to computing as being on a spectrum. At one end of the spectrum are those with an overall goal of deep study of computing theory and methods, rather than their specific application in any particular domain. At the other end of the spectrum are students for whom only general knowledge of computing, necessary for non-expert use of general-purpose computing tools, is required or expected. In the middle is a group that requires some level of in-depth knowledge and understanding of the particular aspects of computing that apply to their primary domain.

Each group has the potential to affect enrollment in and demand for courses in different ways. Because the distribution of students along this spectrum at any given institution is likely unique, both the demand for computing and potential strategies for meeting this demand are likely to affect departments in different ways and therefore should engender different responses from different institutions.

Students who are avoiding all computing courses except those required for their degree may have little impact past the introductory courses; by contrast those students pursuing majors with significant computational content (including minors in computing) will need depth and coherence in their course offerings that will put resource pressure on the units offering the courses. Between these extremes students interested in "some" computing courses will have an intermediate effect. In the subsequent sections course enrollment trends of both majors and non-majors are discussed.

COURSE ENROLLMENT

In the face of increasing CS bachelor's degree production and major enrollment, in 2016 the CRA sent out a supplemental Enrollment Survey to "units" (programs, departments, divisions, schools, and colleges) in the Taulbee (CS Ph.D.-granting) and NDC (CS master's and/or bachelor's degree-granting) groups responsible for serving bachelor's-level majors in computer science. This survey collected supplemental information about undergraduate major enrollments and course enrollments. The results were recently published by CRA in a report titled "Generation CS" (CRA, 2017a).

The CRA Enrollment Survey asked responders for the numbers of students (distinguished by majors and non-majors) in four categories of courses representing different points in computer science education: (1) an introductory course for non-majors, (2) an introductory course for majors, (3) a mid-level course, and (4) an upper-level course.[4] Results were obtained for three years: 2005, 2010, and 2015.[5] Overall, 134 of 190 doctoral-granting institutions surveyed responded, 45 of which reported course enrollment numbers (~24 percent response rate); 93 of the 715 non-doctoral institutions surveyed responded, 20 of which provided course enrollment numbers (~2.8 percent response rate). These are the best quantitative data available; nonetheless, they are not comprehensive, and, because responses were voluntary, they may reflect self-selection bias, and so should be in general interpreted with caution. Furthermore, given the data analyzed are from 2015, it is likely that current enrollment trends and institutional actions taken have evolved in the time that has since elapsed.

Figure 3.3 shows aggregate enrollments, separated by majors and non-majors, for these four course types for the Taulbee and NDC institutions that provided responses for all three years. The impact of non-majors is significant at these institutions: numbers of non-majors are taking courses beyond the introductory level. The data also show that the number of non-majors in courses intended for majors is increasing at a rate equal to or higher than that for majors. Between 2010 and 2015, introductory CS course enrollment increased by an average of 158 percent for majors and 169 percent for non-majors; enrollment in the mid-level course increased by 148 percent for majors and 248 percent for non-majors; and enrollment in the upper-level course increased by 135 percent for majors and 144 percent for non-majors. These data are broken down further in the following sections.

Course Enrollment by Majors at Doctoral and Non-Doctoral Institutions

Course enrollment of CS majors for 2005, 2010, and 2015 at doctoral and non-doctoral institutions responding to the CRA Enrollments Survey is illustrated in Figures 3.4 and 3.5. On average, course enrollments by majors have grown for all course levels for both categories of institution, with the largest growth experienced between 2010 and 2015.

---

[4] Note that not all institutions reported a distinction between introductory courses for majors and non-majors.

[5] The CRA Enrollment Survey surveyed only computer science units, rather than computer engineering or information science. "Non-majors" here refers to students not currently enrolled in computer science degree programs (though it is possible that they may later choose to do so, and become majors).

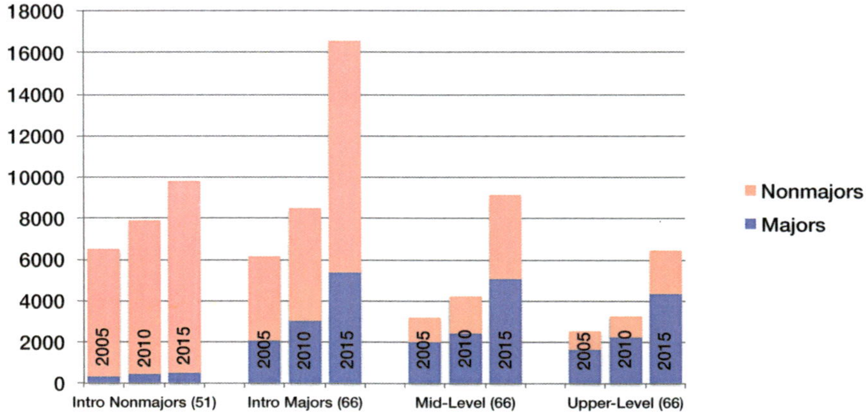

FIGURE 3.3 Non-major enrollment (red) and major enrollment (blue) in computing courses in 2005, 2010, and 2015 at doctoral- and non-doctoral-granting units responding to the CRA Enrollment Survey. The number in parentheses in each category indicates sample size. SOURCE: CRA (Computing Research Association). 2017a. Generation CS: Computer Science Undergraduate Enrollments Surge Since 2006. Online. Available at http://cra.org/data/Generation-CS/.

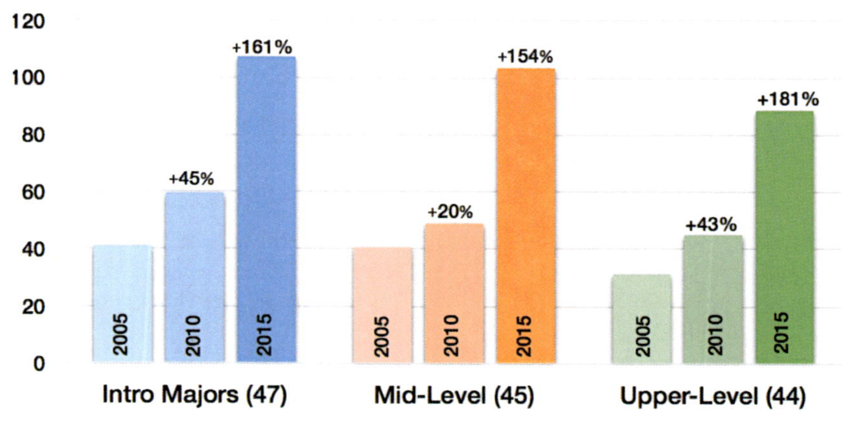

FIGURE 3.4 Average enrollment by CS majors in three representative computing courses at a subset of doctoral-granting units from 2005 to 2015. The number in parentheses in each category indicates the number of institutions responding. The percent increase relative to 2005 appears above bars for 2010 and 2015 for each category. SOURCE: CRA (Computing Research Association). 2017a. Generation CS: Computer Science Undergraduate Enrollments Surge Since 2006. Online. Available at http://cra.org/data/Generation-CS/.

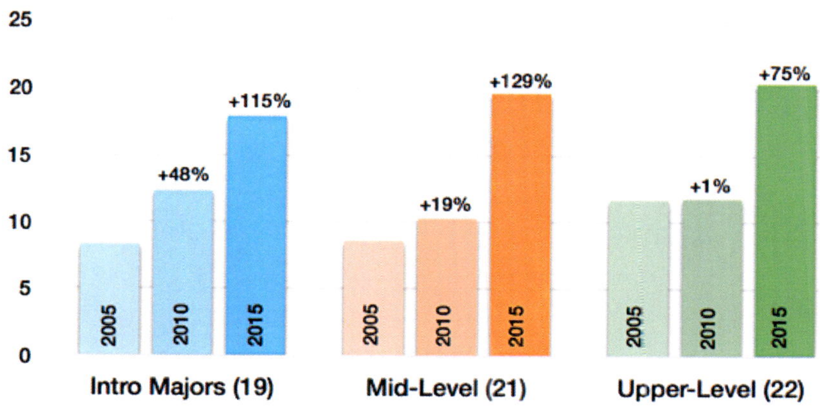

FIGURE 3.5 Average enrollment by CS majors in computing courses at a subset of non-doctoral-granting units from 2005 to 2015. The number in parentheses in each category indicates the number of institutions responding. The percent increase relative to 2005 appears above bars for 2010 and 2015 for each category. SOURCE: CRA (Computing Research Association). 2017a. Generation CS: Computer Science Undergraduate Enrollments Surge Since 2006. Online. Available at http://cra.org/data/Generation-CS/.

Course Enrollments by Non-Majors at Doctoral and Non-Doctoral Institutions

Responding doctoral institutions reported similar growth among non-majors at all course levels. The mean enrollment by non-majors in representative introductory classes not required for the major increased by an average of 55 percent from 2005 to 2015 (among the 38 respondents who reported a distinct course). Enrollment by non-majors in introductory classes required for the major increased by an average of 184 percent (among the 47 respondents). Mean enrollment by non-majors in mid-level courses grew by 265 percent (45 respondents), and the mean enrollment of non-majors in upper-level courses grew by 146 percent (44 respondents) as illustrated in Figures 3.6 and 3.7.

The NDC institutions also reported mean enrollment growth by non-majors in courses at all levels from 2005 to 2015, though not to the extent observed at doctoral-granting institutions: 25 percent increase in introductory courses not required by the major (13 respondents); 92 percent increase in introductory courses required by the major (19 respondents); 133 percent increase in mid-level courses (21 respondents); and 102 percent increase in upper-level courses (22 respondents). However, there is anecdotal evidence that the lack of resources is constraining growth at some non-doctoral institutions, and that interest in enrollment is actually higher than can be accommodated.

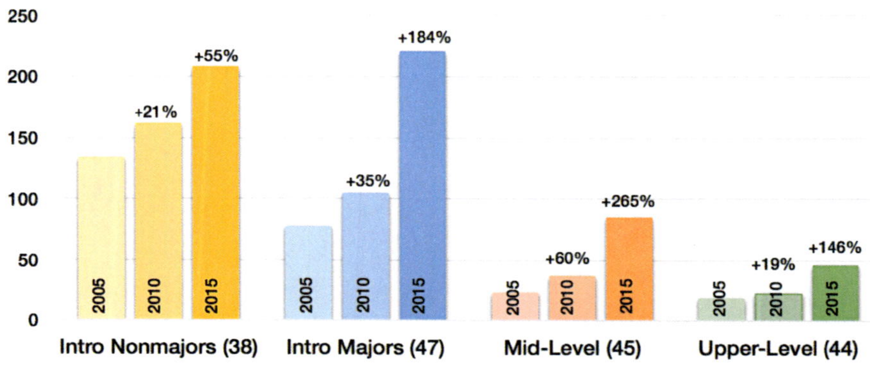

FIGURE 3.6 Growth in the number of non-majors per course at responding doctoral institutions from 2005 to 2015. Numbers in parentheses in each category indicate the number of institutions responding. SOURCE: CRA (Computing Research Association). 2017a. Generation CS: Computer Science Undergraduate Enrollments Surge Since 2006. Online. Available at http://cra.org/data/Generation-CS/.

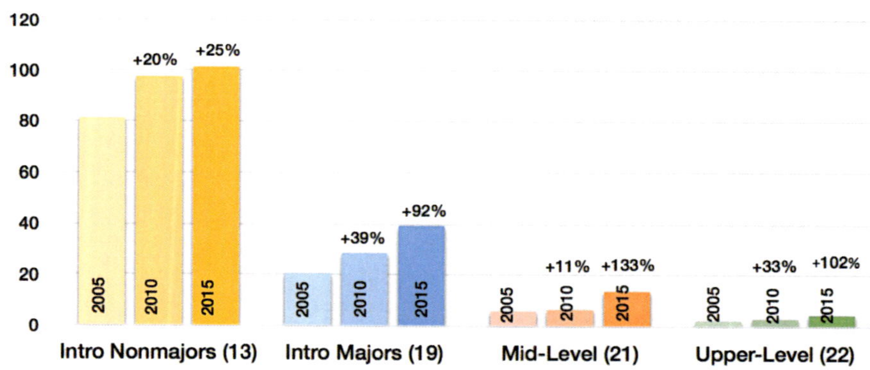

FIGURE 3.7 Non-major growth in computing courses at a subset of non-doctoral institutions from 2005 to 2015. Numbers in parentheses in each category indicate sample size. SOURCE: CRA (Computing Research Association). 2017a. Generation CS: Computer Science Undergraduate Enrollments Surge Since 2006. Online. Available at http://cra.org/data/Generation-CS/.

For example, at Union College, 207 students expressed interest in taking an introduction to programming course for the winter 2017 term, but only 80 seats were available; thus, 127 students were turned away. In winter 2013 (four years earlier), all 80 seats were also filled, but only 47 students were turned away. Furthermore, if Union College favors majors in filling courses, as most institutions do, the enrollment of non-majors would underestimate the demand for these courses among non-majors. Union College, which is an example of a small liberal arts college, has a "small class, high touch" pedagogy; thus, once capacity is reached, which occurred in 2013-2014, demand cannot be met unless faculty are hired and more sections are added.[6] At large doctoral institutions with different pedagogies, on the other hand, computing departments can often meet increased demand by either (1) booking larger rooms to create larger sections or (2) adding more sections and hiring graduate students to teach them.

While these data suggest an "upward trend in the number of non-majors in mid-level and upper-level courses at non-doctoral institutions" (CRA, 2017a), it is important to note again the poor survey response rates, especially for the non-doctoral institutions (approximately 2.8 percent of all surveyed non-doctoral institutions provided course enrollments data, compared to approximately 24 percent for the doctoral institutions). In other words, the data in Figure 3.7 should be interpreted with particular caution.

Enrollments Across Other Institutions

Computing Alliance of Hispanic-Serving Institutions (CAHSI)

Additional evidence of recent program growth is available from the Computing Alliance of Hispanic-Serving Institutions (CAHSI) (Gates et al., 2011, 2016), a coalition of 19 Hispanic-serving not-for-profit institutions that aims "to increase the number of Hispanic students who pursue and complete" degrees in the computing disciplines (CAHSI, 2017a). In spring 2016 CAHSI evaluators convened a focus group with CAHSI leads of the charter institutions to collect data on the challenges and opportunities faced by CAHSI departments in a time of high enrollment growth in computer science departments nationally (Thiry and Hug, 2016a).

Of CAHSI's eight "charter members,"[7] five departments reported CS growth rates among majors ranging from 10 to 25 percent per year from 2013 to 2016, and two departments have experienced more modest increases.

---

[6] Private communication with Valerie Barr.

[7] CAHSI charter members include California State University, Dominguez Hills; Florida International University; New Mexico State University; Texas A&M University; University of Houston, Downtown; University of Puerto Rico, Mayaguez; University of Texas, El Paso, and Northeastern Illinois University. The first seven institutions are the founding CAHSI institutions. CAHSI today includes additional associate and adopting members.

CAHSI departments generally experienced enrollment trends similar to those seen nationwide—years of decline in degree production and enrollments followed by increases in recent years. However, the increase in degree production did not start until about 2013, compared to 2010 for institutions on average (as discussed in Chapter 2), suggesting either that growth at these institutions lags that of those with very high or high research activity, or that the growth is simply not concentrated at these institutions.

The number of students enrolling in CS and CE B.S. degree programs at the seven "founding"[8] CAHSI departments from 2011 to 2016 is illustrated in Figure 3.8, including five CS departments and two computer engineering (CE) departments.

The focus group discussed increases in enrollment in courses and programs, with CAHSI leads attributing recent growth to an increase in CS/CE majors, an increase in students seeking minors in CS/CE, including both science, technology, engineering, and mathematics (STEM) and non-STEM majors, and an increase in the number of post-baccalaureates seeking to improve marketability through continuing studies at the undergraduate level. Some CAHSI institutions also reported an overflow of students from nearby universities that have enrollment caps.

They noted that departments have struggled with insufficient introductory courses/sections to meet demand and have had to increase the capacity of courses, or hire lecturers to cover courses. Almost all CAHSI departments did not have enough faculty to teach key courses, and they were unable to secure new faculty lines in their departments, jeopardizing their ability to manage enrollment growth. In addition, faculty noted that they are less able to advise and mentor graduate students. Faculty also have less time to develop curricula and carry out other essential duties, as noted by half of the focus group participants. Funding to support the additional teaching assistants (TAs) needed to provide student support was another stress point identified.

CAHSI department chairs report that institutional budget cycles and decision making also move too slowly to adapt to rapidly increasing enrollments, creating a weak link between departmental enrollments and actual resources allocated to those departments (Thiry and Hug, 2016a). Administrators and others with financial authority may also be doubtful that increasing enrollments will be sustained, making them less likely to grant extra resources to single departments.

CAHSI departments have implemented multiple strategies to address the challenges inherent in increased undergraduate enrollment, similar to those taken at other institutions (Thiry and Hug, 2016a). Some departments have added undergraduate TAs in addition to the typical graduate student TAs. Others have added more graduate teaching assistants or redirected TAs from upper-division to lower-division courses.

[8] Data are available for all years only at the founding institutions, which include seven of the eight charter members.

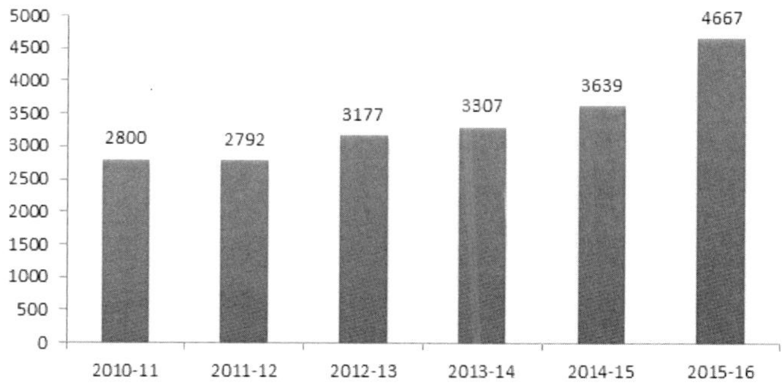

FIGURE 3.8 Total B.S. enrollments in CS and CE degree programs for the CAHSI founding departments, 2011-2016. SOURCE: CAHSI (Computing Alliance of Hispanic-Serving Institutions). 2016. Preview of Award 1042341—Annual Project Report. Online. Available at http://cahsi.cs.utep.edu/about?quicktabs_about=5#quicktabs-about.

With increasing enrollments CAHSI primary investigators reported that some students are entering the major with less preparation and prior experience in computing and advanced mathematics than students in previous cohorts. Departments have used multiple strategies to address student persistence and retention issues, especially related to students' prior academic preparation. Several departments have changed their placement or advising practices. For instance, New Mexico State University has begun to use a placement exam to determine the most appropriate introductory course in which to place students. Some institutions, such as the University of Texas, El Paso, and California State University, Dominguez Hills, are using institutional data to examine student pathways through the major and to identify trouble spots that require interventions. Retention has always been an important focus of CAHSI departments, but increasing enrollments have placed more pressure on departments to meet the needs of students with even more varied academic backgrounds than in the past.

CUSTEMS Institutions

Another view of course enrollments is provided by the Consortium for Undergraduate STEM Success (CUSTEMS), a growing coalition of institutions for which course enrollment data have been collected on a voluntary basis beginning in 2008 in order to track retention of women and underrepresented minorities in STEM degree programs (CUSTEMS, 2017). The CUSTEMS data set includes course enrollment, grades, and admissions records for students at participating institutions. Upon commission from the committee, the CUSTEMS team provided information about enrollment in CS courses at eight historically black colleges and universities (HBCUs), five liberal arts colleges (LACs), and one large public research university—all of the institutions for which the team had student-level data for the years of 2009 through 2014. The identities of the institutions remain confidential for privacy protection.[9]

CS course enrollment data for 2009-2014 at CUSTEMS institutions is presented in aggregate for all institutions in each category. While these plots provide a cumulative rather than time series examination of the enrollment of non-majors in CS courses, and consider only a small set of institutions, they do provide an average picture of the interest in computing classes from non-majors for a 4-year window during the recent growth in CS course enrollments.

Figure 3.9 shows the total number of majors and non-majors enrolled in introductory, intermediate, and advanced CS courses for each category of institution. At the LACs in this sample the majority of non-majors are STEM non-majors (68.7 percent for introductory, 86.3 percent for intermediate, 93.7 percent for advanced CS); the same is true for the public university (68.4 percent for introductory, 93.4 percent for intermediate, 93.2 percent for advanced). At the HBCUs the percentage of STEM non-majors appears to be lower (35.6 percent for introductory, 69.9 percent for intermediate, 46.9 percent for advanced); however, this may be due to the fact that some of the HBCUs have a "tech" major that may not be counted within STEM. The percentages of non-majors (both STEM and non-STEM non-majors) in the three representative courses for the different groups of institutions are illustrated in Figure 3.10.

Minors

One important category of non-majors is minors. While the committee did not find quantitative data that illustrate current enrollment trends for computing minors, it is aware of several institutions where the number of minors has increased substantially in the recent past. For example, the number of computer science minors has more than tripled at the Colorado School of Mines in six short years (from 10 in 2011 to 37 in 2017). In addition, in the CRA Enrollment Survey, only 22 percent of the respondents stated that the number of minors at their institution has not changed in recent years and no one stated that the number of minors has decreased; the remaining 78 percent stated that the number of minors at their institution has increased (50 percent of respondents) or increased substantially (28 percent of respondents) (CRA, 2017a).

The increase in number of minors has an impact on institutions that goes beyond course enrollments; once a student becomes a minor, faculty and staff have responsibilities for that student in terms of advising and ensuring that courses are available. In the CRA Enrollment Survey, 76 percent of institutions that stated the number of minors has increased also stated that the enrollment

[9] See paper appended (Appendix E).

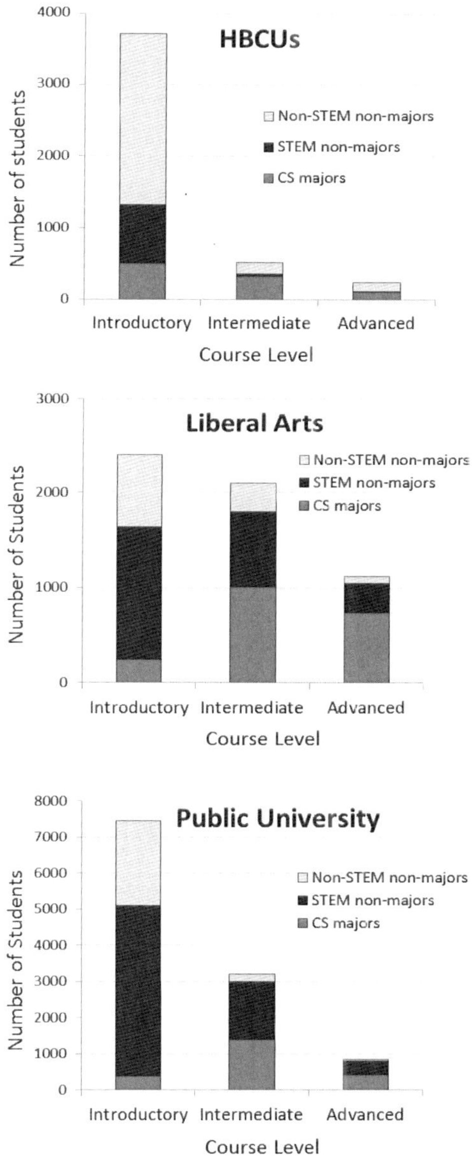

FIGURE 3.9 Aggregate enrollment in introductory, intermediate, and advanced computing courses by course level during the period 2009-2014 for eight historically black colleges and universities (top panel), five liberal arts colleges (middle panel), and one large public university (bottom panel), broken down by CS majors, STEM majors not majoring in CS (STEM non-majors), and students majoring in neither CS nor a STEM field (non-STEM non-majors). SOURCE: Data provided by CUSTEMS.

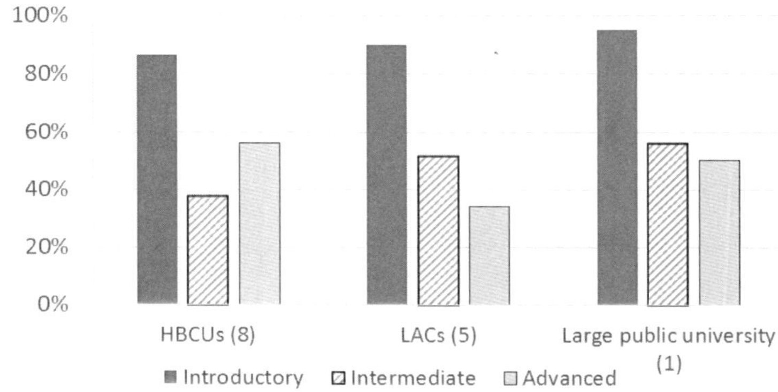

FIGURE 3.10 Percent of non-majors (STEM and non-STEM) in three levels of courses at small samples of different institution types, taken from aggregate (by institution type, averaged between 2009 and 2014) data. HBCUs are historically black colleges and universities; LACs are liberal arts colleges. SOURCE: Data provided by CUSTEMS.

growth is having a big impact on their unit, as did 96 percent of institutions that stated the number of minors has increased significantly (CRA, 2017a).

> **FINDING 2:** Enrollments in CS courses and the number of CS majors have risen markedly since 2005 at many institutions, and there is no indication that enrollments will fall in the near term. Both CS majors and non-majors have contributed significantly to the recent growth in enrollment in undergraduate CS courses. Information about current program enrollment trends suggests that the boom in enrollments has only begun to register in the national data on CS degree production, and that CS bachelor's degree completions will rise sharply for at least the next few years in the absence of institutional actions to limit or discourage participation in the major.

It is clear that enrollments in several computer science courses include a large increase in the number of non-majors taking computing courses. As previously noted these increases are occurring not just at the introductory course level but also at the mid and upper levels. The increased number of non-majors taking computer science courses is not fully explained by an increase in the number of minors. In fact, it turns out that many non-majors are required to take at least one introductory computer science course.

Students from different majors have taken introductory computing courses for some time, because programming is a skill that is increasingly required in many disciplines and sectors of the economy. In fact, as of 2016, programming jobs overall were growing 12 percent faster than the market average (Dishman, 2016), and some companies—for example, GE—have indicated that all new employees will be required to know how to program. Accordingly, some non-computing disciplines now require an introductory programming course, creating a pipeline of non-majors into introductory computing courses.

As part of the CRA Enrollments Survey, a questionnaire was administered to students in representative CS courses at some subset of the Taulbee and NDC institutions to get a better sense of their motivation for enrolling in the course. Of 9,721 students responding to the survey in total, 2,563 were in an introductory course; 405 of these were non-majors. In response to the question "Why did you enroll in an introductory CS course?" 65 percent responded that "it was required for my major/minor"; 54 percent that it was out of "curiosity/interest in computers"; 13 percent that "a teacher/mentor encouraged me"; and 6 percent that "my parents encouraged me." The fraction of students who are neither CS majors nor CS minors who stated that an introductory CS course was required for their major is broken down by discipline in Figure 3.11 for 353 respondents.

To respond to the demand from non-majors, many institutions offer introductory computing courses specifically targeting non-majors, and the interest in these courses is increasing (as illustrated in Figure 3.3, earlier). In such a course, no programming experience is expected. In addition, some institutions (e.g., Harvey Mudd College and Colorado School of Mines) have worked to create a supportive environment for students with no prior coding experience by splitting their introductory programming course into two types of sections: those with prior

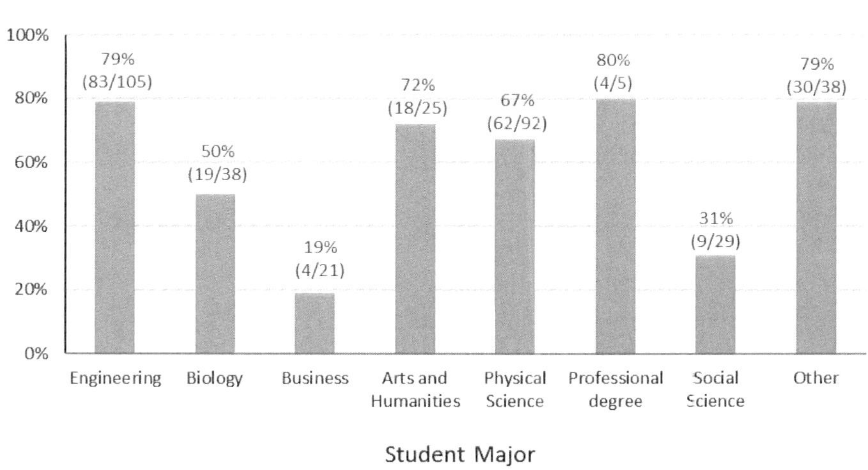

FIGURE 3.11 Percentage of students responding to CRA Student Enrollments Survey in an introductory computing course who stated that the course was required for their degree program, by major. Number responding in the affirmative out of total number indicated in parentheses. SOURCE: Adapted from Camp, T. 2017. Booming Enrollments: Understanding the Surge. Presentation for Computing Research Association Conference at Snowbird. Snowbird, UT. July 17-19.

programming experience and those without. Their efforts aimed to "reduce the intimidation factor" for those without programming experience, by eliminating a "common 'macho' effect, where a few more experienced students intimidate others because they seem to know so much more" (Klawe, 2016). Such programs are particularly important for improving diversity in computing, as students from underrepresented groups are less likely to have prior exposure to the field.

Underlying drivers of the recent increases in interest in computing, both from majors and non-majors, are explored further in Chapter 4.

CHALLENGES WITH FACULTY HIRING

While the number of CS majors has increased dramatically since 2006 and enrollment of non-majors in CS courses has soared, the rate of faculty hiring has grown at a much slower pace, even when departments had open positions and were looking to hire.

One measure of the demand for faculty is the number of ads for open faculty positions. Craig Wills from Worcester Polytechnic Institute has analyzed tenured and tenure-track job postings for CS faculty (excluding dedicated teaching faculty) every year since 2014.[10] His analyses use ads posted on CRA's and ACM's job listing sites, two frequently used and consulted sites for individuals seeking CS faculty positions, as well as mailing lists used frequently by 4-year colleges (e.g., the mailing list of ACM's Special Interest Group on Computer Science Education). His reports examine hiring plans at research, master's, and 4-year institutions and track the research areas departments seek to hire in. His November 2016 report analyzed job ads from 347 institutions seeking to fill hundreds of tenure-track faculty positions in computer science departments. Of these, 313 (90 percent) were from institutions in the United States. The number of positions open at an institution is not always clear from a job ad, as terms like "multiple" or "several" are often used. The study found that the number of open faculty positions in CS departments has increased significantly, and that many departments are looking for faculty in the same research area.

Relevant trends in the 2016 report include the following:

- Interpreting "multiple" as three faculty positions suggests that the 347 institutions posting ads planned to fill a total of 685 positions. Interpreting "multiple" as two faculty positions results in a total of 600 open faculty positions. Subtracting 10 percent of the positions to account for positions outside the United States suggests a conservative estimate of 540 open CS tenure-track faculty positions in 2016.

---

[10] See Performance Evaluation of Distributed Systems Research Group and Worcester Polytechnic Institute; see Wills (2016).

- The number of openings corresponds to a 35 percent increase from the previous year and a 71 percent 2-year increase in the number of open positions.
- About 70 percent of the institutions listed specific research areas. The most frequently mentioned areas in 2016 were information security (21 percent) and data science (15 percent).

CRA's Taulbee Survey collects data on student enrollment, degree production, employment of Ph.D. graduates, and faculty hiring (CRA, 2015). Figure 3.12 shows the relationship between CS majors and faculty growth since 2006 for the Ph.D.-granting institutions that responded to the 2016 Computing Research Association's annual Taulbee Survey. Since faculty hiring needs and student growth trends differ by institution type and other characteristics, the trend does not necessarily reflect the situation across a broader spectrum of institutions.[11]

Figure 3.12 shows that the rate of growth of CS majors exceeds the rate of faculty growth by a large margin. Between 2006 and 2015 the number of computer science majors at these universities has increased by 291 percent (from an average of 192.4 to 753 students), while the growth in tenure-line faculty at those same institutions has grown by just 22 percent (from an average of 23 faculty to 28). Some fraction of the increased teaching needs is filled by teaching faculty, the number of which has grown by 67 percent over that time (from an average of approximately 4 to 6 teaching faculty/instructors).

Institutions use various strategies for growing their faculty size. Institutions typically are reluctant to add new faculty lines quickly due to the possibility that increasing student numbers reflect a temporary phenomenon. In addition, universities, particularly public institutions facing reductions in state funding, may not have had the resources or the authority to hire over this period.[12] Furthermore, some institutions may be reluctant to allow rapid growth in one field, which often occurs at the expense of other academic disciplines.

CS is unique in that it produces a relatively small share of Ph.D.s compared to other disciplines, as illustrated in Figure 3.13.

CRA's Taulbee Survey collects data on the employment of new Ph.D.s and on actual hiring outcomes for Ph.D.-granting departments. According to the Taulbee Survey, during each of the last 3 years about 57 percent of new Ph.D.s accepted employment in industry.[13] It is worth noting that in 2003, 63 percent of all new Ph.D.s accepted employment as a tenure-track faculty member in academia and only 29 percent of all new Ph.D.s accepted employment in industry. Figure 3.14 shows the employment choices made according to the 2016 Taulbee Survey, which are similar to those reported in the preceding 3 years.

---

[11] Although the Association for Computing Machinery has undertaken a new survey of non-doctoral institutions, the response rate is not yet large enough to provide definitive results.

[12] See Leonhardt (2017).

[13] See Figure D6 in Zweben et al. (2017).

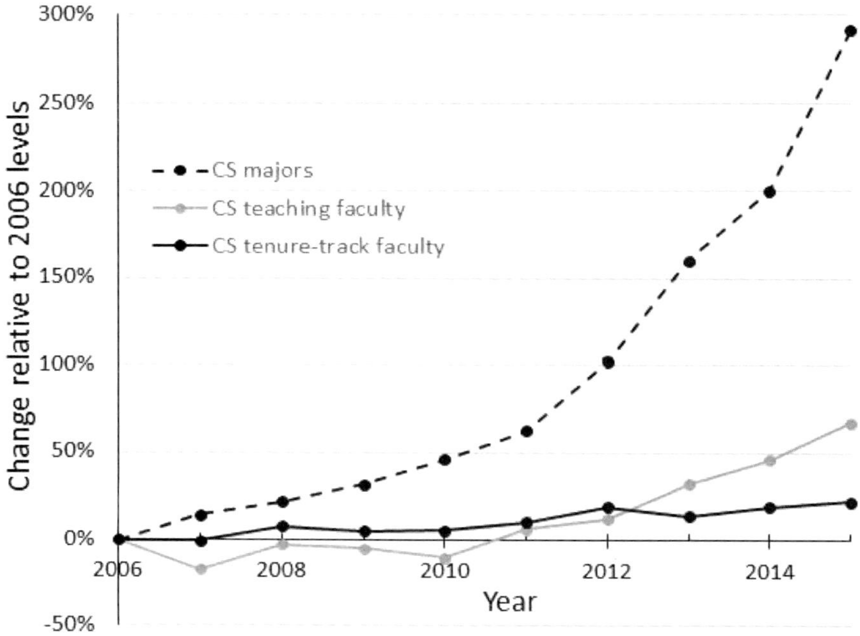

FIGURE 3.12 Change in the average number of CS majors, CS teaching faculty, and CS tenure-track faculty per department relative to 2006 levels, for institutions responding to the 2016 CRA Taulbee Survey. SOURCE: Adapted from Plot B.4 in CRA (Computing Research Association). 2017a. Generation CS: Computer Science Undergraduate Enrollments Surge Since 2006. Online. Available at http://cra.org/data/Generation-CS/.

The following extrapolates this distribution of job choice to all Ph.D.s awarded and relates it to the number of open faculty positions (using Craig Wills's analysis of job advertisements). According to IPEDs 1,903 CS Ph.D.s were awarded from U.S. not-for-profit institutions for 2015; 2,000 is a reasonable estimate for 2016, given the data from the 2016 Taulbee Survey. While some CS departments hire faculty with a Ph.D. in a related field (for example, computer engineering or information sciences) and some CS Ph.D.s take a faculty position in a non-CS department, it is expected that such cases are rare and infrequent compared to the total number of faculty hires.

Taulbee Survey data show that approximately 57 percent of all new Ph.D.s in North America take a position in industry, 11 percent take a tenure-track position (not including teaching positions), and 14 percent take a post-doctorate position (typically for 1 to 2 years). According to the Taulbee Survey, one-third of the new assistant professors hired at Ph.D.-granting institutions are hired immediately after receiving their Ph.D. An approximate estimate, based on the committee's experience, of the number of post-doctorates choosing to become faculty

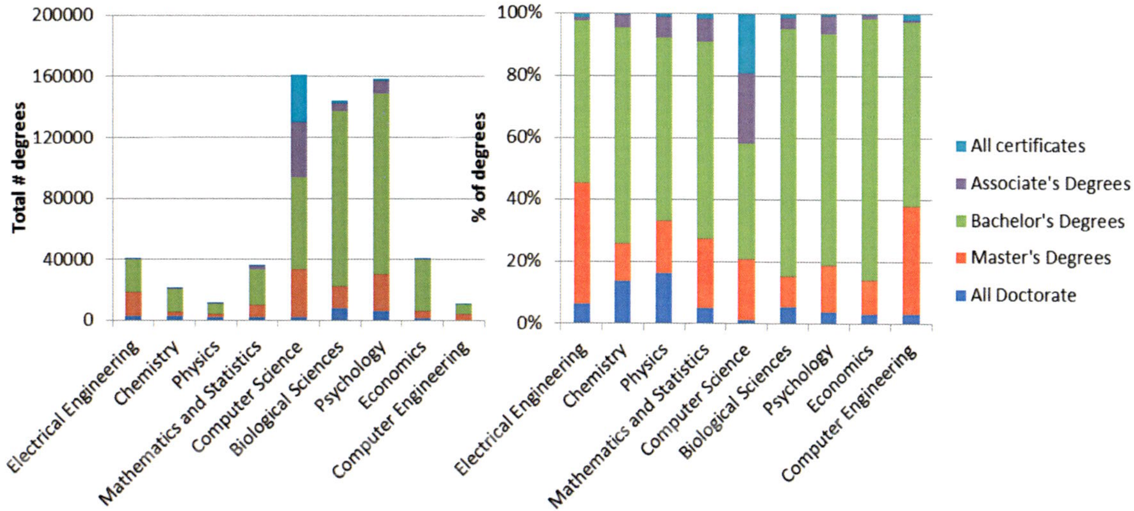

FIGURE 3.13 U.S. degree production for 2015 in several STEM fields, defined using the "detailed" Classification of Instructional Program (CIP) from IPEDS (here, "Computer Science" corresponds to the entire 11 series of CIPs). The left-hand panel displays total number of degrees for each field, broken down by level of degree. The right-hand panel displays the percentage of the total accounted for by each level of degree for each field. Includes degrees and certificates awarded at all institutions; excluding the for-profits does not have a major impact on the distribution of degree types for a given field. SOURCE: Data from IPEDS completions survey accessed via the WebCASPAR online database. See Appendix F for details.

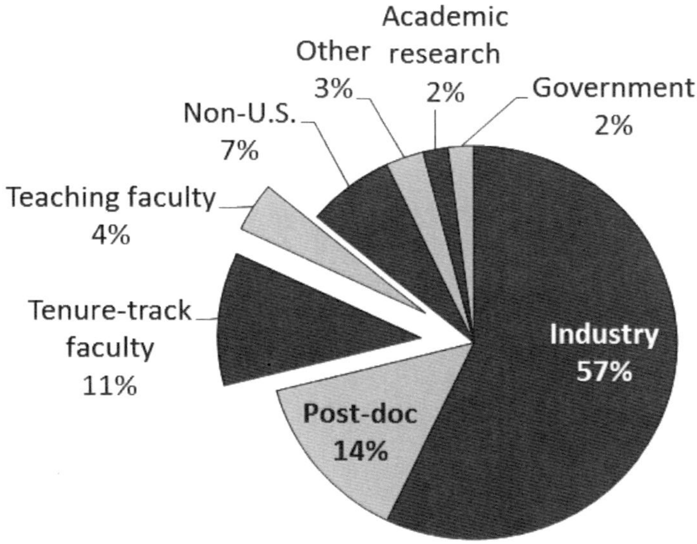

FIGURE 3.14 Employment distribution for 2016 CS Ph.D. graduates at Taulbee institutions. SOURCE: Data in chart obtained from Table D.4 of Zweben, S., and B. Bizot. 2017. 2016 Taulbee Survey, Generation CS Continues to Produce Record Undergrad Enrollment; Graduate Degree Production Rises at Both Master's and Doctoral Levels. *Computing Research News*. 29(5). Online. Available at http://cra.org/crn/wp-content/uploads/sites/7/2017/05/2016-Taulbee-Survey.pdf.

in any given year would be half the number of new Ph.D.s taking post-doctorate positions 2 years prior, corresponding to half of the Ph.D.s pursuing a post-doctorate position in 2014 accepting a tenure-track academic position in 2016.

Based on these percentages, we estimate that about 340 new Ph.D.s took an academic position in the United States in 2016: 11 percent of the about 2,000 new Ph.D.s in 2016 and 7 percent of the 1,884 Ph.D.s from 2014 who took a post-doctorate first.

Comparing this to the conservative estimate of 540 open computer science tenure-track positions in the United States suggests that only 63 percent of the open faculty positions could be filled from this pool. This estimation lacks common additional sources for faculty hires: individuals with a Ph.D. from outside the United States, individuals with a Ph.D. not in computer science, and individuals hired from industry or from another academic institution. At the same time, it ignores loss of CS faculty due to retirements, which are increasingly more common as the age distribution in CS departments gets closer to that of established departments.

The Taulbee Survey estimates that 4 percent of all new Ph.D.s take a teaching position (which corresponds to about 80 hires). Ph.D.-granting departments typically have separate ads for teaching positions also advertised on CRA and ACM job listing pages. As Wills's study does not analyze job ads for teaching faculty, a similar comparison cannot be done. The Taulbee Survey asks departments how many of the open positions were filled.

CS faculty hiring has become a significant challenge nationwide. The number of new CIS Ph.D.s has increased by 21 percent from 2009 (1,567 Ph.D.s) to 2015 (1,903 Ph.D.s), as illustrated in Figure 3.15, while CIS bachelor's degree production has increased by 74 percent.[14] During that time, the percentage of new Ph.D.s accepting jobs in industry has increased somewhat, from 45 to 57 percent according to the Taulbee Survey. Today, academia does not necessarily look attractive to new Ph.D.s: the funding situation is tight and uncertain; the funding expectation of a department may be perceived as unreasonably high; the class sizes are large and not every new hire is prepared to teach large classes and manage TAs effectively; and the balance between building a research program and meeting teaching obligations becomes more challenging. For the majority of new CS Ph.D.s the research environment in industry is currently more attractive. This also translates to challenges with hiring short-term or contract lecturers.

To navigate the difficult situation of increasing enrollments in the near term, departments will need resources other than faculty lines. They may include additional teaching positions, financial support that allows departments to scale classes and programs, and increased TA and staff support. New faculty hires are a valuable resource with a high replacement cost, and effective mentoring is crucial to their success; more emphasis on teaching and classroom management would help to make large classroom and teaching experiences positive.

As institutions assess the role of computer science and the interests and needs of students, the reality of CS faculty hiring challenges and the opportunities available to new CS Ph.D.s, especially in the areas departments want to hire in, are important to consider, as are the environment and workload for faculty in growing programs. Successful researchers may be hired away by institutions with more resources, but a supportive environment may help reduce the retention challenges departments face.

At the committee's public workshop in August 2016, Dr. Greg Morrisett, dean of computing and information sciences at Cornell University, described the faculty hiring situation at his institution as follows:

> We're bringing in money from research, but we're also teaching twice as many students as any other college in the university. . . . We cannot hire fast enough to meet the demand, and it's very clear from these numbers that we should be double the size (Morrisett, 2016).

The growth in student numbers without a commensurate increase in faculty has also led some institutions to impose limits on students entering the computer

[14] At not-for-profit institutions.

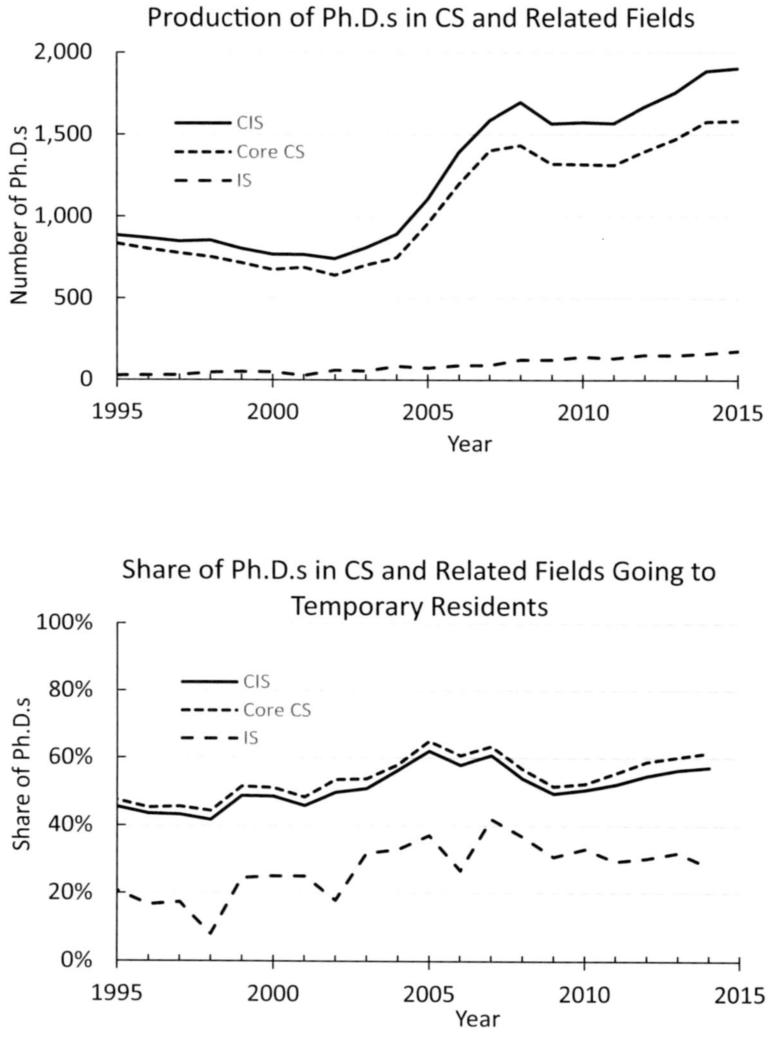

FIGURE 3.15 Ph.D. production in CS and related fields; for-profit Ph.D.s have been excluded. Top panel shows the number of Ph.D.s conferred in a given year in CIS (CIP 11.x series, solid black line), core CS (CIPs 11.0101 and 11.0701, short-dashed black line), and IS (CIP 11.0401, long-dashed black line). Bottom panel illustrates the share of these degrees going to temporary U.S. residents (international students). SOURCE: IPEDS degree completions data accessed via the WebCASPAR online database. See Appendix F for details.

science major, just as in past cycles. Dr. Katherine Newman, former provost of the University of Massachusetts, reported the following situation:

> The extraordinary demand for degrees in computer science, especially relative to our capacity to provide seats in the classroom, means that admission to these degree programs is hypercompetitive. UMass Amherst freshmen who pass through the eye of this needle have extensive preparation in STEM, have often completed a number of CS courses, and offer high school grade point averages in excess of 4.0. These kinds of opportunities for prior preparation are not universal and that poses a challenge to our ability to foster the kind of diversity among computer science students that we are committed to and the field (and the industry) needs.[15]

FINDING 3: With more than half of new CS Ph.D.s drawn to opportunities in industry, hiring and retaining CS faculty is currently an acute challenge that limits institutions' abilities to respond to increasing CS enrollments.

ACTIONS TAKEN OR CONSIDERED IN THE FACE OF CURRENT ENROLLMENT GROWTH

Evidence from the CRA Enrollment Survey shows that many institutions have already taken actions in response to increasing enrollments in CS, and many others are beginning to consider what might be done (CRA, 2017a). The survey asked what actions computing units at the sampled institutions have considered or taken to deal with undergraduate enrollment increases. It should be reiterated that the two sample groups comprised institutions with and without CS Ph.D. programs, respectively, but are not a universal sampling. Furthermore, response was voluntary, so the data are subject to self-selection bias. Nonetheless, the results indicate that demand for CS at some institutions has evoked various reactions to relieve increasing pressure on program resources.

The survey listed the following possible restrictions, and asked respondents to indicate whether they had implemented or considered any of them:

- Tighten requirements for the major.
- Limit enrollments in high-demand classes.
- Advise weaker students to leave.
- Limit advanced courses to declared majors or minors.
- Limit access to advanced courses in another way.

This is not a comprehensive list of all possible solutions, or even all of the solutions currently being deployed; other possible practices include using desired

---

[15] In correspondence with Katherine Newman, following Newman (2016).

choice of major as a factor in freshman admission decisions or capping the major via some other mechanism.

The responses are shown in Figures 3.16 and 3.17. Almost 50 percent of respondents reported limiting enrollments in high-demand courses at both Taulbee and NDC institutions. Nearly half (45.2 percent) of the responding doctoral institutions stated that they have restricted the enrollment in their upper-level courses to majors and minors only. Very few of the responding non-doctoral institutions

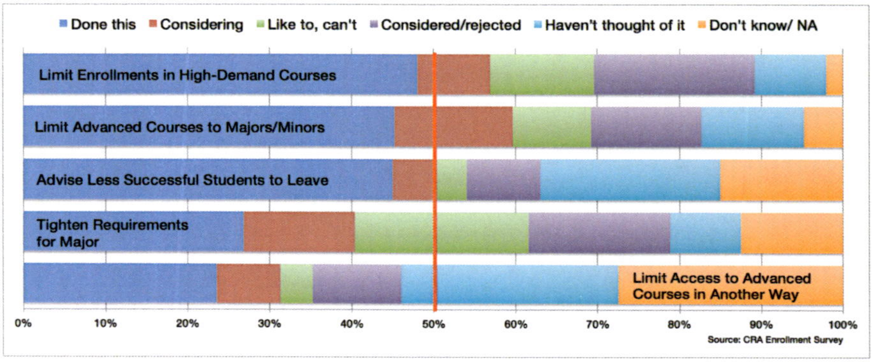

FIGURE 3.16 Actions taken to manage access to courses or major at doctoral-granting institutions. SOURCE: CRA (Computing Research Association). 2017a. Generation CS: Computer Science Undergraduate Enrollments Surge Since 2006. Online. Available at http://cra.org/data/Generation-CS/.

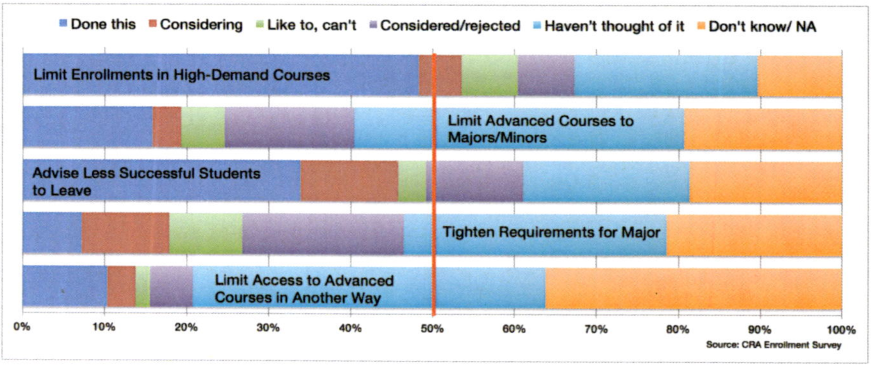

FIGURE 3.17 Actions taken to manage access to courses or major at non-doctoral-granting institutions. SOURCE: CRA (Computing Research Association). 2017a. Generation CS: Computer Science Undergraduate Enrollments Surge Since 2006. Online. Available at http://cra.org/data/Generation-CS/.

tightened their requirements for the major, while almost 30 percent of responding doctoral-granting institutions have done so.

While this survey illustrates actions that institutions are currently taking, it fails to illuminate the impacts that these actions may have on students. The potential impacts of these and other possible actions to respond to demand or mitigate the current strain on computing program resources are discussed in more detail in Chapter 6.

4

Drivers of the Recent Increase in Enrollments in Computing

The trend of increased degree production and course enrollment in computer science (CS) and related fields is prominent across a wide range of institutions, as discussed in Chapters 2 and 3. As with any academic discipline, students' enrollment decisions are informed by a variety of factors, including planned career path, availability of jobs, salary expectations, intellectual interest, appeal of specific degree programs and courses within an institution, and other social or personal factors. In order to shed light on the specific drivers underlying the current growth and how these factors may affect future enrollments, this chapter examines the labor market in computing and discusses the changing role of computing in the economy, in higher education, and in society at large. While it is impossible to know what the future will bring, understanding the drivers of the recent increases in CS enrollment will inform expectations of future demand.

THE LABOR MARKET

Undergraduate students' choices about courses and major field of study may be directly and indirectly influenced by the current state of the labor market. The existence of dynamic adjustment in science and engineering labor markets was recognized as far back as the 1970s, when economist Richard Freeman wrote about the expansion and contraction of opportunities for physicists and engineers.[1]

[1] Writing in 1975, Freeman described the labor market for physicists using this language of cyclical fluctuation: "Although the engineering profession has grown steadily over the past several decades, the labor market for engineers has exhibited marked cyclical fluctuation. A shortage of engineers in the late 1950s and early 1960s was followed by a surplus in the late 1960s and early 1970s" (see Freeman, 1975, 1976).

In essence, degree production in particular fields at colleges and universities can respond to opportunities in the labor market (especially wages) and how they are perceived by students, but the process is not instantaneous and involves lags of multiple years (depending on when students choose their area of specialization and how their expectations change).

Factors affecting the demand for computer scientists in the labor market include changes in technology (in particular, the price and availability of hardware and software), changes in macroeconomic conditions that affect the demand for computer services, and changes in trade or immigration policies (Bound et al., 2013).

Key historical changes in technology with an impact on the labor market and student interests include the rise of the computer hardware industry, concurrent with development of computer technologies for home and business use in the mid-1980s, and the rise of the Internet for commercial purposes starting in the mid-1990s. The latter launched what is often called the "dot-com boom" (Leiner et al., 1997), which increased the demand for computer scientists and included the growth of firms like Yahoo, Amazon, and eBay that helped sustain the boom in the IT sector. (These firms survived the bust that followed; many others did not.) More recent changes in both technology and market conditions include the trends toward data-driven discovery and decision making often referred to as "the Big Data Revolution," fueled by advances in machine learning and computing power; the rise of the smartphone, mobile applications, and social networks; and the ubiquity of software-as-a-service, cloud computing, and the on-demand economy.

Forecasting challenges in science and engineering labor markets are well recognized: data deficiencies, incomplete models, and unanticipated events hinder prediction (Breneman and Freeman, 1974; NRC, 2000). Because of the variety of factors influencing student choice of major, it is not practical to determine causation of past fluctuations in CS and computer and information science and support services (CIS) enrollments, especially given limitations on available data that would help to distinguish between shifts in supply and demand; neither is it possible to predict future trends with certainty. In fact, the committee did not come to consensus on the extent to which economic factors were the decisive cause of past CS enrollment trends, though all agreed that economic trends are one major important factor. Accordingly, in the following, several important economic trends and principles that have played a role in past degree production and enrollment trends are discussed in the context of historical data. Current and projected conditions of the CS labor market are discussed in the context of the current wave of growth in CS undergraduate enrollments.

Historical Data on the Computing Labor Market

Employment in "computer occupations" (including those that do not require a bachelor's degree) has grown significantly since the Bureau of Labor Statistics

(BLS) first introduced this category as one of its Standard Occupational Classifications (SOCs) in 1978, by roughly a factor of 20. According to the BLS Current Population Survey, more than 4.1 million individuals were employed in all computing jobs in 2015. While there are some discontinuities in this data set,[2] it is evident that computing employment has increased significantly, especially during and since the 1990s.[3] Due to discontinuities in data tracking before and after 2000-2002, one must consider a subset of relevant job titles whose definitions do not change (as do some under the unique group of "Computer Occupations").

Employment Levels

In a paper commissioned for the committee (Bound and Morales, 2016, p. 2),[4] economists John Bound and Nicolas Morales tracked computing employment throughout this period by using the categories "Computer Systems Analysts," "Computer Scientists," and "Computer Software Developers."[5] Figure 4.1 shows the overall employment profile in these jobs among those with a bachelor's degree in any discipline. The cumulative number of CIS degrees produced over time is included (dashed line) as a reference. It is apparent that the total number of computer jobs has increased steadily over this time period, with the exception of dips between 2001 and 2002 (coincident with the dot-com bust) and between 2008 and 2010 (at the onset of the Great Recession). According to the plot the cumulative number of CS bachelor's degrees ever produced at any given point in time was roughly half the number of current computer jobs. At the same time, it is unknown how many of the corresponding employers would prefer these positions to be filled by workers with a bachelor's degree in computer science—or if a bachelor's degree is required at all.

Bound and Morales (2016) also considered employment of young college graduates (age 23-29) in computer occupations. The share of young college grad-

[2] The data over this time frame contain inherent limitations. First, the SOCs are periodically adjusted, meaning that some jobs may move between categories at certain points in time, and new job categories emerge with the evolution of the field; computer science in particular has seen significant growth from a single category into a multilevel hierarchy of occupations. In addition, data are unavailable for 2000-2001 on the public-facing site, and discontinuities in collection before and after these times make it difficult to compare trends directly across this boundary for the unique group of "computer occupations" as defined today (in the 2010 SOC revision).

[3] Data from the 2015 Current Population Survey of the Bureau of Labor Statistics, using the SOC of 15-1100, corresponding to "computer occupations." Additional SOCs outside the 15- series may also fall under computing occupations, but they were excluded to avoid overestimating the workforce by including less relevant occupational fields.

[4] See Appendix C for full paper.

[5] These categories correspond to 1990 SOCs of 171 ("Computer Scientists"), 229 ("Computer Software Developers"), 3921 ("Programmers, Business"), and 3972 ("Programmers, Scientific"); the data correspond to individuals with a bachelor's degree in any field who are employed in one of these categories, which accounted for roughly two-thirds of all workers in "Computer Occupations" (15-1100 in the 2010 SOC revision) in 2015.

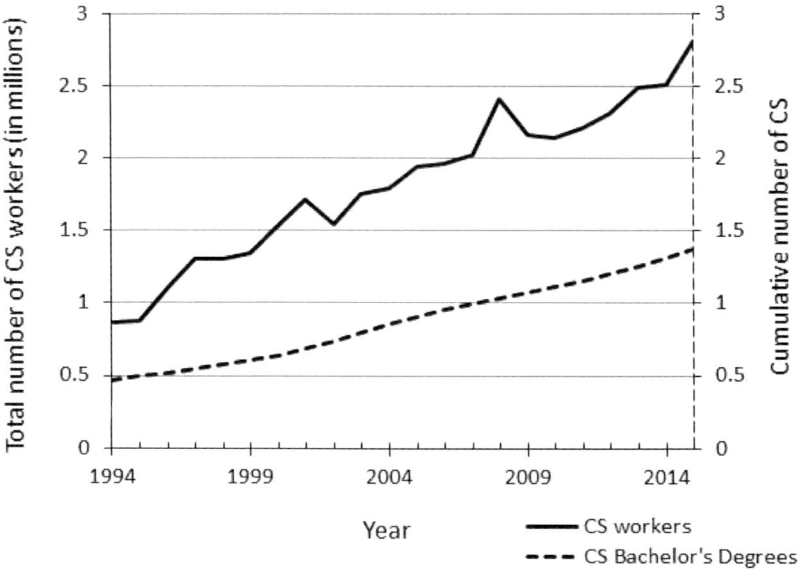

FIGURE 4.1 The number of computer workers (defined as "Computer Systems Analysts," "Computer Scientists," and "Computer Software Developers") holding bachelor's degrees (in any field) over time compared to the cumulative number of CIS bachelor's degrees awarded over time (1994-2015), in millions. SOURCE: Employment data from Current Population Survey, adapted from the Academies-commissioned paper by Bound and Morales (2016), reproduced in Appendix C. Cumulative CIS bachelor's degrees calculated from Integrated Postsecondary Education Data System (IPEDS) completions survey results.

uates employed in computing fields is plotted in Figure 4.2. The share of new graduates with a bachelor's degree in CS is also plotted for comparison. While these two data sets look at different but presumably overlapping populations, they should be related in two significant ways. First, some fraction of CIS graduates contribute to the population of young college graduates in computer occupations, with varying time delays between degree production and entering the workforce. Second, various aspects of the employment prospects in any given field, and how such conditions are perceived by undergraduates in the process of choosing a major, may influence their choice of major and affect the number of degrees produced at the corresponding time of graduation. Neither of these effects can be easily quantified; doing so would require primary research involving rigorous modeling and new mechanisms for further classifying these data, which is outside the scope of this study.

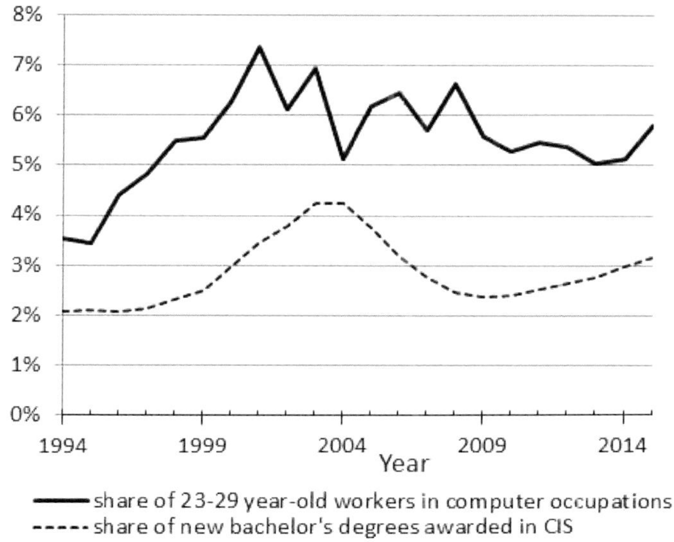

FIGURE 4.2 Share of computer workers who hold bachelor's degrees (in any field) between 23 and 29 years of age (solid line), and share of all bachelor's degrees awarded in CIS (dashed line) each year from 1994 to 2015. SOURCE: Worker data adapted from commissioned paper by Bound and Morales (2016), reproduced in Appendix C. Degree data obtained from IPEDs data, tracked via the WebCASPAR online database.

The plot illustrates that the fraction of young college graduates employed in computer occupations reached 7.4 percent in 2001 (coincident with the dot-com bust), after which they dropped slightly. CIS as a fraction of bachelor's degrees produced in a given year peaked in 2004 at 4.2 percent, dropped to 2.4 percent in 2009, and steadily increased through 2015. While both employment and degree production seem to respond to the dot-com bust (the latter with a lag), no increase in employment in computing occupations among new college graduates is apparent in the years leading up to the recent CS enrollment surge.

In a white paper provided to the committee (see Appendix D), economist Jennifer Hunt examined similar trends, this time using a somewhat broader set of occupational fields for a time series analysis. Figure 4.3 illustrates time series of the share of workers in computer and related occupations. The blue line corresponds to the combination of all computer and mathematics occupations as identified in the Current Population Survey. While this is broader than the set of computer occupations, the trends are consistent with the data from Bound and Morales (2016) and similarly show that CIS and related fields have accounted

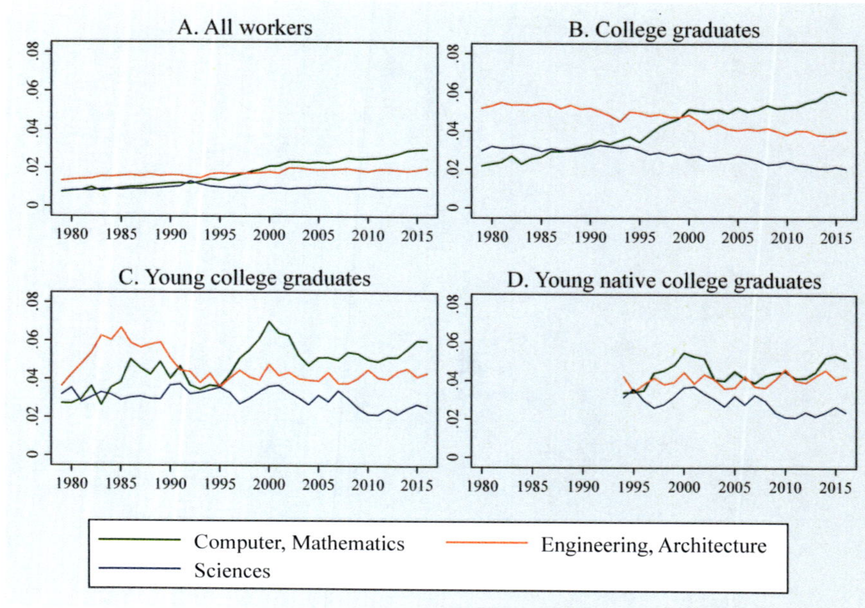

FIGURE 4.3 Share of workers in computer and mathematics and other occupations, for (A) all workers (age 18-64), (B) all college graduates, (C) young college graduates (age 22-26), and (D) young native (U.S.) college graduates. Note that the category "Computer, Mathematics" is broad and includes more than just computer occupations. SOURCE: Hunt, J. 2016. White Paper: Does the Recent Increase in Computer Science Degrees Reflect Increased Demand? Commissioned Study by the Committee on the Growth of Computer Science Undergraduate Enrollments, National Academies of Sciences, Engineering, and Medicine (see Appendix D); data from Current Population Survey Merged Outgoing Rotation Groups 1979-2015.

for an increasing share of occupational fields among all workers and among all college graduates, while those for other sciences and engineering have not.

Wage Trends

Wages in a given occupational field are a dynamic component of the labor market, and their actual or perceived levels can also influence student choice of major. Median wages in computer occupations relative to all occupations held by college graduates are illustrated in Figure 4.4 for workers between 25-29 and 30-34 years of age. This figure shows that median wages for computer occupations in both age groups peaked around the dot-com boom, fell through 2006, and have generally increased with some fluctuations between 2006 and 2012. At their peak CIS occupations offered on average a wage premium of 44 percent and 35 percent for the two age groups, respectively, compared to other fields. This boom and bust cycle does precede that of the fluctuation in CIS bachelor's degree production by several years, which is consistent with the possibility that wages in computer occupations (or conditions connected to wages) may have contributed to student decisions to major in computer science and related fields. Post-2006 wage levels reset to higher than the pre-dot-com levels, similar to the trend observed for year-to-year CIS bachelor's degree production.

Hunt conducted a similar analysis, looking at the absolute median wages for "computer/mathematics" and other occupations, using data from the American Community Survey (ACS). These results are illustrated in Figure 4.5. It is noteworthy that there are historical fluctuations in CS wage trends for young college graduates here as well, though not in recent years. In her white paper Hunt concluded that at least some of the increase in CS degree production since 2008 is in response to something other than wages for computer occupations.

As noted previously, a deeper exploration of the correlations and causalities of these trends is an area for research and beyond the scope of this study. Such

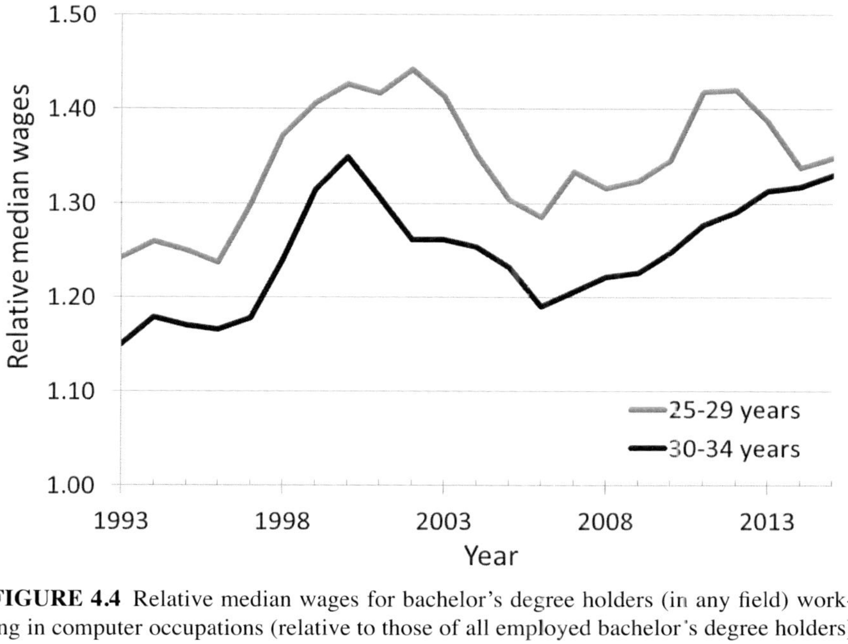

FIGURE 4.4 Relative median wages for bachelor's degree holders (in any field) working in computer occupations (relative to those of all employed bachelor's degree holders) for two age groups: 25-29 and 30-34. SOURCE: Wage data from Current Population Survey; adapted from Academies-commissioned paper by Bound and Morales (2016), in Appendix C.

analysis would ideally involve a clear mapping between the training received in various degree programs with the requirements for a given occupational field, and assessment of whether computer science and related skills or degrees are a primary or preferred requirement for particular jobs. A full model of the complex computing labor market would decompose changes in wages and employment levels into shifts in supply and demand, and connect these to changes in degree production and course enrollments. To do so would require accounting for conditions underlying industry demand as well as factors underlying supply, such as student and parent perceptions of job and earnings opportunities, institutional conditions that affect student interest and the production of degrees and delivery of education leading to computing skills, and federal policies affecting the academic and industrial sectors. These underlying factors, and their relative role in the overall computing labor market, likely change over time.

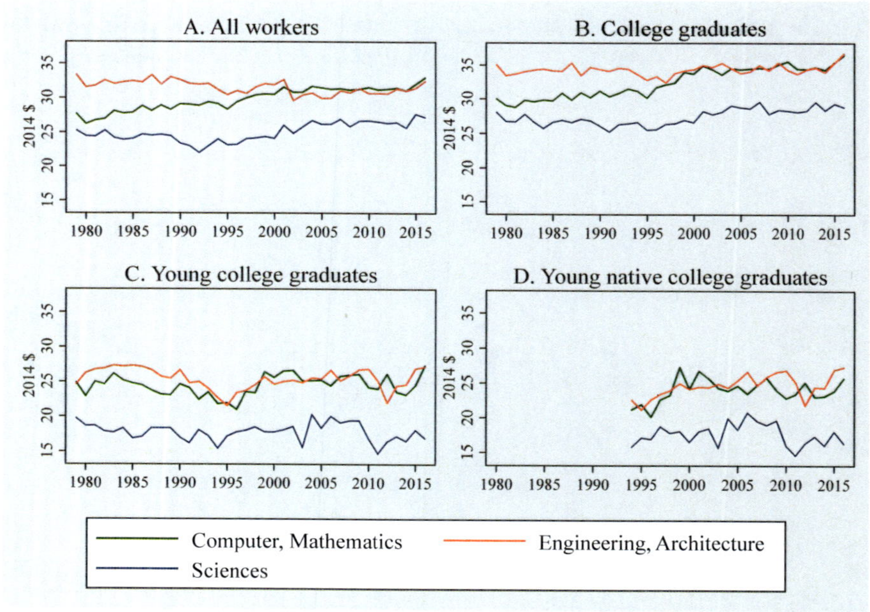

FIGURE 4.5 Median hourly wages of workers in computer/mathematics and other occupations for (A) all workers (age 18-64), (B) all college graduates, (C) young college graduates (age 22-26), and (D) young native college graduates. Note that the blue line includes all computer and mathematics job categories. SOURCE: Hunt, J. 2016. White Paper: Does the Recent Increase in Computer Science Degrees Reflect Increased Demand? Commissioned Study by the Committee on the Growth of Computer Science Undergraduate Enrollments, National Academies of Sciences, Engineering, and Medicine (see Appendix D); data from Current Population Survey, 1979-2015.

The Labor Market for Computing in Recent Years

Labor market supply of computing workers includes computer science majors, students with bachelor's degrees in other fields who have or can obtain sufficient computing skills and knowledge, and those with less than a bachelor's degree. These workers can be domestic or foreign.

Table 4.1 illustrates the top field of degree for bachelor's degree–holding computing workers from 2009 to 2014 according to the results of the ACS. It is noteworthy that only 37 percent of bachelor's degree–holding computing workers age 23 to 39 identified in the ACS during this time reported a degree in a computing field (including the listed categories of computer science, computer engineering, computer and information, or information sciences). This is consistent with the evidence of significant levels of interest in computing among non-CS majors in recent years.

As noted earlier and in previous sections computer science as a field of study and an occupation has demonstrated monumental growth over the last four decades. A closer look reveals that the growth of computing jobs is not limited to employment in the computer services industries; computing occupations have emerged in a range of industries, as illustrated in Table 4.2. These statistics reflect CS degree holders working both in computing occupations and in other occu-

TABLE 4.1 Main Bachelor's Degree for Those Working as Computer Scientists (2009-2014)

Main Bachelor's Degree	Age 23-29	Age 30-39	Foreign 23-39
Computer science	23.9%	22.2%	25.0%
Computer engineering	6.9%	5.0%	11.7%
Computer and information	6.7%	7.5%	5.9%
Electrical engineering	4.4%	4.5%	15.2%
Business management and administration	4.3%	5.6%	1.3%
Management information	3.1%	4.4%	0.5%
Economics	2.6%	1.8%	0.9%
Information sciences	2.4%	2.3%	0.7%
Finance	2.4%	1.7%	0.5%
General business	2.4%	2.9%	2.1%
Mathematics	2.3%	2.3%	3.0%
Other	38.5%	39.7%	33.3%
Number of observations	15,008	26,674	13,167

SOURCE: Data from American Community Survey (ACS); table from commissioned paper by Bound and Morales (2016) (see Appendix C for details).

TABLE 4.2 Share of CS Bachelor's Degree Holders Employed in Select Industries (2009-2014)

Industry	Percentage
Computer and data processing services	21.3%
Professional and related services	17.7%
Finance, insurance, and real estate	11.1%
Colleges and universities	5.0%
Communications	4.8%
Manufacturing—electrical and computing	4.8%
Manufacturing—other nondurables	4.6%
Manufacturing—durables	3.0%
Other	27.7%

SOURCE: Data from American Community Survey (ACS); taken from the Academies-commissioned paper by Bound and Morales (2016) (see Appendix C for details).

pational fields, and illustrate that degrees in computer science and related fields provide skills and background relevant for a range of industries.

Current and Projected Demand for Computing Professionals

Although the committee notes that significant uncertainty must be attached to future employment predictions, the most authoritative forecasts of computing employment show sustained demand for computing workers over the next decade.

Every two years the BLS publishes projections of employment trends for the next decade. In the most recent projections, covering the decade from 2014 to 2024, the BLS predicted that the number of people employed in computing occupations will rise from 3,916,100 to 4,404,700. The addition of nearly half a million computing jobs to the economy corresponds to a growth of 12.5 percent over the decade, compared to an overall projected growth rate of 6.5 percent. This suggests that computing occupations are growing nearly twice as fast as the labor market as a whole.

The centrality of computing to the national science and engineering workforce is reflected in Figure 4.6, which compares the size and anticipated growth in the computing sector to those in other science, technology, engineering, and mathematics (STEM) fields. The left-hand chart in Figure 4.6 shows the current distribution of STEM jobs, of which computing accounts for 62 percent. The middle chart shows that the BLS expects that more than three-quarters of the new STEM positions created between 2014 and 2024 will be in the computing sector. However, as shown in the chart on the right, computing is expected to represent 58 percent of all STEM job openings, reflecting a greater need for replacement

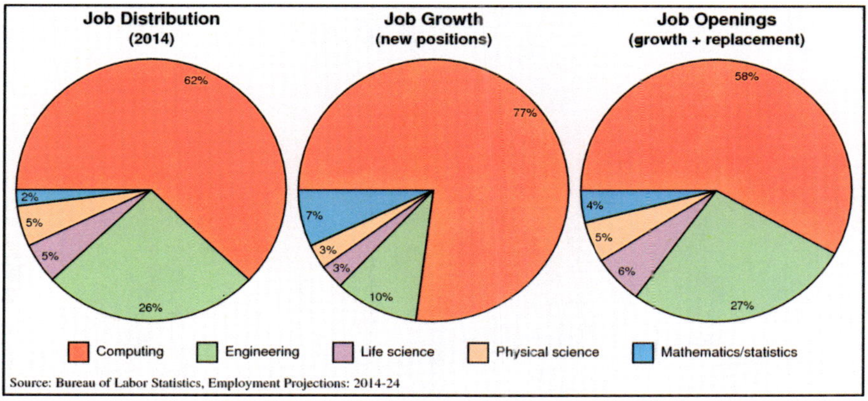

FIGURE 4.6 Projected employment growth for occupations in STEM and STEM-related fields (social sciences not included), 2014-2024. SOURCE: Data from BLS (2015), labor projections, 2014-2024.

of workers in existing positions in other STEM fields, presumably because the workforce in computing is, on average, younger than that in the other STEM disciplines and therefore less likely to lose workers through retirement.

Beyond the growth of the computing sector itself, analyses of job requirements show that employers now expect new hires to have significant levels of computing expertise, particularly at the high end of the labor market. A recent estimate from Burning Glass Technologies[6] estimated that programming skills were important qualifications for nearly half of the job openings in the top quartile of the income distribution in 2015, as shown in Figure 4.7. Burning Glass's analysis also projected that the number of coding job openings will grow faster (8.8 percent net growth for IT jobs requiring coding skills and 7.2 percent for all jobs requiring coding skills) than other career-track jobs[7] (6.4 percent net growth) between 2016 and 2026. This suggests that those without the opportunity to acquire these skills may be less competitive for certain high-paying occupations, and thus potentially at an economic disadvantage. This could have a significant impact on certain underrepresented groups, who are less likely to have experience in computer science in K-12 and college, as discussed in Chapter 5; institutional structures that discourage the acquisition of these skills among some groups could perpetuate economic inequality.

[6] This study was conducted by analysis of 26 million U.S. job postings from 2015 (Burning Glass Technologies, 2016).

[7] Burning Glass Technologies (2016) defines "career-track jobs" as those that pay more than 15 dollars per hour.

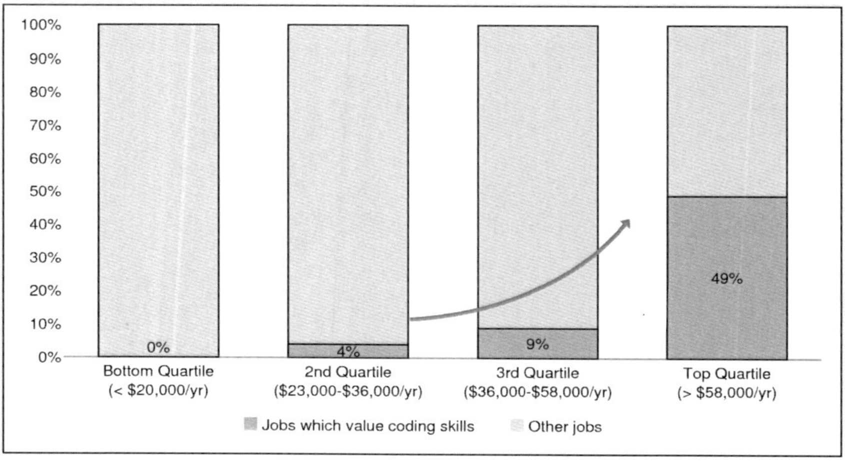

FIGURE 4.7 Percentage of 2015 job openings that value coding skills, by income level. SOURCE: Burning Glass Technologies. 2016. Beyond Point and Click: The Expanding Demand for Coding Skills. Online. Available at http://burning-glass.com/research/coding-skills/.

The current starting salaries for bachelor's degree graduates in computer science often influence the career choices of students. The 2017 National Association of Colleges and Employers (NACE) salary survey reported that computer science graduates received the second highest average salary ($65,540), right after engineering graduates ($66,097).[8] NACE data show wide geographical differences in computer science, with a difference of $14,000 between jobs in the West and the South.[9] For several above-average examples, one may look to the average reported starting salaries for CS graduates from Purdue University ($83,730 for 2015 graduates) (Purdue University, 2017), the University of Illinois at Urbana-Champaign ($85,000 for 2015 graduates) (University of Illinois at Urbana-Champaign, 2017), and the University of California at Berkeley ($99,700 for 2015 graduates and $103,963 for 2016 graduates) (University of California at Berkeley, 2016).

Both employment and degree production have risen substantially in the years since computing became an important component of the national economy. The question of whether a shortfall currently exists—that is, whether contemporaneous production of CS degrees is insufficient for employers to hire as many workers as and when they would like, at the going wage—in computing employ-

[8] See NACE (2017a).

[9] See NACE (2017b).

ment is a challenging one. Many estimates come primarily from sources tied to industry, which could be argued has some incentive to justify a more favorable hiring environment—to expand the pool of potential hires and create more competition, leading to more highly qualified talent and enabling them to offer lower wages.

As of 2014 the number of people employed in computer occupations was 3,916,100 (BLS, 2015). The total number of bachelor's degrees in computer science awarded by U.S. institutions throughout the entire history of the field is only 1,313,034.[10] The number of employees in computing occupations is therefore approximately three times larger than the number of bachelor's degrees in computer science ever produced in the United States.

Another way to examine the relationship between employment levels and degree production is to plot the anticipated employment needs—calculated here by assuming that the projected growth from 2014 to 2024 is distributed equally over the decade—against the number of degrees produced each year in several STEM fields. The resulting graph appears in Figure 4.8, which is an updated version of a graph first presented by John Sargent, senior policy analyst, Department of Commerce, at the CRA Computing Research Summit on February 23, 2004. The leftmost bar in each cluster represents the projected growth in job openings for the most closely related occupational sector. The next four bars represent the number of degrees granted at the associate's, bachelor's, master's, and doctoral levels.

The graphs in Figure 4.8 illustrate several ways in which computer science differs from other STEM fields. First, computer science is the only major discipline in which the projected number of job openings exceeds the rate of bachelor's degree production (Freeman, 2016).[11] Second, computer science is the only STEM discipline that produces a significant number of associate's degrees, which currently account for nearly one-third of computer science degrees. Third, the number of doctoral degrees in computer science is proportionally smaller than it is in any other STEM field. Each of these differences has an effect on the balance between employment needs and degree production. While it is unclear how many of the new computer jobs would require bachelor's degrees in CS (or any degree at all), they are worth observing; it may be that graduates in other disciplines simply go into occupations outside of their major fields, and that this is less common for CS.

In order to meet employment needs, one strategy is to hire employees with computer science degrees below the baccalaureate level. A second strategy is to hire university graduates with degrees in other areas and then provide those employees with whatever additional on-the-job training they require. A third is to hire computer science graduates from outside the United States. Driven by

[10] As computed from NCES (2016).

[11] In the discussion, Dr. Freeman noted that this was a high-level observation, so there may be other fields for which this same imbalance is true if one looks beyond the major disciplinary divisions.

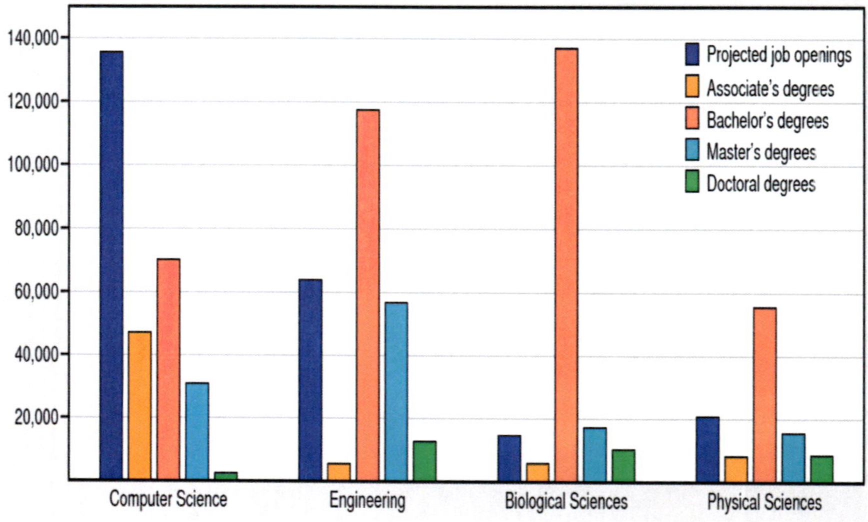

FIGURE 4.8 Projected annual job openings and current degree production in broad STEM fields. SOURCE: Data from BLS (2015) jobs projections and IPEDS completions survey.

its need to fill a rapidly expanding number of positions, industry is pursuing all three of these strategies.

That there is a market for workers with degrees below the baccalaureate level is supported by the unusually large number of associate's degrees produced in the field. In 2014, U.S. institutions awarded 37,643 associate's degrees in CIS, which comprises 31 percent of all CIS degrees. By contrast, associate's degrees constitute an average of 4 percent of STEM degrees in other disciplines. Moreover, the number of associate's degrees has been rising over time, as discussed in Chapter 2, though it has declined in recent years, in large part due to declines at the for-profits. It is worth noting in passing that computer science also produces a large number of certificates compared to other STEM fields, indicating that there is also a market in industry for these credentials.

Understanding the flow of employees both into and out of computing is complicated by the fact that graduates often take positions that would most naturally be categorized as outside their principal area of study. For example, many computer science graduates take positions in occupations other than computing, just as many graduates from other disciplines end up working in the computing field. Such migration is common among graduates in general.

As previously noted less than half of the people with CS bachelor's degrees end up working in a core computer occupation. Conversely, computing occupations have an unusually high rate of in-migration, not only from other STEM fields but also from a wide range of academic disciplines: approximately 67 percent of the bachelor's degree holders in the computing workforce have degrees from outside computer science. This is not necessarily because industry prefers to hire people without computer science degrees—it could also be due in part to their paucity in the labor pool.

The third strategy for meeting workforce needs—hiring highly skilled workers with technical degrees from universities outside the United States—has long been a matter of public controversy. Industry representatives have lobbied for increases in the number of visas available under the H-1B program (though many participants received their degrees at U.S. institutions), which allows companies to employ noncitizens in particular "specialty areas." Under the law employment is on a temporary basis, although many employees who enter the United States under the H-1B program are later qualified to become permanent residents. Industry maintains that they need the ability to hire foreign workers because there are not enough people in the United States with the necessary skills. In their paper commissioned for the committee Bound and Morales report that the percentage of foreigners in the computer science workforce has grown over the last decade, rising from 10.6 percent in 1994 to 26.8 percent in 2015 (Bound and Morales, 2016), which is consistent with insufficient domestic supply to meet industry needs.

The Effects of Competition for Highly Skilled Software Developers

The expansion of the field of computer science has led to both specialization and heterogeneity among computer science graduates.

The intensity of the competition for the best software developers reflects a long-standing recognition that large variations in productivity exist among individual software developers. The original study in this area was published in 1968 by Sackman et al., who found that programmers with the same level of experience exhibited variations of more than 20 to 1 in the time required to solve particular programming problems. Beyond this high variability in coding time, the study revealed that individual programmers showed highly correlated differences in other metrics that contribute to overall productivity, in the sense that the best programmers were not only able to complete the problem in less time but in so doing also typically produced programs that had fewer errors and were more efficient in both running time and utilization of memory. Thus, the best programmers were in fact more than 20 times as effective.

Later studies have reaffirmed the results of the Sackman study and conclude that the best software developers are relatively few in number, but much more productive than the average.[12] There is evidence that the variability in productivity has increased over time. In a *Wall Street Journal* story in November

[12] See, for example, Bryan (1994).

2005, Alan Eustace, then Google's vice president of engineering, said that the best software engineer at Google is 300 times more productive than the average Google software engineer—and this in a company that hires less than one-tenth of 1 percent of its applicant pool (Tam et al., 2005).

The variation in productivity is the critical dynamic that underlies employment policies in the software industry. Companies are under intense competitive pressure to identify and hire those extraordinarily talented individuals at the high end of the productivity curve. Particularly for startups employing a small team of implementers, hiring just one extremely productive person can make the difference between success and failure. After all, if the best software developer can do the work of 10, 100, or even 300 run-of-the-mill employees, a company that attracts such a superstar can compete effectively against a much larger enterprise. Thus, companies whose business depends on software production will try to hire applicants from pools in which the likelihood of finding the most talented individuals is high, such as graduates from top computer science departments, successful participants in collegiate programming contests, or entrepreneurs who have developed successful freeware and shareware systems on their own. Competition to attract employees from these populations is intense. Companies likewise have a strong incentive to avoid problem programmers and are unlikely to hire applicants whom they fear might fall at the low end of the scale.

In a column for the *Los Angeles Times*, Gary Chapman observed that "the software profession is beginning to resemble professional sports or the movie business much more than engineering. Exceptionally gifted programmers are referred to as 'talent,' like movie stars, and some have incomes that make those of film stars look puny" (Chapman, 2000). Images of career paths of computing superstars, which have been visible in contemporary news and media, may also contribute to increased interest among students in pursuing a career in computing. For example, wealthy technology magnates such as SpaceX and Tesla founder Elon Musk, or Facebook founder Mark Zuckerberg—including in films such as *The Social Network*—along with fictional characters on shows such as *Silicon Valley* and *The Big Bang Theory*, may create a glamorous or appealing image of computer science professionals among young people.

Workforce Demand in Key Areas

Another factor that complicates a full understanding of whether the supply of computing expertise is sufficient to meet workforce needs is that demand for particular specialties in computer science varies considerably over time. Some specialties have grown dramatically in importance in recent years. Three areas are commonly highlighted as facing acute demand: cybersecurity, data science, and machine learning.

One of the areas in which a need for skilled workers is most evident is computer security, which today is more often called cybersecurity or abbreviated even further simply to "cyber." Cybersecurity is a high priority for the U.S. government because of the need to protect classified data and other sensitive information. Ensuring that federal agencies are prepared against cyberattacks requires more workers trained in computer security. According to the Department of Homeland Security,

> [a]s technology becomes increasingly sophisticated, the demand for an experienced and qualified workforce to protect our nation's networks and information systems will only continue to grow. Information security and cybersecurity are rapidly growing industries with increased workforce needs (DHS, 2016).

Computer security is also increasingly important throughout the private sector, leading to significant growth in workforce needs in this area. In a report titled *Job Market Intelligence: Cybersecurity Jobs 2015*, Burning Glass Technologies (2015a) noted that

> American employers have realized the vital importance of cybersecurity—but that realization has created a near-term shortage of workers that may require long-term solutions.

The report (Burning Glass Technologies, 2015a) listed the following findings about the cybersecurity job market:

- In 2014 there were 238,158 postings for cybersecurity-related jobs nationally. Cybersecurity jobs account for 11 percent of all IT jobs.
- Cybersecurity postings have grown 91 percent from 2010 to 2014. This is a faster growth rate than IT jobs generally.
- Cybersecurity postings advertise a 9 percent salary premium over IT jobs overall.
- Cybersecurity job postings took 8 percent longer to fill than IT job postings overall.
- The demand for certificated cybersecurity talent is outstripping supply. In the United States employers posted 49,493 jobs requesting a Certified Information Systems Security Professional (CISSP), recruiting from a pool of only 65,362 CISSP holders nationwide.

It is useful to put the first list item in context. American employers posted 238,158 jobs in the cybersecurity area, which is four times the entire production of bachelor's degrees in computer science in that year, even though cybersecurity represents only 11 percent of IT jobs.

Data science is another area that has shown enormous growth in recent years. A 2014 issue brief from the Business Higher Education Forum outlines the growing importance of the field in the following terms:

> The application of data science is pervasive in both the public and private sectors. Companies of all sizes rely on data science and analytics as key transformational components to their core operations. A 2011 report by the McKinsey Global Institute, *Big Data: the Next Frontier for Innovation, Competition, and Productivity*, noted that "big data" is growing at a rate of 40 percent each year and has the potential to add $300 billion of value to the nation's health care industry alone, with broad application in virtually every sector, including scientific organizations and cultural institutions. Projections by Gartner, Inc., indicate that in less than 12 months, 4.4 million information technology (IT) jobs to support big data will be created globally. About 1.9 million of those jobs will be within the United States, and big data has the potential to create three times that number of jobs outside of IT (BHEF, 2014).

Additional recent studies have confirmed high levels of demand for "hybrid jobs" in data science that merge business and technology skills. A report from Burning Glass Technologies (2015b) offered the following assessment of employment demand in this area:

> Data analytics, digital marketing, and mobile development are growing especially fast: Demand for data science skills has tripled over the past five years, while demand for digital marketing and mobile skills has more than doubled.

The Burning Glass report includes surveys of job postings indicating that "more than 250,000 positions were open in the last year for these hybrid technical roles"—again, four times the annual production rate of bachelor's degrees in computer science. Those positions, moreover, offer high salaries and are, in many cases, open to students with less background in computer science than that of a computer science major.

The need for more qualified workers in such hybrid fields has led to an increase in the number of data-science courses, minors, and majors that colleges and universities offer to undergraduates. These trends are difficult to capture in systematically collected national data but are easy to illustrate by example. In recent years more than 25 universities—including Bowling Green State University, Columbia University, Drexel University, Florida State University, Marquette University, Portland State University, Purdue University, Rice University, the University of California at Irvine, University of California at San Diego, the University of Michigan, the University of Rochester, the University of San Francisco, and the University of Vermont—have created majors specifically titled "data science." Other institutions offer similar courses of study under other names. At Stanford University, for example, the website for the major whose official title is Mathematics and Computational Science begins with a heading that describes the program as "the data science major."

At the committee's public workshop in August 2016 several speakers identified machine learning—particularly in applications that use multilayer neural networks to create more sophisticated structures often referred to as deep learning—as an area of intense demand (Wing, 2016).

The emergence of machine learning as a critical technology also changes the prospects for employment of graduates in other fields. Just as new opportunities are created for graduates with the skills to apply machine-learning strategies to automate the analysis of massive collections of data, opportunities are closing in those fields in which such analysis was formerly conducted by people.

> **FINDING 4:** Employment in computing fields has grown steadily since 1975, and the number of jobs in computing occupations far exceeds bachelor's degree production in CS. The Bureau of Labor Statistics (BLS) projects that employment in computer occupations will rise more quickly than overall job growth for at least the next several years.

As discussed in previous sections demand for employees with computing expertise is high and has grown steadily over time. That need has also been projected to grow for the foreseeable future. The number of undergraduates interested in studying computer science—both as majors and as non-majors (as detailed in Chapter 3)—has been increasing rapidly, since about 2005. As computing becomes central to an ever-widening number of disciplines, student interest will presumably continue to grow. Several high-demand areas—including cybersecurity, data science, and machine learning—face labor shortages that academic institutions are currently unable to fill.

Each of these factors suggests a need to expand the nation's supply of workers with sufficient understanding of computer science to meet the needs of the twenty-first-century workforce.

THE CHANGING LANDSCAPE OF COMPUTING

The emergence of new information technology industries, the increased reliance on computation in all parts of society and in research, and shifts in the demand for computing throughout the economy reflect changes in the field and its broad applications (NRC, 2012).

Two areas have been central in the last decade: the continued and increased need for information security, and data as a resource and driver for decision making. The protection of digital information and data; the protection of software and hardware systems and networks from unauthorized access, change, and destruction; and the education of users to follow best security practices are crucial to every organization. We rely upon a connected, networked, and complex cyberspace with vulnerabilities that is almost continuously under attack Teaching safe information security practices to students and similar training of the workforce are increasingly expected. The National Science Foundation (NSF) Secure and Trustworthy Cyberspace program highlights many of the research challenges in the area of cybersecurity involving hardware, software, networks, data, people, and the integration with the physical world.

During the last decade, computing has taken a new, more empirically driven path with the maturing of machine learning, the emergence of data science, and the "big data" revolution. Data science combines computing and statistical methods to identify trends in existing data and generate new knowledge, with significant applications throughout all sectors of the economy, including marketing, retail, finance, business, health care and medicine, agriculture, smart cities, and more. The availability and use of big data sets, combined with computation, simulation, and modeling, has created new academic areas including digital humanities and computational social sciences.

Software tools and systems for animation, visualization, virtual reality, and conceptualization have emerged as a medium for the arts (digital media and multimedia practices) and are driving advances in the entertainment industry (computer-generated graphics in films and video games, and digital methods in music recording), as well as training and education using virtual environments.

The digital age created by computing and information technologies has enabled a new sector of the economy with a wide range of temporary, short-term jobs for independent workers, mediated via the use of digital platforms, including through companies like Uber, Lyft, Airbnb, TaskRabbit, and DagVacay. While a recent study suggests that jobs in this area currently account for approximately 0.5 percent of the U.S. workforce (Katz and Krueger, 2016), they display significant potential for impact on jobs and the economy as a whole (NASEM, 2017).

Computing has become more pervasive among a host of academic disciplines, beyond just the practical use of ubiquitous software tools. New algorithmic approaches and discoveries are helping to drive advances across a range of fields, leading to new collaborations and an increased demand for deeper knowledge of computing among academics and researchers, challenging conventional disciplinary boundaries.

Important examples can be found in the area of computational science, where computational approaches are used to carry out scientific models or simulations to an extent that would be essentially impossible without the aid of a computer. Computational methods have contributed to significant advances and led to new specializations in domains such as chemistry and biology. As one measure of the impact of computing on the advancement of scientific research, the 2013 Nobel Prize in chemistry was awarded jointly to Martin Karplus, Michael Levitt, and Arieh Warshel for development of novel computational models for simulating chemical systems (Nobelprize.org, 2013).

As more and more software systems are used throughout the economy and become integral to daily life, it is becoming increasingly important for individuals to understand how to use them. The fraction of people who need to use software in more targeted ways, write scripts to process and prepare data, and integrate tools and systems is likely to increase. While it is not necessary for all individuals to be computer scientists or professionals in computing in order to succeed or function in society, it is clear that some level of computing skills and knowledge is increasingly necessary, and higher levels of competency can provide a significant practical and professional advantage in many contexts.

> **FINDING 5:** Computing is pervasive, and its penetration is deep and growing in virtually all sectors of the economy, all academic disciplines, and all aspects of modern life. The broad opportunities in computing, both in the labor market and for enabling a host of intellectual pursuits, will continue to be drivers of increasing enrollments in undergraduate computer science, from both majors and non-majors. While there will probably be fluctuations in the demand for CS courses, demand is likely to continue to grow or remain high over the long term.

Increased Participation in Computing in Primary and Secondary Environments

Another potential driver of recent (and possible future) increases in CS undergraduate enrollments at the undergraduate level is increased engagement of students with computing in K-12. Throughout the history of the field, student exposure to computer science has been small compared to that of other STEM disciplines. Many high schools do not offer CS courses,[13] and most do not require students to take a course in computing. Currently, 13 states do not allow CS courses to be counted toward high school graduation requirements.[14] The changing role of CS in society, including the pervasive exposure of students to new technologies such as smartphones, along with the historically low and uneven access of K-12 students to computing (Google, Inc. and Gallup, Inc., 2016), has prompted a series of efforts to enhance the exposure of primary and secondary students to CS in recent years.

For example, in 2003, the Association of Computing Machinery established the K-12 Computer Science Task Force, and founded the Computer Science Teachers Association (CSTA) in 2004. CSTA produced the K-12 Computer Science Standards, which became the de facto national standards for the discipline, and produced and disseminated a host of classroom resources designed to develop student interest in computer science as an education and career pathway.

Universities have also participated in outreach to students in K-12 to help build interest in the field and break down stereotypical attitudes about computing. In particular, Carnegie Mellon University and Indiana University pioneered these efforts via a series of "roadshows."[15]

---

[13] Note that computing courses that teach computational thinking and/or coding are distinct from basic computer training courses that teach proficiency with word processing or other computer applications.

[14] In particular, teacher training has been a major challenge. See, for example, Code.org (2017).

[15] See Cottam et al. (2010).

The NSF has sponsored such projects through its CS education programs. NSF's Computing Education for the 21st Century was founded in 2011 with the aim of helping to reverse the decline in undergraduate computing majors that occurred after the dot-com bust "by engaging larger numbers of students, teachers, and educators in computing education and learning at earlier stages in the education pipeline" (NSF, 2012). Its Broadening Participation in Computing program track (building on alliances developed between 2006 and 2009) (NSF, 2016a) aims "to significantly increase the number of U.S. citizens and permanent residents receiving postsecondary degrees in the computing disciplines, with an emphasis on students from communities with longstanding underrepresentation in computing" (NSF, 2009). Another track, CS10K, "aims to have rigorous, academic computing courses taught in 10,000 high schools by 10,000 well-prepared teachers" (Cuny, 2015).

In 2016 the College Board introduced a new Advanced Placement (AP) course, Computer Science Principles (CSP), developed in part with NSF support, in 2,700 high school classrooms nationwide, "with the goal of creating leaders in computer science fields and attracting and engaging those who are traditionally underrepresented with essential computing tools and multidisciplinary opportunities" (College Board, 2017). This launch followed 10 years of development of course materials and other resources for high school teachers, and phased pilot efforts at dozens of high schools in the United States and Canada. In May 2017 it was announced that the implementation of this course has helped to increase high school student participation in AP computer science. In particular, the number of students sitting for any AP computing exam was approximately 111,000 in 2017, with approximately 51,000 of these students coming from the new CSP course, compared to approximately 57,000 in 2016 before CSP had launched (CRA, 2017b). Because participation in AP courses in general (and CS in particular) has been found to correlate to increased probability of majoring in the corresponding field (Mattern et al., 2011), the introduction of this new AP program is likely to newly contribute to an increase in the number of computing major enrollments in 2018 and computing degrees beginning in 2022.

In 2016 President Obama announced a national effort for "Computer Science for All," to be led by NSF and the U.S. Department of Education in partnership with other federal agencies to boost K-12 students' CS knowledge and skills. This persists as a non-profit, the CS for All Consortium.[16]

In addition, many industry-sponsored efforts have focused on supporting professional development and providing resources for CS teachers. For example, Google's CS4HS aims "to provide CS teachers globally with an opportunity to improve their technical and pedagogical skills." This program, launched in 2009 after several years of pilots, supports CS education professionals in providing professional development opportunities and educational resources to high school

[16] See http://www.csforall.org/.

CS teachers around the world.[17] Google has also made a variety of learning resources available online. Another example is Oracle's Oracle Academy, an initiative to assist teachers in preparing secondary students for college and careers, through the provision of educational resources online.[18] Microsoft's Technology Education and Literacy in Schools program works to connect U.S. high schools with technical expertise and support to help build and sustain computer science courses; specifically, the program connects volunteers to teach or support high school introductory or AP computer science courses and instructors.[19]

Several private-sector technology and engineering companies also have launched initiatives to boost exposure to CS courses and skills. For example, IBM's Pathways in Technology Early College High Schools (P-Tech), launched in 2011, created grades 9-14 technology-focused early-college high schools that culminate in an associate's degree. The program promotes postsecondary degree completion and career readiness and provides engaging academic courses and work-related experiences through partnerships with industry partners. Several states and cities have launched networks of P-Tech schools.[20]

Raytheon teamed with the Science and Innovation Center of Pinellas County Florida, SRI International, and St. Petersburg College to create an innovative cybersecurity educational program that prepares high school students for testing in industry-recognized certifications and earning credits toward a 2- or 4-year degree in network security from St. Petersburg College.

Combined, these and related activities indicate significant momentum toward earlier exposure of students to computer science. Impacts from efforts begun in 2009 could already be contributing to enrollment growth. Moving forward, continued increases in the level of exposure of students to computing before they enroll in college could have multiple possible effects on undergraduate enrollment. First, this earlier formal education in computing could provide some of the skills that certain students might otherwise seek in a postsecondary computing course. On the other hand, early exposure to computing could have the opposite effect of increasing course or major enrollments by stimulating student interest early and prompting further exploration in the postsecondary environment. Finally, the need for more teachers to administer these courses could also lead to increased demand on CS undergraduate education and training in order to meet it. These and related programs also have implications for student diversity, as discussed in Chapter 5.

---

[17] See https://www.cs4hs.com/.

[18] See https://edu.google.com/cs/learn.html.

[19] See https://www.tealsk12.org/.

[20] See https://www.ibm.com/thought-leadership/ptech/index.html.

5

Impacts of Enrollment Growth on Diversity in Computing

Diversity is critical to success in any field. Diversity of perspectives and experiences results in robust thinking and approaches that can help yield solutions and products that meet the needs of a diverse customer base, which often improves the value of a product across the spectrum of users. Diversity is often linked to positive outcomes, such as greater innovation, productivity, and profit.[1]

A recent industry report identified a "massive economic opportunity" associated with increasing the ethnic and gender diversity in the U.S. technology workforce, with the potential to add $470 to $570 billion to the U.S. tech sector and support the creation of jobs and the improvement of products. The report identifies underrepresentation of African American and Latino/Latina workers in the tech industry compared to the U.S. workforce as a whole, accounting for 7 and 8 percent of tech workers, respectively, compared to 12 and 16 percent of all U.S. workers, as illustrated in Figure 5.1. The gap is even larger for women, who represent only 28 percent of the tech workforce compared to 47 percent of the overall labor force.[2]

The lack of diversity in computer science and in the information technology sector of the economy, especially among women and underrepresented minorities, is a well-recognized challenge.[3] These representation rates are even smaller than those reported for the tech industry as a whole when considering diversity in computing occupations among all U.S. bachelor's degree holders. According to data from the American Community Survey, between 2009 and 2014, 25.1 per-

[1] See NCWIT (2014).

[2] See Intel Corporation and Dalberg Global Development Advisors (2016).

[3] See, for example, Cereijido and Selyukh (2016); Donnelly (2017); Margolis and Fisher (2002); Wiener (2016).

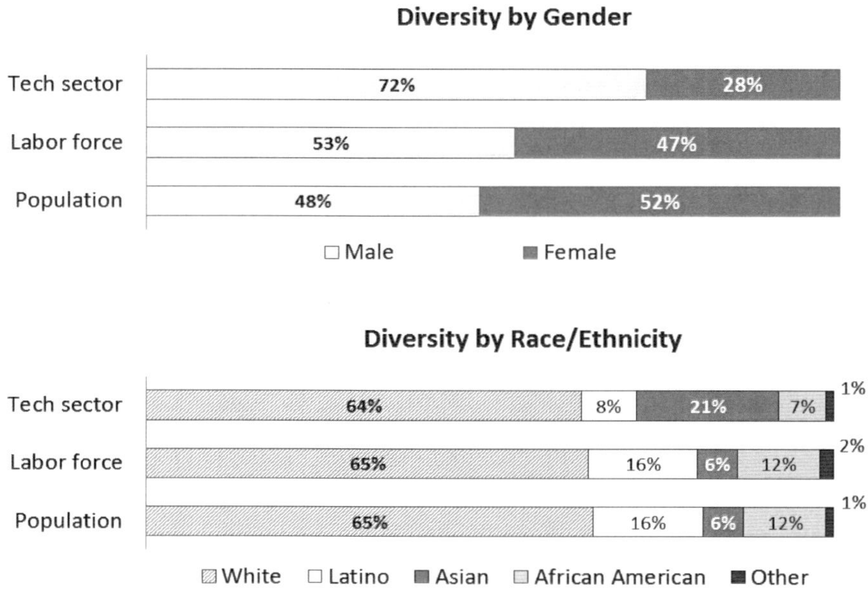

FIGURE 5.1 Overview of diversity in the U.S. tech workforce.
NOTE: Numbers may not add to 100 percent, presumably due to rounding, SOURCE: Data from Intel Corporation and Dalberg Global Development Advisors. 2016. Decoding Diversity: The Financial and Economic Returns to Diversity in Tech. Online. Available at https://www.intel.com/content/www/us/en/diversity/decoding-diversity-report.html.

cent of these workers were female, 5.9 percent were African American, and 4.6 percent were Hispanic or Latino/Latina (Bound and Morales, 2016).

For these reasons the participation of women and underrepresented minorities in computing is of unique interest to many in higher education, government, and industry, and it is of particular importance to the future of the discipline.

The recent enrollment growth in computing presents a unique opportunity for departments to increase student diversity. However, to accomplish this increase, it is important for departments to be *intentional* about the increase—that is, to put into place programs, policies, and partnerships to increase diversity. For the purposes of this report, "underrepresented minorities" are defined as including the following groups: black or African American, Hispanic, and American Indian or Alaska Native; other (including two or more races) are included in the category of "other or unknown" in the Integrated Postsecondary Education Data System (IPEDS) data. The committee recognizes that people with disabilities comprise an important community that is underrepresented in computing; however, due to the lack of sufficient data, this dimension of diversity is not discussed in this report.

This chapter revisits the national statistical data on undergraduate degree completion (discussed in Chapter 2) with an eye to diversity trends in computer science (CS). Then, current enrollments data from multiple surveys are examined to elucidate recent diversity trends in student enrollment in CS courses and degree programs for available samplings of institutions. Potential diversity challenges and opportunities related to the current enrollment surge are explored.

HISTORICAL DIVERSITY OF UNDERGRADUATE CIS DEGREE RECIPIENTS

As context for thinking about diversity in computing in the current enrollment boom, it is instructive to consider the historical participation of women and underrepresented minorities in computer science and related majors. These trends are explored for women and underrepresented minorities in the following sections based upon available data.[4]

Representation of Women among CIS Degree Recipients

The relative share of computer and information science and support services (CIS)[5] bachelor's degrees reported going to women at all institutions increased until 1985, during the first historical surge in CIS degree production, peaking at 37 percent 2 years before the mid-1980s decline in overall annual CIS bachelor's degree production, as illustrated in Figure 5.2. At that time this share decreased abruptly, leveling off somewhat in the mid-1990s, then dropping again precipitously beginning in 2004, one year before the 2005 onset of the decline in overall CIS bachelor's degree production during the dot-com bust. After 2008 the share of CIS bachelor's degrees awarded to women leveled off, remaining steady near 18 percent overall through 2015. While representation of women is slightly less at not-for-profit institutions, this gap narrowed somewhat between 2011 and 2015.[6]

CIS Degrees by Race/Ethnicity

Figure 5.3 illustrates the relative share of all U.S. (CIS) bachelor's degrees conferred each year to all categories of race/ethnicity from 1977 through 2015 at all institutions (left) and at not-for-profit institutions.[7] While representation of

---

[4] Note that there is some degree of uncertainty in the participation rates discussed in this section. In particular, race/ethnicity is not reported for all national degree production data from IPEDS; a significant number are reported as "other" (which includes two or more races) or "unknown."

[5] According to the IPEDS "detailed" classifier, corresponding to the entire 11 series of Classification of Instructional Programs (CIPs). See NSF (2016b, Chapter 2) for additional discussion of this classifier.

[6] There is some evidence that the rate of participation among women has begun to increase at many institutions in recent years. This is discussed in more detail later in this chapter.

[7] According to the IPEDS "detailed" classifier, corresponding to the entire 11 series of CIPs. See NSF (2016b, Chapter 2) for additional discussion of this classifier.

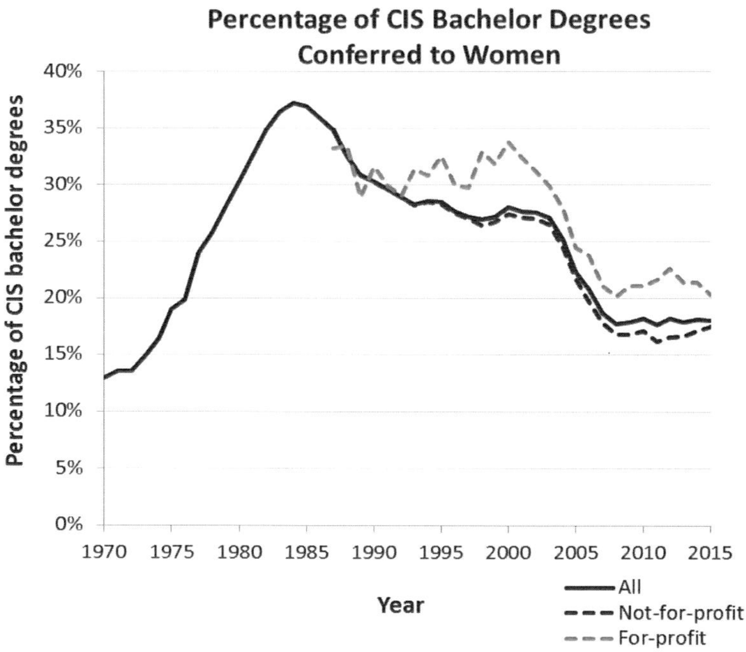

FIGURE 5.2 Percentage of reported CIS bachelor's degrees conferred to women at for-profit (dotted gray line), not-for-profit (dotted black line), and all (solid black line) institutions. SOURCE: Data from IPEDS degree completions survey accessed via the WebCASPAR online database. See Appendix F for details.

underrepresented minorities is higher at for-profit institutions, the share of CIS bachelor's degrees reported for underrepresented minorities has increased both in general and at not-for-profit institutions since 1975.[8] However, this increase has not been uniform across all underrepresented groups.

CIS Degree Production for Women and Underrepresented Minorities

The time series trends for Hispanic or Latino, black (non-Hispanic), and American Indian or Alaska Native (non-Hispanic) students at all institutions and at not-for-profit institutions only are illustrated in Figure 5.4. The share of all CIS bachelor's degrees going to Hispanic students has increased steadily, as has

[8] It should be noted that a significant fraction of students do not identify a race/ethnicity each year, contributing to significant uncertainty about the accuracy of the apparent trends for any particular race/ethnic group.

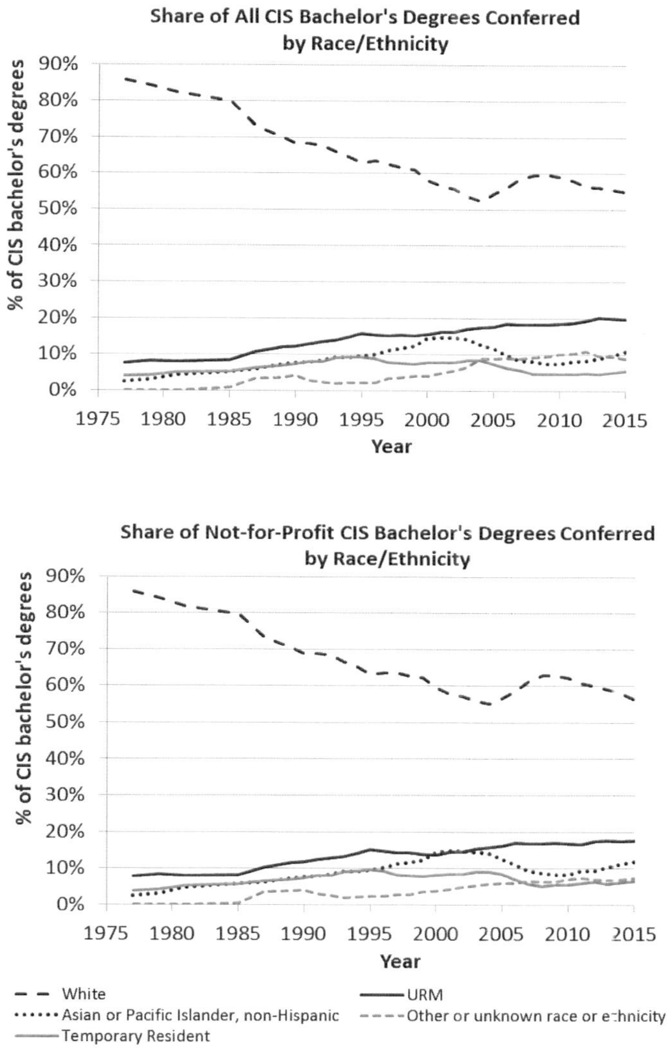

FIGURE 5.3 Share of all reported U.S. CIS bachelor's degrees conferred, by race/ethnicity for all institutions (top panel) and not-for-profit institutions (bottom panel). The curve labeled "URM" is the combined share of the following underrepresented minority groups: black, non-Hispanic; Hispanic or Latino; and American Indian or Alaska Native. "Other/unknown race/ethnicity" includes students of two or more races and students for whom race/ethnicity is unknown. "Temporary resident" corresponds to foreign students, and is exclusive of the other categories, as defined by the National Center for Education Statistics (NCES). Categories displayed add to 100 percent at any point in time. SOURCE: Data from IPEDS completions survey accessed via the WebCASPAR online database. See Appendix F for details.

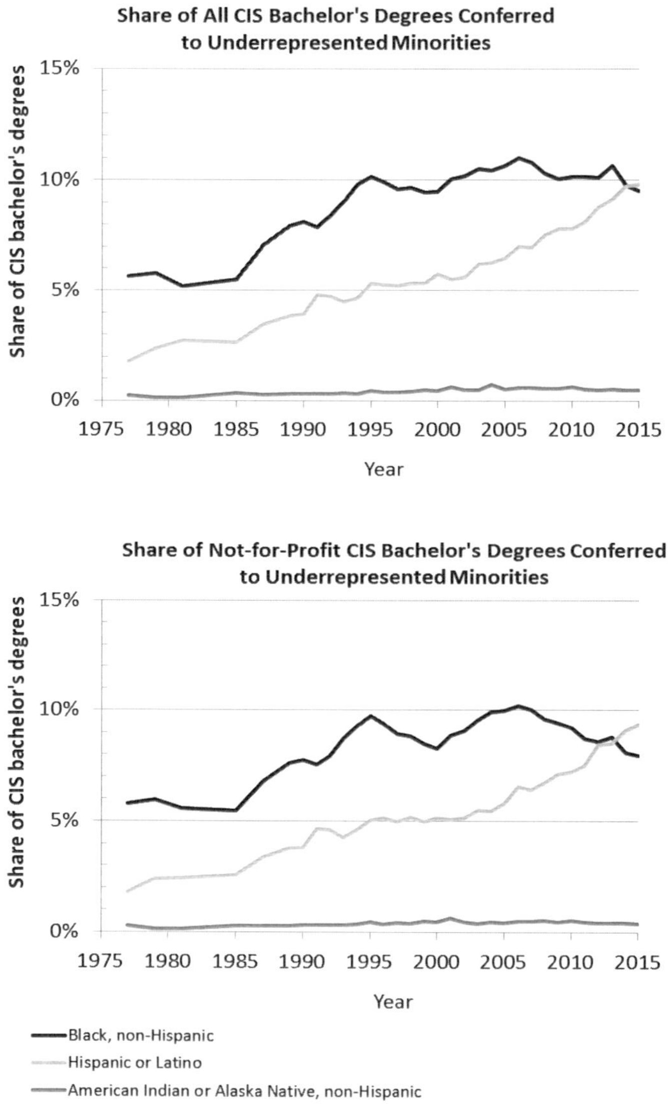

FIGURE 5.4 Share of reported CIS bachelor's degrees conferred to underrepresented minority groups at all (top panel) and not-for-profit (bottom panel) institutions. SOURCE: Data from IPEDS completions survey accessed via the WebCASPAR online database. See Appendix F for details.

the share of all U.S. bachelor's degrees[9] and the representation of Hispanics in the U.S. population.[10] While the share of CIS bachelor's degrees going to black, non-Hispanic students has increased over the long term with some fluctuations, it has decreased somewhat in recent years (from 10.1 to 9.5 percent overall between 2010 and 2015, and from 10.2 to 7.9 percent at not-for-profit institutions between 2006 and 2015).

The absolute numbers of degrees conferred to students of each underrepresented race/ethnic group are illustrated by institution type (public, private, for-profit) in Figure 5.5, and for women in Figure 5.6.

For all ethnicities and genders, public institutions provide the largest number of graduates, with the exception of American Indian or Alaska Natives in 2004 where more graduates came from for-profit institutions. For African Americans and American Indians or Alaska Natives, for-profit institutions produced the second largest number of graduates in recent years (and did until 2015 for women and Hispanics); for white, non-Hispanic students, non-profit, private institutions produce the second largest number of graduates.

It is notable that, for white students, public institutions have been by far the top CIS degree producers, accounting for more than twice as many degrees as private or for-profit institutions (which produced similar amounts) since 2012. In contrast degrees awarded to Hispanic or Latina females, American Indian or Alaska Native students, and black or African American students have a much more significant contribution from for-profit institutions, which typically do not provide exposure to research or the environment of institutions with advanced degrees, or access to top recruiters and job opportunities.

Data on recent CS/CE degree production by race and gender is also available for Computing Alliance for Hispanic-Serving Institutions (CAHSI) institutions, illustrated in Figure 5.7; a recent increase in degree production is apparent (as discussed in Chapter 3). While the sample size is quite small compared to the national data, it is worth noting that degree production is notably high for Hispanics; overall the relative participation of women, Hispanics, and other underrepresented minorities (in this case, identified as African Americans, Native Americans, and Pacific Islanders) has also increased somewhat in recent years (Hug et al., 2017).

FINDING 6: CS and CIS have historically had low representation of women and underrepresented minorities. This trend of underrepresentation in bachelor's degree completions had not improved significantly as of 2015, but there is some evidence that representation is improving among students currently majoring or interested in majoring in CS.

---

[9] The share of all bachelor's degrees conferred to Hispanic students has similarly increased over time (NSF, 2016b).

[10] See Flores (2017).

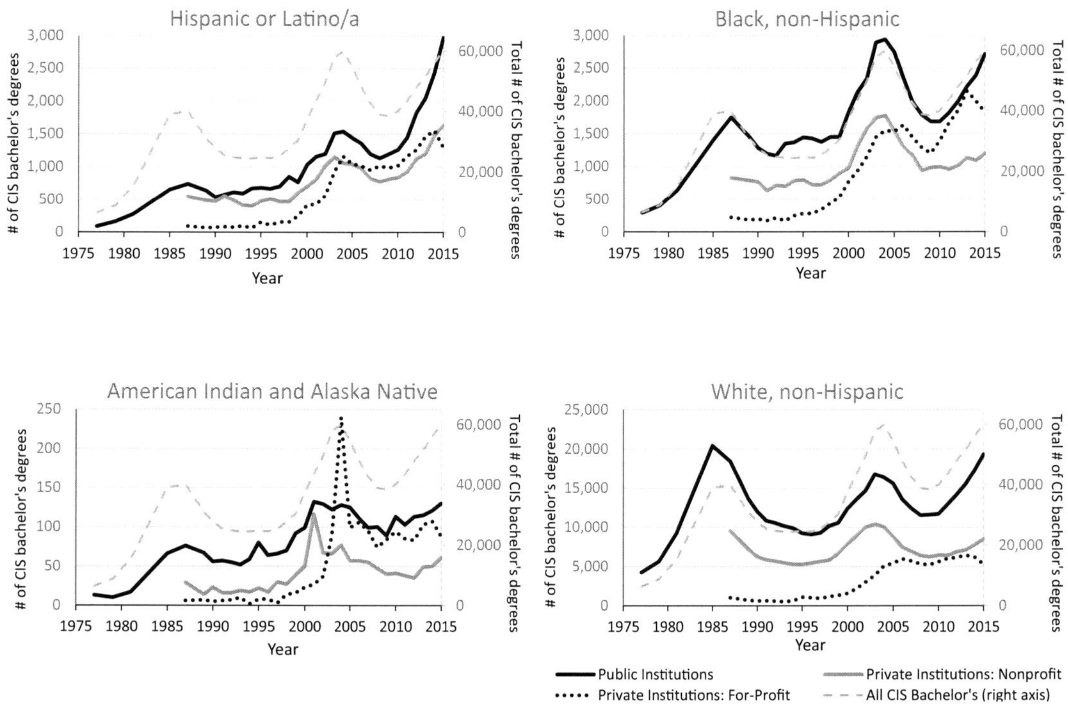

FIGURE 5.5 Number of CIS bachelor's degrees reported (solid lines, left vertical axis) from 1990 to 2015 for Hispanic or Latino, non-Hispanic black, American Indian or Alaska Native, and non-Hispanic white students, by "institutional control," including for-profit status of institution. The total number of CIS bachelor's degrees produced over time for all races/ethnicities is plotted as a reference (dashed line, right vertical axis).
SOURCE: Data from IPEDS completions survey accessed via the WebCASPAR online database. See Appendix F for details.

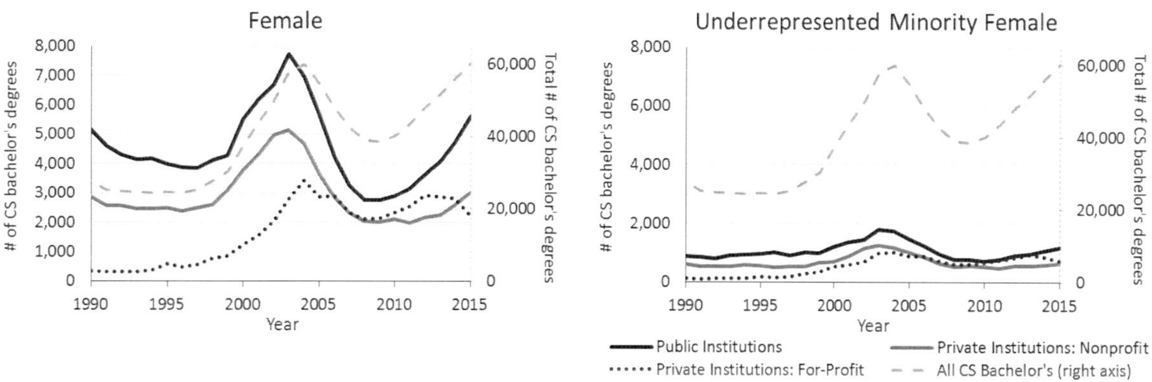

FIGURE 5.6 Number of CIS bachelor's degrees reported (1990-2015) for female (left panel) and underrepresented minority female (right panel) students, by for-profit status of institution. The total number of degrees produced over time for all races/ethnicities is plotted as a reference (dashed line, right vertical axis). SOURCE: Data from IPEDS completions survey accessed via the WebCASPAR online database. See Appendix F for details.

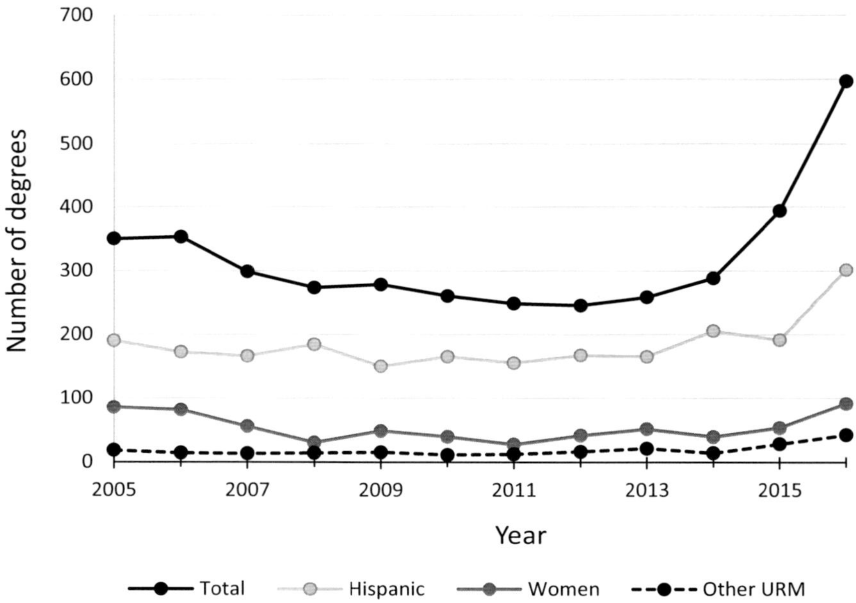

FIGURE 5.7 Number of computing bachelor's degrees awarded by CAHSI institutions: total and broken out for women, Hispanics, and underrepresented minorities, 2005-2016. SOURCE: Hug et al., 2017. CASHI External Evaluation Report, 2016-2017. Online. Available at http://cahsi.cs.utep.edu/cahsifiles/Reports/evaluation/2015-2016CAHSI AnnualEvaluationReport.pdf.

RECENT DEGREE PRODUCTION FOR WOMEN AND UNDERREPRESENTED MINORITIES IN CORE CS, CE, AND IS

The data discussed in the previous sections provide a useful picture of historical diversity trends in CS and related fields. As noted in previous chapters the CIS categories include some fields that may be outside traditional or core CS disciplines, and do not include computer engineering (CE). In order to examine the participation of underrepresented minorities in core CS, CE, and information science (IS) at not-for-profit universities since the recent enrollment surge began, the share of degrees in each of these fields going to women, and black or African American, American Indian or Alaska Native, and Hispanic/Latino students are plotted in Figures 5.8, 5.9, 5.10, and 5.11. For the purpose of these analyses, these three fields are defined as follows: (1) core CS corresponds to the IPEDS CIPs

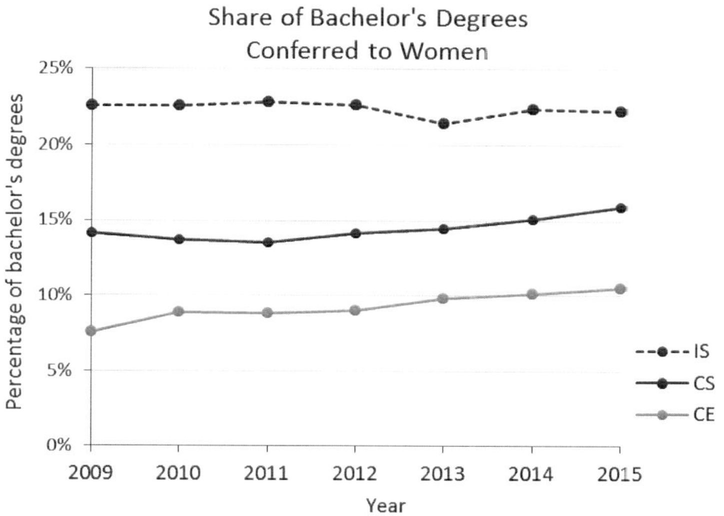

FIGURE 5.8 Reported share of bachelor's degrees in core CS, CE, and IS at not-for-profit institutions conferred to women between 2009 and 2015. SOURCE: Data from IPEDS completions survey accessed via the WebCASPAR online database. See text and Appendix F for details.

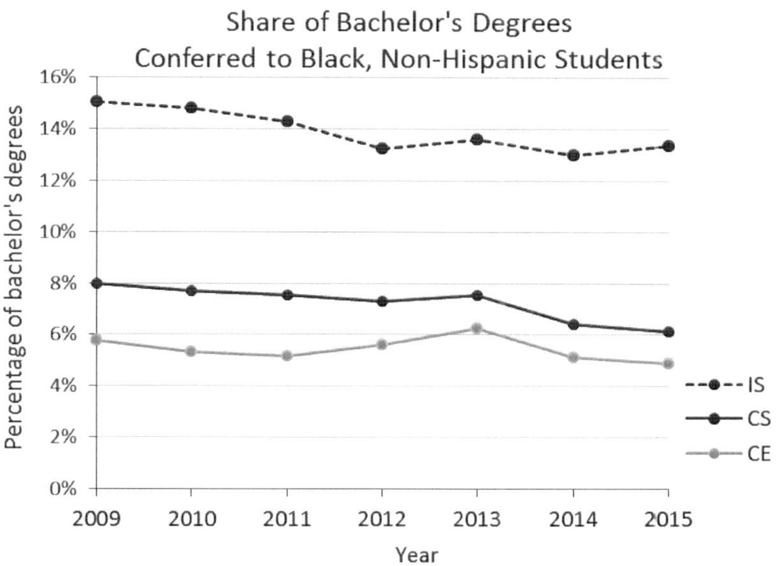

FIGURE 5.9 Share of bachelor's degrees in core CS, CE, and IS at not-for-profit institutions reported for black, non-Hispanic students between 2009 and 2015. SOURCE: Data from IPEDS completions survey accessed via the WebCASPAR online database. See text Appendix F for details.

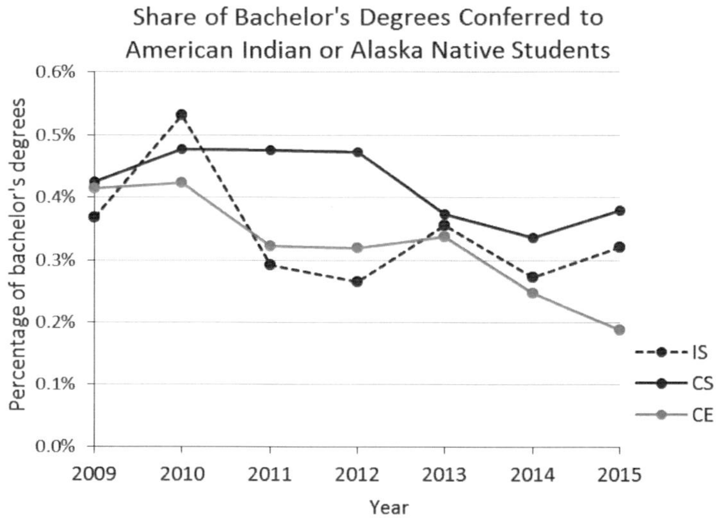

FIGURE 5.10 Share of bachelor's degrees in core CS, CE, and IS at not-for-profit institutions reported for American Indian or Alaska Native (non-Hispanic) students between 2009 and 2015. SOURCE: Data from IPEDS completions survey accessed via the Web-CASPAR online database. See text and Appendix F for details.

of 11.0101 and 11.0701, (2) CE corresponds to the IPEDS CIP of 14.09xx, and (3) IS corresponds to the IPEDS CIP of 11.0401.[11]

It is noteworthy that women are much better represented in information science/studies than in core CS, and not surprising that they are more poorly represented in CE, as engineering overall generally has the lowest representation of women among science, technology, engineering, and mathematics (STEM) fields. While the share of women in IS has been relatively constant at around 22 percent since the recent enrollment surge began, the share in core CS has increased from 13.6 percent in 2011 to 15.9 percent in 2015.

In their Generation CS report, the Computing Research Association (CRA) broke down the trends for core CS further, to compare the representation of women at doctoral (CS Ph.D.-granting) and non-doctoral (CS non-Ph.D.-granting) institutions, approximately corresponding to those polled in the Taulbee and NDC surveys, respectively. They found that the share of bachelor's degrees going to women at doctoral institutions rose from 11.4 percent in 2009 to 15.3 percent in 2015; representation of women was higher overall at non-doctoral institutions,

[11] See the section "Data Used in the Development of This Report" in Chapter 1 for additional discussion of the IPEDS classifiers for computer science and related fields.

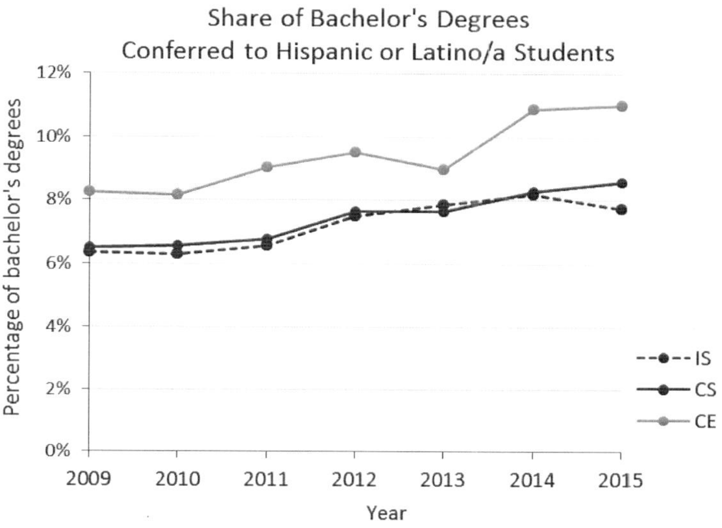

FIGURE 5.11 Share of bachelor's degrees in core CS, CE, and IS at not-for-profit institutions reported for Hispanic or Latino students between 2009 and 2015. SOURCE: Data from IPEDS completions survey accessed via the WebCASPAR online database. See text and Appendix F for details.

where they accounted for 17.0 percent of CS degrees in 2009, dropped to slightly below 16 percent from 2011 to 2014, and rose to 16.6 percent in 2015. This shows that, while the representation of women in core CS has been higher at non-doctoral programs than at doctoral programs, the latter has improved steadily since 2011, and nearly bridged the gap by 2015.

Black or African American students also have much higher representation—by approximately a factor of 2—among IS bachelor's degree recipients than for core CS or CE at not-for-profits. At the same time, while the absolute number of black or African American students completing computer science and related degrees has increased in the current surge, this increase has been slower than that of other race/ethnic groups. As a result, the share of CS, CE, and IS degrees going to African Americans actually decreased between 2009 and 2015, falling from 8.0 to 6.1 percent (CS), 5.8 to 4.9 percent (CE), and 15.0 to 13.4 percent (IS). According to the IPEDS analysis in the Generation CS report (CRA, 2017a), representation of this group dropped both at doctoral-granting (from 5.5 to 4.3 percent) and non-doctoral-granting (from 10.6 to 8.6 percent) institutions between 2009 and 2015; representation of black or African American students completing CS bachelor's degree programs at non-doctoral institutions was double that at doctoral institutions.

American Indian or Alaska Native students have also seen declining representation in core CS, CE, and IS. Overall representation is similar between the three fields, and the low numbers make it difficult to analyze further.

Hispanic or Latino students have seen increasing representation in all three fields, with very similar shares of the degrees produced in both core CS and IS. Unlike the other groups discussed in this section, the share of degrees conferred to Hispanic or Latino students is markedly larger for CE than for CS or IS.

According to the further CRA analysis of bachelor's degree production in core CS, increasing representation of Hispanic/Latino students has occurred at both doctoral and non-doctoral units over this time, with a consistently lower share but larger growth (from 5.8 to 8.4 percent) at doctoral units compared to non-doctoral (from 7.0 to 8.5 percent).

DIVERSITY OF COMPUTER SCIENCE ENROLLMENTS

In order to better understand the relationship between diversity in both CS degree program and course enrollment in the context of the recent surge, it is instructive to consider available surveys, given the lack of national-scale data about degree enrollments and course enrollments, as discussed in Chapters 2 and 3. The committee turned to five data sources, three of which were discussed in more detail in Chapter 3: (1) data on freshman intent to major in CS from the Freshman Survey Trends of the Cooperative Institutional Research Program (CIRP) of the Higher Education Research Institute (HERI) at the University of California, Los Angeles; (2) CS program enrollment data from Ph.D.-granting institutions surveyed by the CRA during the time period of 2012 through 2015, as part of the Taulbee Survey; (3) the CRA and Association for Computing Machinery (ACM) Enrollment Surveys, including data on course enrollments; (4) data collected and analyzed by the Consortium for Undergraduate STEM Success; and (5) enrollment data for members of CAHSI. While these case studies represent a small subset of U.S. institutions, they nonetheless allow for a unique and in-depth look at diversity of enrollment in CS majors or courses, which complements that provided by the degree production data presented in the preceding section. In the following, gender diversity and the representation of underrepresented minorities in undergraduate computing are explored using the available data.

Intent to Major in Computer Science

While the fraction of CIS bachelor's degrees awarded to women remained relatively flat from 2009 to 2015, the fraction of female baccalaureates whose degrees were in CIS did increase slightly (from 0. 74 to 0.99 percent of female bachelor's degree recipients) during this time, meaning that the participation rate in CS among women has increased at the same time as it has for men (from 4.57 to 6.02 percent of male bachelor's degree recipients). Among respondents to the

HERI CIRP survey (discussed in Chapter 3), the share of female freshmen intending to major in CS increased from 0.3 to 1.7 percent between 2011 and 2015, compared to an increase from 2.1 to 6.3 percent for male freshman. These data, illustrated in Figure 5.12, suggest that the relative growth in the share of students interested in enrolling in CS as a major is higher for women than for men.

Similar data for underrepresented minorities, shown in Figure 5.13, show that these groups have also begun to participate at increasing rates in computer science bachelor's programs at not-for-profit institutions. However, unlike for women and Hispanics, the rates of intent to major in CS among black and American Indian or Alaska Native students have not yet reached dot-com-era levels.

The HERI CIRP survey is based on a sampling of students at a subset of all not-for-profit institutions of higher education, whereas the IPEDS degree completions are extracted from all not-for-profit institutions, and the specific data presented may include more disciplines than those counted in the HERI CIRP survey. In addition, students change majors during their undergraduate careers for a number of reasons; it remains to be seen whether the faster increase in interest among women (according to the survey) will translate to an increase in the share of CIS degrees going to women when the freshmen of 2011-2015 graduate, and how increased participation among underrepresented minorities will affect the overall diversity among CS bachelor's holders.

Computer Science Program and Course Enrollments

As discussed in Chapter 3 the CRA conducts an annual survey of Ph.D.-granting institutions to collect data on CS degree production (bachelor's, master's, and doctoral), faculty demographics, faculty salary, and Ph.D. graduate placement. The Taulbee Survey is distributed to 266 Ph.D.-granting departments annually. Because CRA is focused on computing research, it only recently began collecting data on undergraduate enrollment in the degree program, with data broken out by ethnicity and gender beginning in the 2012-2013 academic year. In the first 3 years, 121 departments responded to this section of the survey (though not necessarily the same 121 departments each year); 155 responded for the 2015-2016 academic year.

Overall, average CS program enrollments per department more than doubled in this time period. At the same time, upward trends were observed in the percentage of Hispanic (7.8 to 9.5 percent), multiracial non-Hispanic (2.1 to 3.0 percent), and female (13.9 to 18.3 percent) subgroups. The percentage of black or African American students fluctuated around 5 percent, most recently decreasing, and the percentage of American Indian or Alaska Native and Native Hawaiian or other Pacific Islander was small, below 0.5 percent. The shares of major enrollments for women and for all race/ethnicity groups are displayed in Table 5.1.

The corresponding statistics for the non-doctoral institutions responding to this survey are listed in Table 5.2. While these data are less complete, the

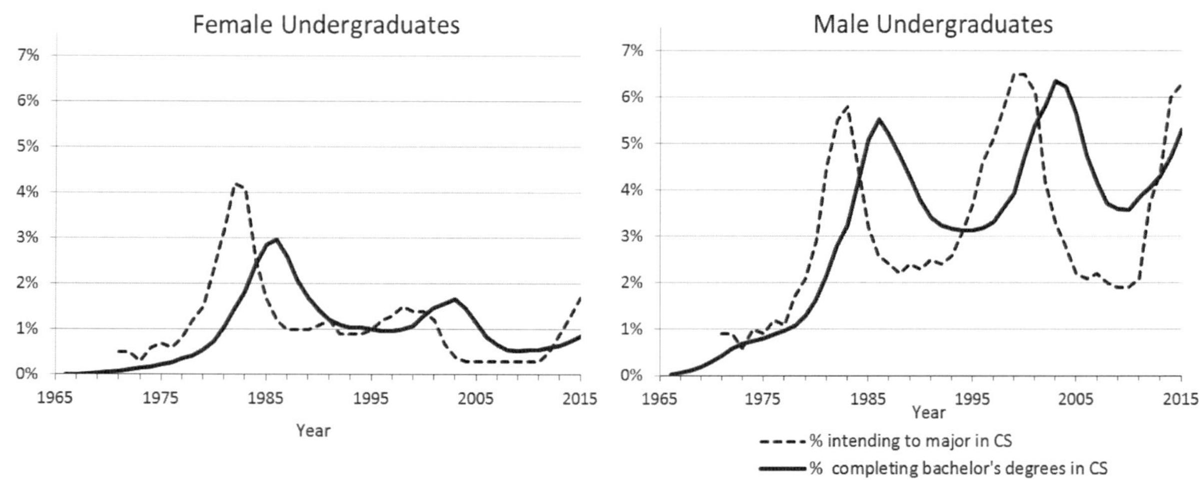

FIGURE 5.12 Share of female (left panel) and male (right panel) undergraduates at U.S. not-for-profit institutions participating in CS bachelor's degree programs at the beginning and end of the undergraduate career. The dotted lines indicate the fraction of female (left panel) and male (right panel) freshmen intending to major in CS from 1970 to 2015, according to the HERI CIRP survey. The solid line indicates the fraction of female (left panel) and male (right panel) bachelor's degree recipients from 1966 to 2015 whose degree was in CIS, according to the IPEDS NCES completions data for all not-for-profit institutions. SOURCE: Data from Eagan et al. (2016) and IPEDS completions survey accessed via the WebCASPAR online database (see Appendix F for details).

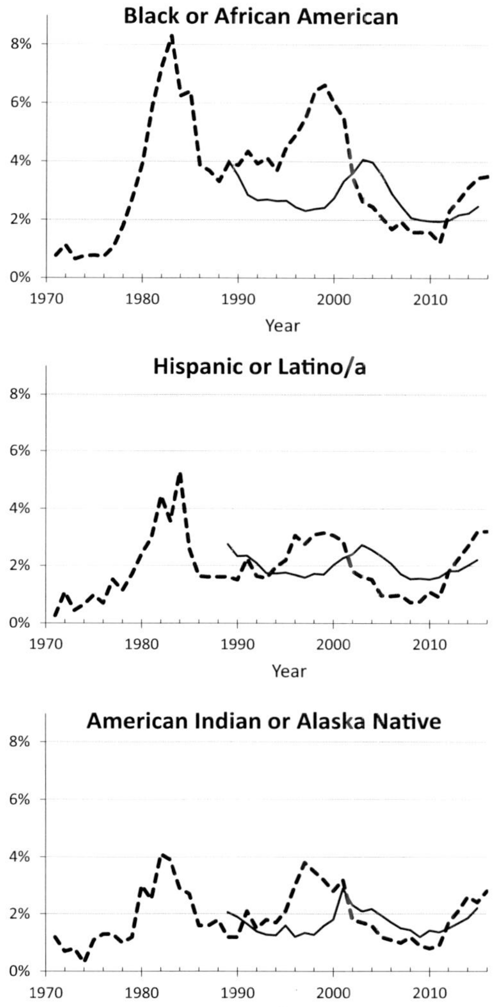

FIGURE 5.13 Percentage of students in underrepresented groups at U.S. not-for-profit institutions participating in CS bachelor's degree programs at the beginning and end of the undergraduate career. The dotted lines indicate the fraction of freshmen of the corresponding group intending to major in CS from 1970 to 2015, according to the HERI CIRP survey. The solid line indicates the fraction completing a bachelor's degree in CIS in the year indicated, according to IPEDS completions data. SOURCE: Data from Eagan et al. (2016); IPEDS completions survey accessed via the WebCASPAR online database (see Appendix F for details).

TABLE 5.1 Demographics of CS Undergraduate Program Enrollments at Taulbee (Subset of CS Ph.D.-Granting) Institutions

	2012-2013	2013-2014	2014-2015	2015-2016
Total enrollment	*43,391*	*72,447*	*90,604*	*104,634*
Women	13.9%	15.3%	16.5%	18.3%
American Indian or Alaska Native	0.4%	0.4%	0.4%	0.1%
Native Hawaiian or other Pacific Islander	0.2%	0.2%	0.3%	0.3%
Multiracial not Hispanic	2.1%	2.7%	2.8%	3.0%
Black or African American	4.9%	5.0%	5.4%	4.8%
Hispanic, any race	7.8%	8.8%	9.0%	9.5%
Asian	16.1%	19.5%	21.6%	23.8%
White	58.9%	54.4%	51.0%	47.4%
Nonresident alien	9.6%	8.9%	9.5%	11.0%

NOTE: Students with no or unknown race/ethnicity listed were excluded from the total in calculation of the corresponding percentages. SOURCE: CRA Taulbee Survey.

TABLE 5.2 Demographics of CS Undergraduate Program Enrollments at NDC (Non-CS Doctoral) Institutions

	2012-2013	2013-2014	2014-2015	2015-2016
Institutions reporting	*101*	*163*	*132*	*121*
Total enrollments reported	*6,659*	*14,061*	*12,759*	*11,864*
Average enrollments per institution reporting	*66*	*86*	*97*	*98*
Women	12.6%	11.0%	16.1%	16.0%
American Indian or Alaska Native	0.3%	0.3%	0.4%	0.4%
Native Hawaiian or other Pacific Islander	0.2%	0.2%	0.2%	0.2%
Multiracial not Hispanic	1.3%	2.0%	1.7%	2.4%
Black or African-American	5.3%	4.4%	4.8%	5.5%
Hispanic, any race	7.0%	8.3%	7.1%	6.6%
Asian	6.3%	6.1%	9.5%	8.7%
White	53.3%	52.0%	51.4%	46.3%
Nonresident alien	3.3%	4.1%	4.3%	5.1%

NOTE: Students with no or unknown race/ethnicity or gender listed were excluded from the total in calculation of the corresponding percentages. SOURCE: ACM NDC Survey; unpublished data courtesy of ACM.

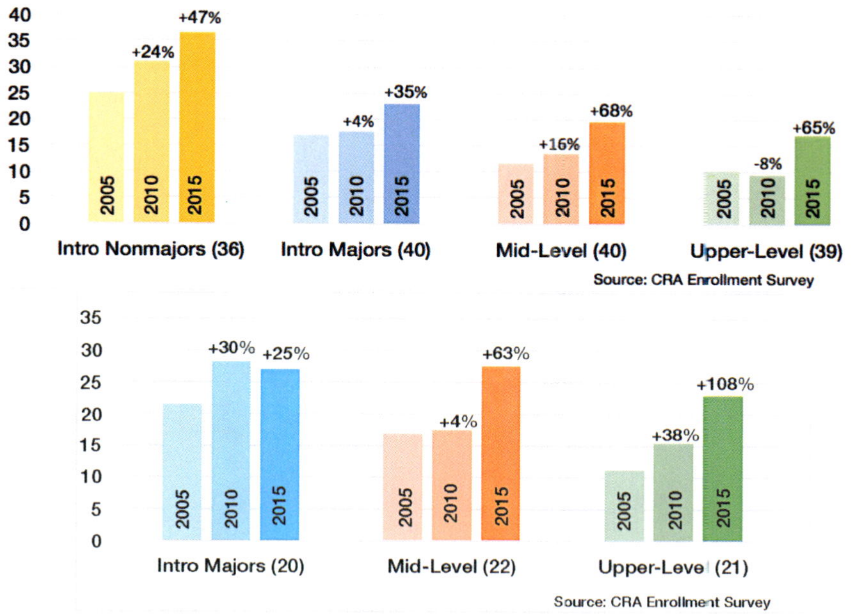

FIGURE 5.14 Median percentage of female students in courses surveyed—doctoral (top) and non-doctoral (bottom) granting units. SOURCE: CRA (Computing Research Association) 2017a. Generation CS: Computer Science Undergraduate Enrollments Surge Since 2006. Online. Available at http://cra.org/data/Generation-CS/.

reported representation levels are similar, though generally smaller for women and Hispanic students.

As discussed in Chapter 3 the CRA conducted in collaboration with ACM a special survey of institutions to obtain detailed evidence of the extent and impact of the current enrollment surge at CS departments. The overall goal of this 2015 survey was to measure, assess, and better understand enrollment trends, with a focus on undergraduate degree programs.[12]

In addition to total course enrollment numbers, institutions were asked to provide the demographics of the students enrolled in courses that are representative of the four course categories: introduction for non-majors, introduction for majors, mid-level, and upper-level computer science courses (CRA, 2017a).

Figure 5.14 illustrates the median percentage of female students in each category of class at the doctoral (top panel) and non-doctoral (bottom panel) institutions that responded to the survey. The median response for doctoral institutions

[12] See Chapter 3 for additional background on this survey.

indicated a slight increase in representation of women in all but the upper-level course between 2005 and 2010, and a more pronounced increase across all course types between 2010 and 2015. The median response for non-doctoral institutions showed similar trends for mid- and upper-level courses (this category does not include courses directed at non-majors, as few non-doctoral institutions reported courses of this type). This suggests that there is reason to expect that the fraction of CS degrees awarded to women will increase in upcoming years unless something disrupts the trends in the pipeline. The illustrated decrease in participation of women along the course progression could be due in part to the time lag between courses (e.g., trends in introductory classes would take a few years to propagate as students advance), but it nonetheless illustrates that attrition rates are higher among women than men.

For CS Ph.D.-granting institutions, the data are further broken down by private versus public institutions in Figure 5.15, which indicates that women make up a larger percentage of CS students at private institutions than at public ones, and the rate of increase is higher.

The median number of underrepresented minority CS students at responding institutions increased for all course levels between 2005 and 2015, as illustrated in Figure 5.16. It is worth noting that minority-serving institutions (MSIs) contribute

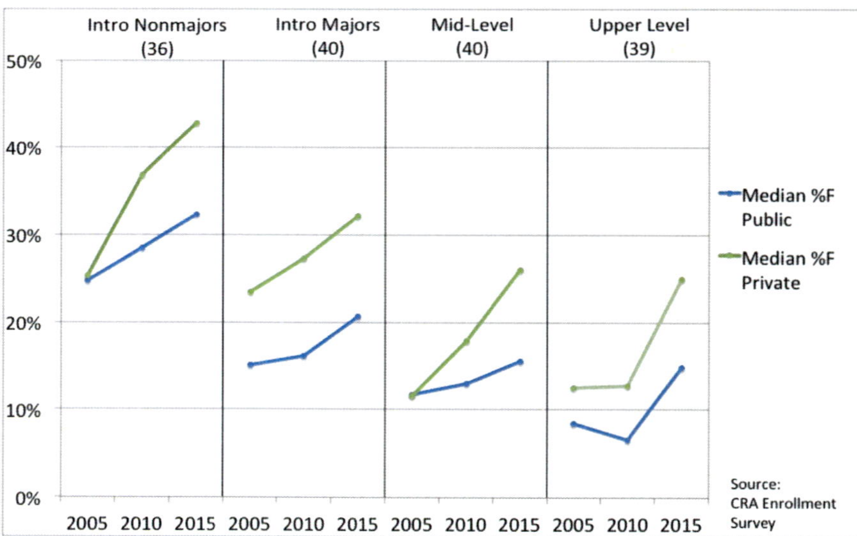

FIGURE 5.15 Median percentage of female students in courses surveyed in doctoral-granting units—public versus private. Number in parentheses in each category indicates sample size. SOURCE: CRA (Computing Research Association). 2017a. Generation CS: Computer Science Undergraduate Enrollments Surge Since 2006. Online. Available at http://cra.org/data/Generation-CS/.

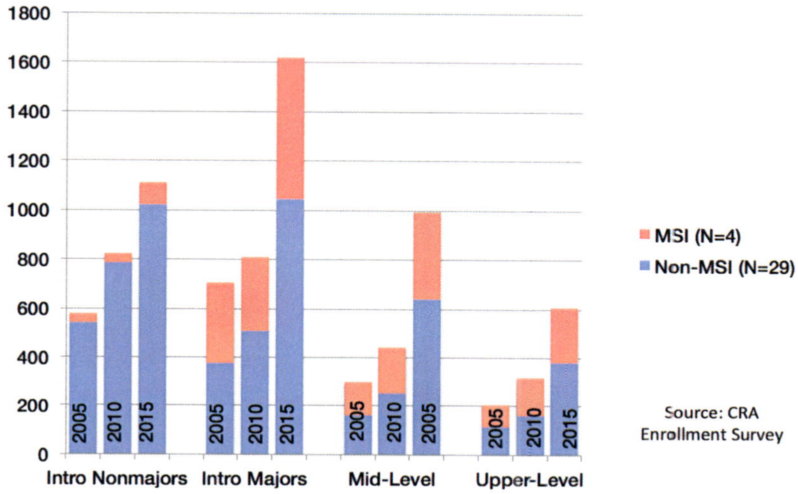

FIGURE 5.16 Number of underrepresented minority students in representative courses in doctoral-granting units. SOURCE: CRA (Computing Research Association). 2017a. Generation CS: Computer Science Undergraduate Enrollments Surge Since 2006. Online. Available at http://cra.org/data/Generation-CS/.

to these numbers disproportionately. The median percentage of underrepresented minority CS students at non-MSI institutions is illustrated in Figure 5.17 for all course levels at doctoral (top panel) and non-doctoral (bottom panel) institutions. For each course category the fraction is higher in 2015 than in 2010 or 2005, though an increase did not necessarily occur during each 5-year interval.

DIVERSITY IMPACTS ASSOCIATED WITH ENROLLMENT GROWTH

Representation of Women

Interest in CS as a major among both the female and male freshmen populations rose significantly in the lead-up to the surge in CS degree production in the 1980s; the corresponding representation of women among CS degree recipients increased. In the dot-com era, interest again increased among freshmen of both genders, but the increase was less pronounced among women than among men. However, in the wake of this growth, the share of female undergraduates intending to major in CS seemed to drop much more than it did for male undergraduates, according to Figure 5.12. Because these trends in freshman interest in the major were surveyed within the first few weeks of students' undergraduate education, student interest as measured by the survey is likely informed by a

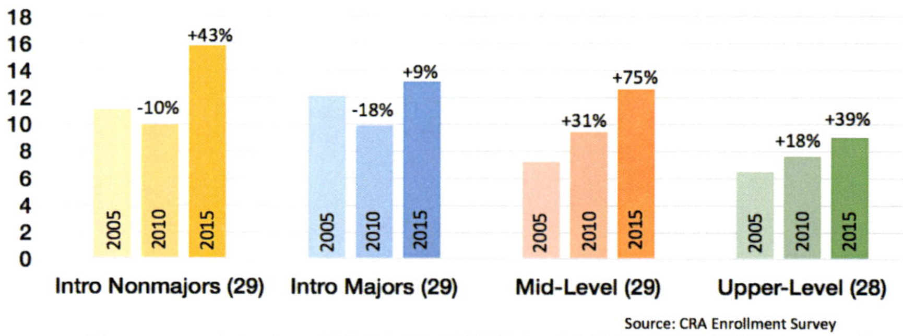

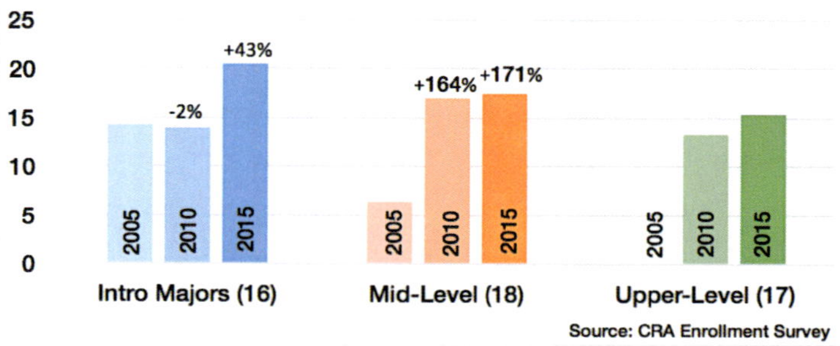

FIGURE 5.17 Median percentage of underrepresented minority students in courses surveyed (excluding MSI)—doctoral-granting (top) and non-doctoral-granting (bottom) units. The number of institutions responding in each category is indicated in parentheses. SOURCE: CRA (Computing Research Association). 2017a. Generation CS: Computer Science Undergraduate Enrollments Surge Since 2006. Online. Available at http://cra.org/data/Generation-CS/.

student's preexisting understanding, and affinity for the substance of the discipline, knowledge of the requirements of the major, perception of the culture of the academic program compared to that of other fields, and expectations of career opportunities. Several recent studies have identified factors that may contribute to women's interest levels in computer science. In general women's awareness or perception that STEM fields tend to be male dominated can affect their participation rates or interest level (Sax et al., 2017). For example, the existence of masculine stereotypes in the environment of a computing classroom can decrease a woman's sense of ambient belonging in the environment, and discourage interest in the environment, whether or not there are any males present (Cheryan et al., 2009).

Because many factors influence these decisions, it would be difficult to define a single cause for the decreasing representation of women in CS and related fields after past surges.[13] Nonetheless, there is a very real possibility that the state or culture of academic computer science was or became somehow uniquely discouraging to women at times when enrollments surged. Thus, with the onset of the current surge, it is critical to consider the potential impacts of enrollment growth—and the actions that institutions take in response to this growth—on the inclusiveness of academic programs.

Representation of Underrepresented Minorities

During the increases in overall enrollment in the mid-1980s and late 1990s, participation among black, Hispanic/Latino, and American Indian/Alaska Native students increased as well. In the wake of both past increases, the share of CIS degrees conferred to students from these groups also increased. In the recent period of enrollment increases, the share of CIS degrees awarded to Hispanic students has increased, but the share going to black and American Indian or Alaska Native students has decreased. While these results are mixed, there may be opportunities to harness the current enthusiasm for the field to build and sustain new interest in computing among individuals from underrepresented or disadvantaged groups by considering best practices described in the next section and collaborating with organizations focused on broadening participation in computing.

Capitalizing on enrollment growth is of particular importance, given that computing jobs offer higher wages on average for new college graduates and throughout one's career, computing skills are more commonly valued in the highest-paying occupations, and computing jobs are expected to grow at twice the rate of all U.S. jobs through 2024, as discussed in Chapter 4.

Best Practices for Diversity

An institution's actions to respond to increased demand for computing courses has the potential to affect its alignment with best practices for diversity. At the same time, the need to respond to increased demand also provides an opportunity for institutions to rethink and redesign practices to increase diversity.

The subject of diversity in STEM-related disciplines has been well studied and reported on for many years. Factors that affect diversity are broad ranging and include institutional and departmental policies on admissions, dedicated retention programs and support structures, pedagogical approaches, perceptions of the value of a discipline, identity with the major, and the nature of the learning environment (Eagan et al., 2010).

[13] For some historical context on forces affecting the participation of women in computer science, see Misa (2011) and Ensmenger (2012).

A review of literature suggests the following best practices for recruitment, retention, and success of diverse student populations in STEM and computing disciplines:

- Minimize or remove the presence of ambient stereotypes in the classroom (Cheryan et al., 2009).
- Include service learning and real-world context in the curriculum (Brinkman and Diekman, 2016; Davis and Finelli, 2007).
- Build meaningful relationships with faculty and peers in the field (Chang et al., 2014; Cole and Espinoza, 2008; Conrad et al., 2009; Gates et al., 2016; Newhall et al., 2014; Peckham et al., 2007; Wilson et al., 2012).
- Emphasize collaborative problem solving and interdisciplinary projects (Peckham et al., 2007; Pulimood and Wolz, 2009).
- Provide multiple pathways to attract computing majors (Peckham et al., 2007).
- Enable student participation in undergraduate research programs (Chang et al., 2014; Conrad et al., 2009; Davis and Finelli, 2007; Gates et al., 2016; Villa et al., 2013; Wilson et al., 2012).
- Provide introductory course options that separate students with prior experience in computer science from those with no experience (Cohoon and Luther, 2011).
- Provide learning environments other than those expected in the normative culture of computer science (Simon et al., 2015).
- Enlist a diverse team of faculty, instructors, and mentors.
- Finally, active assessment and refinement of institutional culture and practices with an eye to inclusivity is an obvious—but not trivial—step for improving diversity.

While such practices reflect the current state of thinking about diversity, it is worth noting that many of these studies are based on single-institution or single-time-point cases. Thus, much of the available literature has been somewhat limited in causally attributing positive trends to these practices. There is a great need for more broad and longitudinal studies on the efficacy and underlying mechanisms of such actions for increasing participation and retention among women and underrepresented minorities.

Diversity and Institutional Responses to Increasing Enrollments

As computing departments face pressures created by rapidly increasing enrollments in computing majors and courses, decisions about how to deal with these pressures must be made. Availability of faculty, graduate/undergraduate teaching assistants, classroom space, and financial resources influence the responses of individual institutions. Some of the possible responses do not curb demand for courses but accommodate it, such as by hiring additional faculty (tenure-track, non-tenure-track, visiting, or adjunct), making wider use of teaching assistants to teach classes and provide instructional support, or increasing the number and size of course sections offered. In other cases restrictions are placed on the number and type of students being serviced by the department. These actions include imposing enrollment caps on the major, tightening admission requirements for the major, restricting registration in high-demand courses to majors and minors only, and reducing offerings of courses that are not as highly demanded or that service students outside the computing major, as identified by the CRA and ACM Enrollments Surveys discussed in Chapter 3.[14] Less than half (46.5 percent) of the responding doctoral institutions reported considering potential impacts on diversity when choosing what actions to take; 79.8 percent of respondents reported that they are not monitoring for diversity effects at these transition points.

Deploying new admissions policies as a way of managing enrollment demands poses the potential to negatively impact diversity in computing programs—indeed, one explanation proposed for the sudden drop in the participation of women in computing in the 1980s is that the practices put in place at many universities to manage that boom in enrollments created an unfriendly or even hostile climate that was found to be less welcoming or appealing by female students.

While there is evidence that diversity of CS enrollments has been increasing at many of the institutions currently experiencing surges in enrollment (as discussed earlier in this chapter), there is no guarantee that tactics recently (or soon to be) deployed for managing large enrollments will not disrupt this trend.

For example, overreliance on past measures of knowledge or success, such as standardized testing, for decisions about acceptance into courses and majors could be limiting to diversity. The ethnicity breakdowns of scoring on the SAT (NCES, 2015) and ACT (NCES, 2010b) exams reported by the NCES show that underrepresented minorities score lower on these exams than their white and Asian counterparts, which may be due to disparities in the opportunities available to different populations at the K-12 level. In particular, studies have found correlation between SAT performance and socioeconomic factors (Geiser, 2015). Several authors have made the case for broadening admissions decisions in general beyond such narrow quantitative measures (Aguinis et al., 2016; Manning, 1989; Nunez, 2015; Soares, 2012).

Expectation of K-12 exposure to computer science can also have a negative impact on diversity. This expectation may manifest as an element of the admissions decision process, or it may be implicitly included in the expectations of student skill level in the first required computer science course. For example,

[14] This list of possible restrictions corresponds with the actions identified in the questionnaire for the CRA Enrollments Survey and is not necessarily comprehensive. For example, another restriction would be to prohibit students already declared in another major from switching into CS as a major, regardless of any other mechanism of capping the major.

TABLE 5.3 Number and Mean Scores of AP Computer Science-A Test Takers by Ethnicity (2010-2015)

	# of Test Takers		% of Test Takers		Mean Score	
Race/gender	Male	Female	Male	Female	Male	Female
White	21,779	4919	40.1	9.0	3.09	2.91
Asian	11,110	4803	20.4	8.8	3.36	3.28
Hispanic	4820	1436	8.9	2.6	2.35	2.03
Two or more races	1770	645	3.3	1.2	3.15	2.99
Black	1415	612	2.6	1.1	2.10	1.81
No response	651	177	1.2	0.3	3.15	2.79
American Indian	79	9	0.1	<0.1	2.80	1.89
Native Hawaiian	56	15	0.1	<0.1	2.38	2.20
Other	57	26	0.1	<0.1	3.14	3.19
Total	41,737	12,642	76.8	23.2	3.05	2.90

SOURCE: Data from the College Board.

reliance on participation or performance in Advanced Placement (AP) Computer Science-A (illustrated in Table 5.3) as a means of limiting the number of students in courses or degree programs would also have the effect of limiting the diversity (that is, participation of women and underrepresented minorities, with the exception of students who declared two or more races) in undergraduate enrollments.[15] In 2015 girls represented only 22 percent and underrepresented minorities only 13 percent of AP test-takers. In nine states, not a single African American student took the exam (Heitin, 2015).

However, introduction of the new AP CS Principles (CSP, discussed in Chapter 4) resulted in a near doubling of the number of students taking an AP CS course between 2016 and 2017 to approximately 111,000 in 2017 (Chatlani, 2017; College Board, 2017; CRA, 2017b). CSP has also been credited with increasing the number of minorities and women taking a CS AP exam, with minority students accounting for 20 percent and women for 27 percent of 2017 test takers; however, this representation has not yet reached parity with the general population.[16]

The discussions in previous sections focused on institutions that offer 4-year undergraduate degrees. It is important, however, to note that minority, first-generation, and low-income students disproportionately attend 2-year institutions

[15] Data obtained from https://research.collegeboard.org/programs/ap/data/archived/ over the years 2010-2015.

[16] See Chatlani (2017); Kamenetz (2017); Partovi (2017); Purdue (2017).

for economic reasons. In 2011 nearly half of all students at the undergraduate level attended 2-year colleges (Kena et al., 2014; Mooney and Foley, 2011), and approximately 18 percent of individuals who received bachelor's degrees in science and engineering between 2007 and 2011 had previously earned associate's degrees. The share of CIS degrees accounted for by women and underrepresented minorities is higher for associate's degrees than it is for CIS bachelor's degrees, as illustrated in Figures 5.18 and 5.19.

A recent study by Excelencia in Education found that today's college students no longer fit the perceived "traditional" student profile of a full-time student transitioning directly from high school to a 4-year college or university (Santiago et al., 2015). This is true, for example, of CAHSI students, who often take a longer path to graduation because of financial constraints and responsibilities for families and dependents. A survey of CAHSI institutions (Thiry and Hug, 2016b) revealed that 23 percent of CAHSI students temporarily left the university (i.e., did not enroll for one or two semesters) because of economic hardship, 50 percent worked outside their studies, and 53 percent were first-generation college students. Many of the CAHSI institutions receive transfer credits from 2-year colleges for approximately 30 to 40 percent of their students.

CAHSI is now piloting efforts to extend peer-led team learning (PLTL) to 2-year feeder colleges with the intent to increase the computing pipeline to 4-year colleges. PLTL has significantly contributed to students' persistence in their chosen major. Prior to the implementation of PLTL in "gatekeeper" courses in the major, merely 77 percent of the enrolled students finished the course, while 87 percent of students completed the course after PLTL implementation (Thiry and Hug, 2016b). In addition, over the years, CAHSI departments have made an effort to foster student participation in computing clubs and professional chapters of computing groups. Indeed, CAHSI students report that they participate in computing-related organizations at slightly higher rates than the national sample of computing students. Likewise, CAHSI students report much higher rates of participation in computing-related groups for minority students than the national sample of students (Thiry and Hug, 2016b).

FINDING 7: There is no guarantee that the representation of women and underrepresented minorities in CS will improve without a focused effort. Retention is always a challenge, and adverse conditions associated with high demand for courses—as well as actions taken by institutions in order to manage enrollments—could negatively impact the inclusiveness of undergraduate computing programs.

ACTIVE EFFORTS TO INCREASE DIVERSITY IN COMPUTING

As discussed in previous sections the recent increases in degree production (2009 to present) and computing enrollments (roughly 2005 to present) have

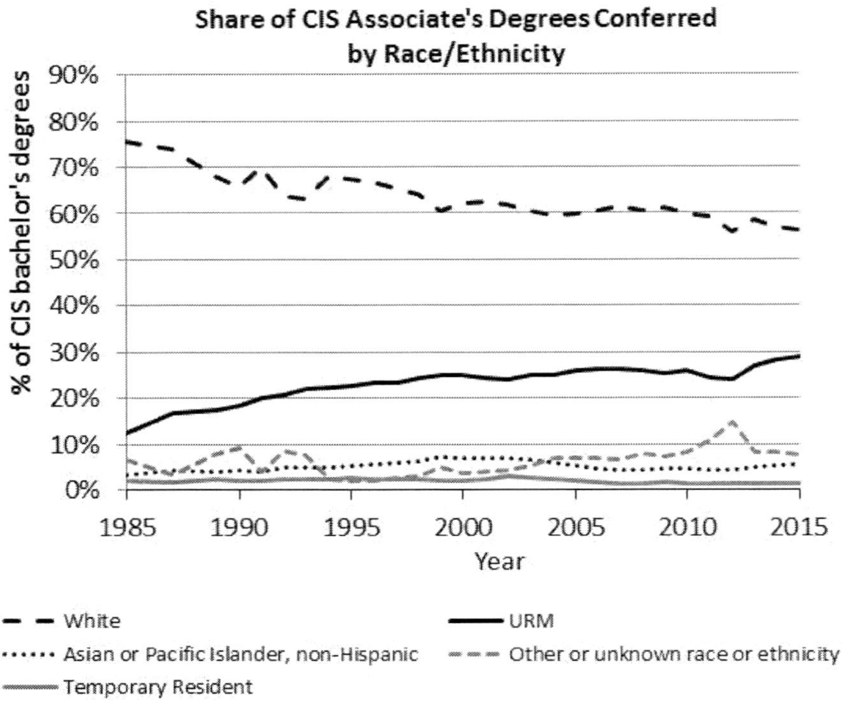

FIGURE 5.18 Share of all U.S. CIS associate's degrees conferred by race/ethnicity. The curve labeled "URM" is the combined share of the following underrepresented minority groups: black, non-Hispanic; Hispanic or Latino; and American Indian or Alaska Native. "Other or unknown race or ethnicity" includes students of two or more races and students for whom race/ethnicity is unknown. "Temporary resident" corresponds to foreign students, and is exclusive of the other categories, as defined by NCES. The sum of all curves is 100 percent in any given year. SOURCE: Data from IPEDS completions survey accessed via the WebCASPAR online database. See Appendix F for details.

coincided with increases in the total number of women and underrepresented minorities participating in computer science and related fields. While the share of CIS degrees going to women has not increased during this time, there is some evidence to suggest that participation among women in CS has begun to rise. These trends may be due in part to recent efforts to broaden participation in computing, including activities aimed at increasing diversity in computing and to increase the participation of students in CS at the K-12 levels.[17]

[17] See the section "Increased Participation in Computing at Primary and Secondary Levels" in Chapter 4 for additional discussion of increasing CS exposure in K-12.

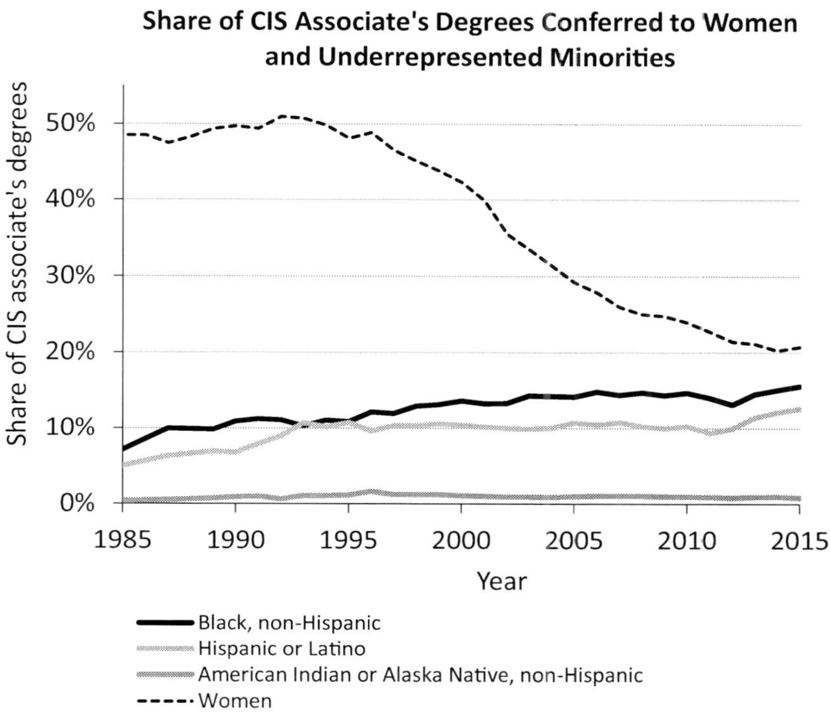

FIGURE 5.19 Share of all U.S. CIS associate's degrees conferred to women and to underrepresented minority groups. SOURCE: Data from IPEDS completions survey accessed via the WebCASPAR online database. See Appendix F for details.

Organizations such as the Computing Research Association Committee on the Status of Women in Computing Research, the Association for Computing Machinery Council on Women in Computing, the Anita Borg Institute, and the National Center for Women & Information Technology (NCWIT) support a range of such initiatives and provide useful resources, such as mentoring and guidance on mentoring practices for women in computing. Efforts to support and increase gender and racial/ethnic diversity in computing include the Grace Hopper Conference (Anita Borg Institute, 2017a), organized by the Anita Borg Institute; the ACM-W Celebrations of Women & Computing conferences (ACM-W, 2017); the Richard Tapia Conference (ACM, 2017), organized by the Center for Minorities and People with Disabilities in IT (CMD-IT) and sponsored by the ACM; the CMD-IT University Award, which recognizes institutions for effective retention of underrepresented minorities in undergraduate CS programs; the

Building, Recruiting, and Inclusion for Diversity Initiative (Anita Borg Institute, 2017b), co-led by the Anita Borg Institute and Harvey Mudd College; the CAHSI Summit, co-located with the HENAAC Conference organized by Great Minds in STEM;[18] and NCWIT's Aspiration program for high school girls (NCWIT, 2017). Sustained success in these and related programs will likely contribute to future increases in diversity in computing.

In addition, many CS departments today have support and outreach programs for women and underrepresented minority students in their departments and broader communities. Such efforts are expected to improve the environment for these students and help decrease attrition among these groups.[19]

A constellation of public and private efforts to boost high school students' CS skills and knowledge may increase the numbers and diversity of undergraduates enrolling in CS courses and majoring in CS over time. However, such an increase may further contribute to the enrollment pressures that many institutions are currently experiencing and intensify demands for solutions. Furthermore, attrition among women and underrepresented groups remains a challenge in computer science and related fields; while increasing interest shows promise, deliberate efforts may be needed to translate this into increasing representation of these groups in these fields.

LEVERAGING BOOMING ENROLLMENTS TO INCREASE DIVERSITY IN COMPUTER SCIENCE AND RELATED FIELDS

Increasing enrollments in CS courses pose a range of challenges for CS units and the students seeking these courses. Much emphasis has been placed on the negative implications for diversity—in particular, due to increasing competition for courses and higher student-to-faculty ratios for these courses, which could lead to less-welcoming, even hostile environments. As discussed in previous sections, this is a serious risk.

At the same time, the recent boom does present some opportunities for improving diversity. Even if representation levels of women and underrepresented minorities have not increased much, on average, the absolute number of students from these groups has. As these numbers continue to rise there will be a larger critical mass for creating or strengthening supportive peer communities and networks, and for the successes of women and underrepresented minorities to become visible and inspirational to their peers. There will be more women and underrepresented minorities to serve as peer mentors and undergraduate teaching assistants, which may help to evolve the image of the field.

Furthermore, where demand is increasing, institutions will adapt in response, whether in the near term, the long term, or both. Any changes to policies, prac-

[18] See CAHSI (2017b).

[19] For example, see CSWN (2017); CS Women UMass Amherst (2017); PWiCS (2017); Women@CC (2017); Women@SCS (2017).

tices, and pedagogies that ensue have the potential to change the culture of the program for the better, but only if institutions make such cultural shifts a priority. In the following chapter, the range of options available to institutions are discussed, along with their advantages and risks; diversity implications are a key dimension.

6

Institutional Strategies

Institutions facing significant increases in demand for computing courses have several options for how to proceed, as discussed in Chapter 2. In the near term, the options are to accommodate the demand, or to restrict access to majors or courses. Over time, these decisions may have an impact on the nature of the program and the institution's character and diversity, even as demand continues to change. Thus, it is important for institutional leaders to take the long view, and to act strategically in ways consistent with the institution's values and mission.

This chapter discusses institutional resources and constraints, ways in which institutional character and goals can inform decision making, and a range of options for dealing with the computer science (CS) enrollment increases and underlying drivers, as well as the risks and advantages of specific strategies.

INSTITUTIONAL RESOURCES AND CONSTRAINTS

For academic institutions, responding to substantial and rapid changes in student demand is challenging. This is not unique to CS—and CS is not the only academic field that has experienced rapid enrollment increases—but the rate and magnitude of the recent change in demand for CS courses, from both majors and non-majors, appear to be extreme. Furthermore, the relatively small number of CS Ph.D.s pursuing an academic career, coupled with the broad opportunities for CS faculty in the private sector, has made faculty hiring especially difficult, which limits what institutions can do and further exacerbates the challenge.

The key resources in support of a department's teaching mission are faculty, teaching staff, teaching assistants (TAs), facilities, and support staff, all of which are dependent on a department's budget. An institution's capacity to respond to increased student demand for computing courses will be limited by constraints on any one of these resources, as discussed here.

Faculty and Teaching Staff

The most significant resource constraint in CS departments is the faculty and professional teaching staff. This includes tenured and tenure-track faculty, teaching faculty, lecturers, instructors, professors of practice, and other titles for faculty with a primary teaching role. Tenured or tenure-track faculty have multiple additional responsibilities, such as research and institutional or other professional service requirements. Teaching faculty with an academic rank may have their own research program, often in the area of CS education. All teaching staff typically take on a variety of additional roles, including managing other teaching staff or TAs, or advising, tutoring, or mentoring students. Faculty workload can be increased to respond to greater demand, but only so far before additional instructors become necessary to accommodate increasing numbers of students.

Academic growth in computer science has historically aligned with times of industrial opportunity, as is the case presently. Thus, even if there is institutional commitment to expand CS faculty, it may be difficult to attract competitive candidates, as discussed in Chapter 3. This challenge may be exacerbated when faculty are recruited into a climate of extremely high teaching loads or high student stress.

The mix of faculty types—not just the number—is a significant factor that relates to institutional values and mission. CS departments at research universities have primarily tenured and tenure-track faculty. Adding large numbers of faculty not on the tenure track can create administrative and cultural issues, including the perception of "classes" of faculty, though it may help improve the diversity of instructors which can in turn have positive impacts on student diversity. While this is an especially acute issue at research universities, it is a potential problem at all institutions and underscores the importance of considering long-term consequences and institutional values.

Teaching Assistants

TAs—drawn from either the graduate or undergraduate student bodies—are crucial for the successful delivery of education in many institutions. TAs lead small lab sections and discussion sessions, prepare projects, grade projects and assignments, and provide individual instruction.

Ph.D. students are an experienced and preferred source of TAs in Ph.D.-granting departments, providing the primary source for help with higher enrollment courses. Ph.D. students in computing are typically supported through non-TA sources of funding such as fellowships and research assistantships. Departments have to balance the need for an experienced TA against the adviser and student goal of making progress on research. As CS enrollment has surged, the Computing Research Association (CRA) Enrollment Survey suggests that graduate students have increasingly been asked to teach courses in departments with CS Ph.D. programs.[1] However, the increase in enrollment has not been matched with an increase in doctoral students to serve as TAs.

As illustrated in Chapter 2, master's degree production in CS is an order of magnitude greater than Ph.D. production, and has increased rapidly in recent years as students have sought skills in high demand in industry. Many institutions have relied upon these master's programs as a source of revenue, and over 55 percent of all master's degrees were awarded to foreign students in 2015. Although CS master's students are commonly admitted with no promise of financial support and they have a higher concentration of coursework, drawing TAs from the master's student body is crucial for many departments.

Undergraduate CS students are another source of TAs.[2] As enrollment increases, the size of the undergraduate TA (UTA) pool scales linearly with the undergraduate enrollment. At many institutions that do not offer graduate programs, UTAs are already supporting instruction, but this is an increasingly common practice at research universities as well. Serving as a grader, lab assistant, peer instructor, mentor, or tutor can be a valuable part of an undergraduate's educational experience. These opportunities provide motivated UTAs with a strong connection to the student body and can allow valued interaction with graduate TAs. Undergraduate TAs can also be inspirational to other undergraduates, who may become inspired to pursue academic or teaching careers. Teams of early-stage UTAs require careful management and oversight by the instructor, as well as institutional support and training, and may not be appropriate at all institutions.

Support Staff

Support staff play a crucial role in maintaining a healthy and well-managed learning and work environment, and can play a role in easing the pressure of growth in student demand. The responsibilities and level of support vary by institution, but can include undergraduate advisors and course or technical support staff, who may be tasked with addressing exceptions and points of potential confusion among students.

As the number of students increases, various factors may lead to increases in the demand for staff time and attention. For example, the number of exceptional situations (such as illness, accidents, time conflicts, or family issues) likely

[1] See Figure F3 in CRA (Computing Research Association). 2017a. Generation CS: Computer Science Undergraduate Enrollments Surge Since 2006. Online. Available at http://cra.org/data/Generation-CS/.

[2] See, for example, Figure F3 in CRA (Computing Research Association). 2017a. Generation CS: Computer Science Undergraduate Enrollments Surge Since 2006. Online. Available at http://cra.org/data/Generation-CS/.

increases with a larger student population, as does the potential to be lost in the crowd. In addition, the efforts required for routine course management tasks—preparing exams, supporting assignments and projects—increases with size. With larger class sizes, the demand on teaching and support staff to handle issues such as cheating and harassment likely also increases. Some aspects of staff work exhibit scale easily, while others do not, such as student advising, which requires one-on-one time, and depends on advisors' knowledge of students.

Facilities

Facilities, such as classrooms, lecture halls, and computer labs, and associated equipment are also a necessary resource. In computing lectures and labs, computers and projectors are generally a key requirement; students need computers to complete programming and other assignments, whether their own or university-issued laptops or desktops.

Increasing student enrollments present a host of facilities challenges that can impact the character and attractiveness of the program. At some institutions there are simply no lecture halls big enough to accommodate all students, and, when such rooms do exist, they may be so large that they are an impediment to teaching and learning. For example, at the University of California, Berkeley, in the fall 2016 semester, more than 1,800 students initially enrolled in the introductory computer science course for majors, dropping to 1,567 students after the first several weeks. Early in the semester the course was taught in the Zellerbach Auditorium for Performing Arts, which has a seating capacity of 2,525. Even dividing such very large courses into multiple sections can challenge the capacity of larger lecture halls—and such large class sizes can have a negative impact on the students' experience—or challenge the availability of a larger number of smaller rooms. These pressures are not necessarily limited to introductory courses or non-major offerings; major enrollment is up and non-majors are progressing more deeply into computer science programs at many institutions.

Video capture and replay, or even studio preproduction,[3] of large lectures can help to mitigate facilities constraints and help to tailor large lecture presentations to a diversity of students and learning styles. The ability to go back and review particular aspects of a presentation, especially when learning computational techniques or problem solving is involved, allows students to absorb material at their own pace. It can also help to mitigate demands that might otherwise be placed on staff if a student misses class.

Computer science courses often have substantial laboratory components, which are not typically present in large social science and humanities courses, but not as specialized or complex as large biological or physical science courses. With growth in enrollment, more sessions in lab facilities (or more seats during lab ses-

[3] This is distinct from online courses, though there may be overlap in methods.

sions, as many students increasingly use their own laptops) must be provided. At the same time, lab sessions may offer a more personalized small-course setting where individual hands-on learning takes place. In this case the quality of teaching assistants and support staff may become even more critical to the quality of the course, as does the lead instructor's guidance and management of teaching support staff. In addition, content distribution and collection, grading, and approaches to resolving errors and disputes must scale. Of course, all these benefits of labs are contingent on the availability of lab facilities and equipment, which are subject to similar space constraints as are lectures. Expense also obviously goes up with the scale of lab facilities.

In general, tiered instruction—with large lectures, smaller discussion or lab sessions, small group or peer advising, and one-on-one tutoring—can assist with the efficient allocation of resources when dealing with large numbers of students.

INSTITUTIONAL MISSION AND CHARACTER

One of the reasons that U.S. higher education is the envy of the world is its unique diversity. The nation's more than 4,000 institutions of higher education range from technical institutes and community colleges that award certificates or associate's degrees to Ph.D.-granting, research-intensive universities; and from small, private liberal arts colleges with a few hundred students to gigantic flagship public universities with tens of thousands of students. Each has important roles to play in supporting the nation's need for computing professionals and innovation and CS's need for the faculty and research that sustain the discipline.

Given this institutional diversity, it is likely that one institution's response to the growth in CS will be inappropriate—if it is even feasible—for another. A reliance on doctoral student TAs is obviously infeasible at a liberal arts college or master's institution, for example. Less obvious, but of potentially profound importance to the institutions, are actions that would push against long-standing institutional practices and core values. For example, for an institution that allows admitted students to major in any field they choose, it would be precedent setting, even mission altering, to impose limits on the number of CS majors.

Beyond institutional diversity, there are also important considerations related to student diversity. U.S. higher education institutions value contributions from a demographically diverse group of students and faculty with a range of experiences and perspectives. The offerings and atmosphere of any institution will attract different types of students, and institutional actions—including admissions and enrollment practices—play a major role in determining who is drawn to the institution and to specific programs, including the participation of underrepresented communities, and can impact the success and retention rates of different groups.

Every institution has its own distinct distribution of intellectual endeavors. In the face of increasing demand for a specific discipline, ensuring the vitality of less-populated disciplines might be a priority. Too much migration to popular fields could decrease the level of interest in the smallest programs to a level below a critical mass. For institutions that prioritize a broad, liberal arts education for their students, requiring early declaration of major, in particular during admissions, could inhibit the tradition of discovery during the first years of a broad education. Institutions that prioritize deep technical training in science and engineering may find it detrimental to the institution's character to limit student access to experience in computer science, which is increasingly important for a range of science and engineering disciplines. Alternatively, they may want to maintain or increase the academic profile or ranking of the institution by maintaining or introducing high entrance requirements.

It is crucial that institutions be thoughtful and intentional in choosing strategies to respond to growth in computing enrollment. This includes a consideration of mission and values, and the consequences of actions—or inaction.

INSTITUTIONAL RESPONSES TO INCREASING COMPUTER SCIENCE ENROLLMENTS

While the challenges of increasing enrollments in undergraduate computing courses are very real and some institutions are in dire need of relief, it must be noted that resources at academic institutions may be limited. In particular, investments in one area typically mean that cuts must be made to another. Accordingly, strategic decisions about how to respond to the surge in demand for computing must be made based on an analysis of the overall costs and benefits for the institution of the various possible actions.

In this section the range of responses available to academic institutions are reviewed, including those listed in the CRA survey and discussed in the previous section. In general there are four categories of responses available to institutions: (1) limit participation, (2) leverage resources in new ways, (3) grow programs and the resources that feed them, and (4) restructure the nature of computing education within the institution. The categories range from relatively inexpensive and nondisruptive actions to major changes in organization and resource commitments.

The responses are briefly evaluated in terms of their advantages and risks. Because the needs and priorities of U.S. institutions of higher education are diverse, even among members of any given category of institution, the committee does not believe it would be appropriate or effective to prescribe any single strategy or combination of strategies to any given institution or institution type. Instead, institutions must identify how the advantages and risks will translate to their individual circumstances, and decide how to proceed. What is best for any particular institution depends on many factors, including and especially the institution's mission and vision.

Limit Participation

Limit the Number of Majors

Institutions can take actions to limit the number of majors in their computer science program. These limits could be imposed at the point at which students are formally accepted into a major program, which occurs either before (if students must apply directly to a degree program at the time of application, as at Carnegie Mellon University, for example) or after they enter the college or university (whenever the institution requires major declaration). Enhanced restrictions to limit enrollment could be made by imposing a set of threshold performance requirements for entry into the program based, for example, on high school or college grades, grades in particular courses, performance on exams in certain courses, entrance or qualifying exams, or other factors. Alternatively, caps could be imposed with acceptance into the major based upon lottery, first-come-first-served, or some other non-performance-based prioritization.

Advantages: Imposing limits would prevent potentially unmanageable growth in computer science degree programs, and alleviate the associated pressure on departmental resources. Depending on how the restrictions are implemented, limiting enrollment should be administratively expedient. There is the additional benefit of near certainty about student numbers, making it much easier for units to plan.

Risks: Limiting the number of students who may declare as CS majors at any point in the student's undergraduate experience may cut them off from their true passion, or prevent others from discovering theirs. Depending upon where in the process the limit is imposed, it may also introduce stress or an environment of real or perceived competition for students who desire to enter a CS program, which could discourage participation among underrepresented groups. A ranking-based approach for determining eligibility would promote head-to-head competition based on the chosen requirements, which could cause students to focus on these requirements rather than other educational objectives. This strategy could also affect the climate for faculty, instructors, TAs, and support staff, by requiring them to respond to enhanced student stress, angst, or competitive attitudes, which risks diminishing the talent within the university.

However, some of these challenges could be overcome by introducing the limits at the time of acceptance of prospective students into the college or university, so students would have advance knowledge of whether a given institution will permit them to major in CS or another computing field. At the same time, in the extreme, limiting CS enrollments at all institutions would not be in the national interest, as it would restrict the total production of CS degrees feeding into the economy at a time when demand for computing professions is expected to grow.

Measures to limit major admission or declaration would likely result in reduced demand for more advanced courses or major-only introductory courses, but would not necessarily limit the number of non-majors who want to enroll in courses. On the other hand such limits could affect the overall climate in such courses, and thus the level of interest in the course.

Limit Course Enrollment

Another action, which is not mutually exclusive with limits on majors, is to simply limit course enrollments. Decisions on whom to allow into courses could be made based upon a student's major (or intended major), their class (e.g., seniors before underclass students), via performance requirements, by lottery, or on a first-come-first-served basis.

Advantages: This approach will remove the pressure on departmental resources associated with growth in student course enrollments, and would enable more individual attention to be paid to students than would be possible in larger classes or cohorts.

Risks: Again, this approach risks barring students who may have a sincere passion for the field, or who may need the course or associated skills for their major area or intended career path. It also limits the ability of a student population to be exposed to computing. These limitations restrict the potential of a student's experience, and the measures imposed could make students feel their future is determined by factors beyond their control, especially if students are performing or achieving at the required level but are still unable to enroll in desired courses, which can affect a student's ability to complete his or her program in four years. Students may try to influence enrollment decisions by pleading with or pressuring faculty responsible for enforcing limits, which can lead to a negative environment for the department and the institution.

This option carries many of the risks associated with limiting majors. In particular, capping course enrollment based on past performance or experience could disproportionately affect women and underrepresented minorities. It could also create a competitive environment among non-majors, which discourages participation and exposure to CS in ways that are becoming increasingly important for a range of disciplines, thus limiting students' educational experiences.

Redirect Demand for Courses and Majors

Restrictions on course enrollment or declaration of major are often associated with efforts to redirect students into alternative courses or majors. This can be done by communicating (e.g., via advising or in presentations to potential future students) how difficult it is to get into courses or majors and other associated challenges, and encouraging them to consider alternatives.

Advantages: This approach has the benefit of clearly presenting the challenges of the program to the students before they decide to pursue them. It may also prompt students to look more closely at what is best for them.

Risks: This approach could also serve to discourage students who might otherwise enjoy and succeed in computing courses or the major, and close what might have been successful pathways. In addition, telling students who are still deciding which institution of higher education to enroll in about the challenges or limits associated with CS at a given institution may cause them to lose interest in the institution. In particular there is a risk (as discussed in previous chapters) that limiting access to courses could lead to declines in participation of women and underrepresented minorities.

Grow Programs

Growth is an obvious response to increased demand, but growth may have its own disadvantages, including potentially large opportunity costs for other university programs and priorities.

Increase Class Sizes

One response to increased course demand is to allow class sizes to grow to accommodate the demand.

Advantages: This has the benefit of allowing all interested students access to the courses that they want to take, and would likely help to avoid the sense of scarcity and competition that comes with the imposition of limits.

Risks: Larger class or lab sizes may or may not align with pedagogical needs or goals, depending on the nature of the course, and could negatively impact learning outcomes. Larger classes will be less agile in meeting individual student needs. They could also affect the student experience further by limiting individualized interactions with faculty and teaching staff, creating the sense of being lost in the crowd, and heightening competitive pressures, which could also have a negative impact on student diversity. A larger number of students per class or lab will increase the workload on faculty or teaching staff and the required management skills may limit who can teach these effectively. Even if additional hires are made, junior faculty with less experience are generally not effective instructors for large classes. In addition, physical resources such as classroom space may be stretched beyond capacity.

Strategies can be deployed to mitigate the negative aspects of large lecture classes, such as recording lecture material to permit student replay at a later time, expanding tutoring or office hours, and optional special sessions to provide further challenge or enrichment. Additional actions may be necessary to manage the burden of larger classes on academic resources. For example, course management staff could help to reduce a primary instructor's management load. Technology can be leveraged to support grading and course communications, including online forums, and is already quite common at many institutions. Faculty teams, rather than individual faculty, may offer courses collaboratively, enabling greater scheduling flexibility or specialization. In addition, new pedagogical strategies such as collaborative projects and peer-to-peer instruction (discussed earlier in this chapter) could also ease some of the workload associated with teaching larger classes. New teaching arrangements may require initial investment of time and resources, especially at the onset.

At the same time some aspects of teaching do not scale easily, such as accommodating exceptional situations that arise in students' lives. The ability to handle exceptions effectively or not can contribute significantly to the climate of a course and the program, either positively or negatively.

Increase the Number of Sections or Courses

Departments may offer additional lecture sections for a given course, or offer similar courses that address the same student needs, rather than simply increasing the class size of one offering.

Advantages: This approach meets student demand without the downsides associated with increased class sizes. If the same instructor is simply teaching additional sections of the same course, the additional time required for preparation of materials is minimal.

Other benefits of scale may derive from this approach. Multiple offerings provide an opportunity to specialize individual sections toward different student backgrounds and the freedom to respond to student interests in a given course. For example, an introductory course with two sections could target students with prior programming experience in one section, and those without in the other. Similarly, the need to offer more sections could provide an opportunity to offer more distinct courses to better explore the specific interests of a diverse group. It could also augment the course schedule by making sections available at alternative times, such as evenings, weekends, or summers, which would make better use of existing facilities, provide benefits to students with nontraditional schedules, perhaps due to commuting distance and job schedules, and additionally help students to avoid conflicts with other courses. In particular, summer offerings not only expand capacity, they can also alleviate difficulties in satisfying prerequisites in the presence of over-enrollment.

Risks: In the absence of additional faculty or teaching staff, an increased number of course sections serving a larger number of students will increase workload in the form of lecture hours, advising time, grading responsibilities, and other individual interactions with students. The question of how teaching load is counted for an instructor teaching multiple instances of the same course needs to be addressed. Proper synchronization between sections of the same course taught by the same or a different instructor is often needed. This approach is also constrained by the number (rather than size) of available classrooms to accommodate additional sections.

Hire More Faculty

Advantages: Increasing the number of faculty or teaching staff makes it easier to offer more courses or course sections, and provides more opportunity for students to interact one-on-one with instructors. Adding faculty also leads to an expansion of research and related activities which benefits both the institutions and the regions that they serve.

Risks: Other than the issues associated with adding faculty in any field—such as institutional budget constraints and the costs associated with a faculty search—computer science faces an acute shortage of Ph.D.s pursuing an academic career, as already discussed in previous sections. In addition, the number of qualified individuals interested in a teaching faculty or other instruction position may be similarly low. The availability of short-term or contract instructors varies considerably, often driven by the geographical location and other employment opportunities around an institution. Furthermore, the same pressures make current faculty more difficult to retain, as they are recruited by both industry and other institutions.

Leverage Resources Creatively

Rather than maintaining the status quo and continuing to conduct computing instructional programs in the manner of past decades, programs have the opportunity to embrace change and make use of existing resources in new and more flexible ways. Several examples follow.

Use Technology for Teaching

Technology for education is rapidly growing, affording many potential pathways for responding to the demand for CS coursework and degrees. In addition, computer science material is some of the most amenable to technological enhancement, and CS instructors are likely to have the knowledge to wield and even develop such technology. This includes online course materials such as lecture videos and automated administration and grading of homework, exercises, and tests.

Advantages: Technology-based education offers many advantages, and when blended with more traditional teaching methods, may improve the quality of the educational experience while reducing the workload of instructors. Online, automated processes can provide instant validation of correctness, and repetition can solidify mastery, enabling faculty-student and TA-student interactions to focus on strategic approaches to problem solving. Online material frees students in both time and place, allowing them to learn material at their own pace and in their own space. Students with CS experience may move through course material more rapidly, and those with less precollege experience or exposure to CS may work more slowly. The freedom to complete coursework in a self-paced manner can be especially powerful for those constrained by job, family, and financial obligations, and to those who may need to spend more time with the material to achieve mastery due to lack of prior exposure to the subject; these students are more likely to be underrepresented minorities.

Beyond online material for a lecture or a course, a number of high-quality online degree programs in CS exist. A master's in CS is offered by Georgia Tech wholly online. While the program is still relatively young, the response to it has been huge, reaffirming the large demand for CS degrees and the appetite for online programs.

Risks: Technology-based learning is important and growing, but it is not a panacea, at least not yet. Experience with massive open online courses (MOOCs) and other online material shows that great attention must be paid to the learning experience and to the variation in the individual needs of students, and that their effectiveness varies; some analyses suggest that they may further exacerbate educational inequalities rather than mitigating them.[4] While one can be confident that technology in the hands of a successful instructor will enhance student learning, this cannot be assumed for online material unsupported by a learning infrastructure. As the reliance on technology for education increases, overall issues related to the sociology of learning must be addressed: academic integrity, the nature of online interaction and collaboration and the role of social media, the appropriate mix of virtual and physical, and no doubt more, currently unanticipated issues. Finally, it may be more difficult to automate elements of advanced courses, which are also seeing high demand, in particular due to the need for deep mentoring and supervised research.

Leverage Undergraduates as Nontraditional Teachers and Mentors

In addition to the traditional departmental teaching resources, undergraduates may provide valuable support in formal and informal capacities, as teaching assistants, discussion leaders, peer graders, project collaborators, and online forum discussants (though this approach is more commonly recognized as a strategy for MOOCs). As noted earlier the use of undergraduate students as TAs is a long-standing practice at many institutions, but it is a relatively recent or an underused resource at others. One prominent example is the Megas and Gigas Educate (MaGE) program at Mount Holyoke College, a women's liberal arts college, which was launched in 2015 with support from Google's CS Capacity Program to help meet demand for CS courses during the current enrollment surge in the face of limited resources. This program trains undergraduate students to teach and mentor each other in supportive and inclusive ways in order to increase CS enrollment capacity and diversity in the program.[5]

[4] See, for example, Emanuel (2013) and Kizilcec et al. (2017).

[5] See MaGE (2017).

Advantages: Undergraduates have the potential to provide significant help and reduce the workload for graduate TAs and for faculty and other instructors. Undergraduates are typically paid per hour of effort, which can cost significantly less than graduate TAs. In addition, the shared experience of undergraduates may make them particularly attuned to understanding the problems and the challenges facing their peers around specific content. Furthermore, from a pedagogical perspective, peer teaching and evaluation can be valuable learning experiences in and of themselves, and can help empower students and build their confidence with the material. Finally, the undergraduate pool is larger than those of graduate students or faculty, and typically more diverse, presenting an opportunity for a more diverse set of instructors, which could contribute to a more inclusive culture.

Risks: Undergraduates who are unclear on the material may cause confusion among their peers. In addition, not all undergraduates have the knowledge or maturity to successfully teach, assess, or mentor their peers, or understand conflict-of-interest situations. If poorly implemented or not properly supervised, this approach can place additional strain on course instructors.

Retrain Faculty and Graduate Students from Other Fields as Computing Instructors

As computing becomes increasingly important in a range of academic disciplines, many Ph.D.s in non-CS fields are emerging with knowledge and experience in computer science. At the same time, Ph.D. production in a number of fields exceeds the number of academic opportunities, and many Ph.D.s seeking an academic position are passionate about teaching. One approach to expanding the instructor or teaching faculty pipeline in CS is to create rigorous training programs for such non-CS Ph.D.s with the goal of preparing them to teach undergraduate CS courses, possibly aimed at students in domains close to that of their Ph.D. research. Stanford University recently started an M.S. program for this purpose,[6] and Ph.D.s in math, physics, and engineering are known to have pursued CS teaching positions successfully in the past.

Advantages: Training for non-CS Ph.D.s to become computer science instructors could attract individuals with research experience who are passionate about teaching, and increase the pool of CS instructors. Such individuals could provide especially valuable experience and insights in the context of a relevant X+CS program. Teaching computing outside of CS would also seem to offer institutions more flexibility if there are significant fluctuations in student demand in the future.

Risks: Creating successful M.S. programs targeted at individuals with Ph.D.s in areas outside CS comes with a number of challenges, given the fact that such

---

[6] See Starkman (2017).

individuals likely have varied backgrounds and experiences with CS. Entry into such programs might need to be contingent both on demonstrated success in teaching and some threshold background or performance in CS. The curricula would need to be flexible to enable tailoring to the range of backgrounds and thinking that come with primary training in other fields. Furthermore, professional development of such instructors would also require special attention and mentoring, and consume already limited faculty time.

Leverage External Teaching Resources

There may be additional resources outside the institution (experts, teaching spaces, etc.) that can be leveraged with minimal overhead. For example, regionally co-located institutions could pool teaching resources; local industry or government experts could teach or support college/university classes; or public or private facilities could be found to serve as additional, low-overhead course meeting sites.

Advantages: Collaboration with private industry could provide additional, nonacademic perspectives on computing and insights into the workings of industry to students, and help them form connections with potential future employers. Similarly, those in industry and government may find value in contributing to undergraduate education, and see it as an opportunity to recruit new talent. Leveraging local experts and facilities could be a low-cost tactic, if of mutual interest to the parties.

Risks: Using outside resources could limit the institution's control and ownership over its own program. Quality control is important and can be especially challenging with external teaching resources. Furthermore, the availability or quality of such external resources varies by region, and may not be feasible for institutions in rural areas. Finally, it is possible that reliance on external resources could deplete the pool of resources available for meeting K-12 CS needs, to the extent which they may overlap. Finally, contract instructors of any sort are difficult to hire in CS, given the current landscape of opportunities in industry, as discussed in Chapters 3 and 4.

Build Mechanisms for Continuously Aligning Resources with Workload and Demand

More responsive resource allocation strategies, such as adoption of Responsibility Center Management (RCM) models (Carlson, 2015), enhanced use of more flexible resource pools, or institution of differential fees that scale with program or course enrollment, can encourage and enable programs to accommodate increasing enrollments.

Advantages: Many of the challenges associated with increasing enrollments relate to budget constraints or a lack of flexibility of resource allocations. Faculty and teaching and support staff are not easily transferred between units, teaching budgets often do not track enrollments, and staff to expand the capacity of such faculty when needed are difficult to hire. Physical, administrative, financial, and human resources are often bound to decanal or departmental units for decades with no processes for reallocating or sharing them, or for clearly understanding how they are utilized.

An RCM model is one approach to increasing the flexibility and alignment of resources, giving computing units more control over the resources they have available, and better enabling them to respond to the demands of increasing enrollment. Using more flexible pools of teaching resources, such as undergraduate TAs, rather than relying on a more limited number of graduate students, is another strategy. In some situations differential fees could both moderate some of the demand and provide additional resources to expand capacity. These measures can regularize administrative decision making, allowing resource availability to be anticipated well in advance and avoiding the stress and inefficiency of ad hoc responses.

Risks: RCM and other approaches to tying departmental resources directly to teaching activities create barriers to interdepartmental cooperation and collaboration. If a department receives funds for each student it teaches and must pay for each course that its majors take in other departments, it is inevitable that barriers to student enrollment will be erected. It must also be recognized that changing budget models and processes reallocates resources, it does not increase them—that is, some units will lose resources, while CS is gaining them, which could result in the weakening of units with fewer students that are nonetheless highly valued or central to an institution's mission or character. Furthermore, it is unlikely that the specific issue of responding to demand in CS would be sufficient to stimulate a shift in an institution's budget model if it was not already the best choice for the institution.

In general the use of market mechanisms as a way to allocate resources or to manage demand must be pursued with caution and with an appreciation for its impacts. As with any market-based approach, which by definition puts an emphasis on willingness to pay, there are impacts on those who may be willing but unable to pay. This is an especially important issue for underrepresented minority students.

Interdisciplinary Collaboration

Given the rapid evolution of computing disciplines, and the increase in non-CS disciplines as a source of student enrollment in CS courses and research opportunities, institutions should look outside of CS as they contemplate responses to enrollment growth. There are several possibilities that range from relatively modest changes in courses to the creation of new interdisciplinary programs that could alter in profound ways the relationships among units. Such strategies go beyond administrative reordering, requiring institutions to engage in important intellectual questions about the role of computing in the future of other disciplines and the role and use of computing in the careers that all graduates will pursue.

Much of the increase in enrollments in computer science courses has come from non-majors, and we can expect the demand from these sources will increase in the future as computing becomes an integral part of more disciplines and is expected by employers from a wide range of more industrial sectors. Here, we identify several specific approaches for the non-major.

Increase the Presence of Computer Science in Non–Computer Science Courses

Incorporating computational and computer science knowledge, skills, and experience into non-CS courses could provide non-majors who are primarily interested in obtaining computing skills with sufficient exposure to computing to meets their needs, or enough of an introduction to computational methods relevant to their coursework or career. This approach would leverage the computational knowledge of instructors or faculty in other fields if and when it is available. It would create more pathways for non-CS students to incorporate computing into their education and future careers, as well as providing appealing hooks for CS students to learn more about other disciplines. Shared courses with other domains can enrich the experience of CS faculty and TAs, especially if approached as a collaborative effort, rather than a service relationship. The non-CS faculty and TAs may welcome the opportunity to incorporate new methods and create new partnerships with CS faculty and TAs.

Tailor Introductory Computer Science Courses to the Needs of Non-Majors

Incorporating more of what non-majors need into introductory or specialized CS courses could reduce the need to take additional upper-level courses. For example, after learning basic programming skills such as iteration, abstraction, flow of execution, data structures, and functions in an introductory course, non-majors can focus on additional concepts and projects related to applications in their major. The use of systems, packages, tools, and environments may also be targeted to relevance and use in their major. Successful tailoring of offerings to non-majors in this manner is an open and important area for further research and exploration.

All of these approaches with the non-major in mind offer similar advantages and risks.

Advantages: Shifting CS content to courses in other departments, which obviously provides direct relief to CS, and tailoring CS coursework to the non-major both have the merit of providing a targeted and more efficient educational experience for the student and the institution. If done well and timed effectively, such approaches can also provide a more effective way for non-majors to learn computing concepts, as well as an environment enriched by the issues and examples from the student's major. Rigorous instruction in computing outside CS courses would also seem to address some of the underlying demand for computing skills throughout the workforce while offering institutions more flexibility in the event that there are significant fluctuations in student demand for CS programs at some point in the future.

Risks: It is possible that these approaches merely shift the burden from one department to another, although that can be viewed as beneficial by the institution if it serves to distribute the burden more evenly. It is also likely to be more difficult to ensure the quality of CS courses for non-majors, whether taught inside or outside CS departments or related units. Such courses must balance the needs of non-majors with instruction of the relevant CS principles. This can be achieved through interdisciplinary collaboration on teaching strategies, and possible co-teaching. At the same time, strengthening CS offerings for non-majors could deter some students from selecting CS as a major, thus depriving the field of their contributions. Finally, it is possible that these measures could backfire by stimulating even greater demand for CS courses.

Develop a Wider Range of Computing-Related Programs

Computing is important in all aspects of the economy and plays a crucial role in science, technology, engineering, and mathematics fields. Many institutions have included a computing requirement (typically a programming course) for all or a selected subset of majors. However, to be prepared for the workforce or future research, one programming course is generally not enough. Today's students understand the job market and where the opportunities are. Students majoring in CS or pursuing a double major with CS may actually be more interested in another field but are pursuing CS because they see it as the best way to achieve the opportunities they seek. Creating new programs of study targeted at students interested in CS for its applications to another domain could help to reduce the number of majors and enrich offerings available to students.

Data science, naturally spread over computer science, statistics, applied mathematics, and various application domains, provides a compelling, focused opportunity in which to develop such institutional capacities. Other established majors can be approached computationally as well, such as cognitive science, operations research, econometrics, computational biology, digital media, and others. Several institutions have established or are exploring new CS+X and X+CS blends with synergistic fields, such as computational anthropology, computational linguistics, computational advertising, and so on, as discussed in Chapter 3. Importantly, computational coursework in other domains can provide significant value to other fields and enable a more customized undergraduate experience for students while reducing some of the burden on CS programs. Such blends could also be effective at improving the diversity of computing-related programs, even if they are not housed in CS units.

Assessing the advantages and risks of these approaches is not straightforward. Unlike the efforts focused on non-majors, creating new computing and interdisciplinary programs goes beyond merely dealing with the excess demand for CS instruction. But, of course, that is the point. Such new programs bring intellectual progress and excitement that go well beyond the administrative benefits of shifting teaching loads.

New Organizational Structures for Computer Science

Historically, computer science programs were formed as departments in colleges of engineering, science, or arts and sciences. Increasingly, colleges of computing or schools of information and computer science or similar organizations, with CS being one of the units, are being formed. The emphases and character of these programs vary widely; Table 6.1 provides a sampling of institutions whose computing organizations are representative of a range of such models.

Concomitant with the increase in the number of students seeking to take CS courses, the reasons for taking these courses have become more diverse, new computing-related programs and majors are being created, and other disciplines are incorporating computation into their own courses. In any such environment placing a CS department into a more autonomous organizational structure that can respond effectively to emerging needs becomes increasingly important. Given the vast diversity of programs, this larger step is certainly not merited for the majority of institutions, but for the 10 percent of the institutions that produce 50 percent of the degrees it ought to be considered, and for the 3 percent of the institutions that produce 25 percent it cannot be ignored.

The organizational placement of a CS department can have significant impact on the undergraduate students choosing the program and courses most appropriate to their interests and abilities, and can affect the diversity of students choosing to enroll in the program. The organizational structure impacts approval and reporting channels, and can have significant impact on how quickly and effectively a program can respond to changes in course demand and reallocation of resources. The appropriate structure could also reduce duplication in courses and programs, and coordinated programs can lead to better graduation rates. The organizational structure typically does not directly affect the research conducted or courses taught by individual faculty.

Computer science departments in a college of science find that their programs differ from many science programs in a number of significant ways: (1) A bachelor's degree in CS has a wide range of high-paying job opportunities immediately after graduation and students have well-paid internship opportunities. (2) CS Ph.D.s and CS faculty have a wide range of high-paying opportunities outside of academia;

TABLE 6.1 Partial List of Schools and Colleges of Computing That Include a Computer Science Department

Arizona State University	School of Computing, Informatics, and Decision Systems Engineering	http://cidse.engineering.asu.edu
Carnegie Mellon University	School of Computer Science	https://www.cs.cmu.edu
Clemson University	School of Computing	http://www.clemson.edu/cecas
Cornell University	Computing and Information Science	http://www.cis.cornell.edu/
DePaul University	College of Computing and Digital Media	https://www.cdm.depaul.edu
Drexel University	College of Computing and Informatics	http://drexel.edu/cci
Georgia Institute of Technology	College of Computing	http://www.cc.gatech.edu/
Indiana University	School of Informatics and Computing	http://www.soic.indiana.edu
Long Island University	College of Information and Computer Science	http://www2.liu.edu/CWIS/cwp/cics/cics2.html
Montana State University	Gianforte School of Computing	https://www.cs.montana.edu/
New Jersey Institute of Technology	College of Computing	http://ccs.njit.edu
Northeastern University	College of Computer and Information Sciences	http://www.ccis.northeastern.edu
Pace University	Seidenberg School of Computer Science and Information Systems	http://www.pace.edu/seidenberg/
Rochester Institute of Technology	College of Computing and Information Sciences	https://www.rit.edu/gccis
State University of New York, Albany	College of Computing and Information	http://www.albany.edu/ceas/
University of California, Irvine	School of Information and Computer Sciences	http://www.ics.uci.edu/
University of Massachusetts	College of Information and Computer Sciences	https://www.cics.umass.edu/
University of Nebraska, Omaha	College of Information Science and Technology	http://www.unomaha.edu/college-of-information-science-and-technology/
University of North Carolina, Charlotte	College of Computing and Informatics	http://cci.uncc.edu
University of Pittsburgh	School of Computing and Information	https://sci.pitt.edu/

NOTE: A number of institutions have information schools that currently do not include the CS department. These include the University of Washington; the University of Maryland; the University of California, Berkeley; Pennsylvania State University; the University of Michigan; the University of Illinois, Urbana-Champaign; Rutgers University; and the University of Texas, Austin.

in certain areas faculty are actively recruited by industry. (3) Increasingly, professional M.S. degrees in specialized computing fields (e.g., security and data science) are being created and have significant enrollment providing a source of income to the department. (4) CS faculty tend to be more entrepreneurial than science faculty.

Computer science departments in schools or colleges of engineering also find their discipline to be increasingly different from the other engineering fields: (1) CS departments offer courses taken by undergraduates across all majors; increasingly, the courses taken by non-majors include higher level ones. (2) Computing is immediately relevant to almost every area and domain outside engineering. (3) CS departments increasingly offer undergraduate and graduate degrees jointly with non-science and non-engineering departments. Undergraduate curricula increasingly allow more flexibility and choices depending on the students' interest.

Advantages: There are many additional advantages. In a new college or school of computing, a dean represents departments with commonalities not found in other arrangements which allow for better-focused arguments to be made to the higher administration. The departments included in addition to CS can vary considerably and are institution dependent.[7] New undergraduate and graduate programs are created in an environment bringing relevant groups together earlier in the needed approval process, allowing for better collaboration and communication. A college offering different undergraduate programs can create a curriculum with a common first year, allowing students to choose among different computing majors after the first year. Programs and majors in one organizational structure have the potential to lead to better course enrollment management and better understanding of objectives students have.

Risks: The risks of creating a new college would seem to be institutionally specific and derive mainly from distributional issues within the university. If a new college gives CS a more direct line to university leadership, for example, that presumably means that the leadership has another direct report, which could dilute the attention it can provide to any single college. There are unavoidably some costs of change and these must be weighed against the benefits. Furthermore, while deans of colleges of computing may be on equal footing with deans of other colleges, this may not change the potential for allocating resources to the new college.

FINDING 8: Departments facing sharp increases in demand for computing courses have experienced significant strain on a wide range of resources. Failure to respond thoughtfully to the demand and the resource deficits will result in adverse conditions for students, faculty, the programs, and the

[7] They may include statistics, information sciences, library sciences, computational biology, information technology programs, management information systems, communication, policy, media, and computational social sciences. Alternatively, areas sometimes considered computer science—such as human-computer interaction, machine learning, and robotics—may have their own departments within colleges of computing.

institution as a whole in the near or long term. Conditions such as an unwelcoming academic climate and loss of faculty members can be especially harmful in the long term.

A TEMPLATE FOR ASSESSING THE CURRENT COMPUTER SCIENCE ENROLLMENT CHALLENGE

There is no single approach—a "silver bullet"—for responding to enrollment growth that will be optimal at all institutions. Every tactic has benefits and costs. Leaders will need to select strategies and make trade-offs that are appropriate to their circumstances and to their institution's mission and values.

> **FINDING 9:** U.S. institutions of higher education have differing missions, priorities, and business models, and serve different populations with different needs. There is no one-size-fits-all solution for responding to enrollment increases. However, all institutions need to assess the role of computer science and related fields and make strategic plans to address realistically and effectively the high demand for courses, student interests and needs, faculty and staff workloads, research and teaching allocations, and physical resources. At all institutions there is an opportunity to reassess the role of CS and computing and to consider changes that go beyond the current challenges and position the institution for future success.

Yet, this is a time of opportunity. It is a time for institutions to consider their missions and the constituencies they serve, and to determine what role computing should play in the experience, knowledge, and skills of its graduates of 2025 and beyond. Institutions should take action to meet these goals, and metrics should be defined and monitored to determine progress and unintended consequences.

Institutions may start by performing a self-assessment to establish current facts, feasible actions, and strategic goals. This knowledge will help to elucidate a path forward that is consistent with the institution's goals. The key questions to consider are as follows:

1. Situation and trends
   a. How has student demand for and access to computing changed in the past 5 years?
   b. How have the demographics—including motivation for enrolling—of computing majors and course enrollees changed?
   c. How have the number and workloads of faculty and teaching and support staff changed?
2. Impacts of past actions
   a. How has the institution dealt with enrollment growth in the past? What can be learned from these experiences?

   b. What were the effects of past changes on program character and climate, and student and faculty demographics?
3. Role of computing and computer science
   a. At what points throughout the process of student application, acceptance, declaration of major, enrollment in courses, is access to computing limited? How is this done? What are the effects of these access controls on students and staff, including on the participation of women and underrepresented minorities?
   b. What are student and faculty perceptions about the program? How does this vary based on student and faculty backgrounds and interests? How is the program viewed outside the institution?
   c. What is the perceived relationship of programs to job prospects?
   d. Are class sizes affecting student stress factors and climate? Do these effects vary by student background and demographic?
   e. Why are students enrolling in computing courses at your institution?
   f. What is the educational mission of your computing program for majors and for non-majors? Is this consistent with the interest of these students?
   g. What are the institution's target goals for longer-term program growth? How many major, mixed-major, and non-major students should be accommodated in 5 years? 10 years?
   h. How will these goals impact the preparation of students for their professional lives, students' intellectual growth within the college/university experience, and the culture and climate for students and faculty in computing programs and throughout the institution?
4. Non-major interest and engagement with computing
   a. What are academic fields and career goals of the non-majors enrolling in your computing courses?
   b. Are these courses required for their degree program?
   c. Do computing courses provide a necessary or competitive skill in the student's chosen field(s)?
   d. What other departments or programs on campus offer courses with some computing content?
   e. Are there opportunities for collaborative blending of computation with other fields that might help to meet student interest?
5. Faculty, staff, and other resources
   a. How do the growth of undergraduate CS enrollment, TAs, faculty, instructors, and academics compare since 2006?
   b. How many new faculty and teaching positions were authorized since CS enrollments have begun increasing? How many of the positions were filled?
   c. If the department faced faculty retention issues, how were they handled? Did they have an impact on the morale and climate in the department?

   d. How does the institution provide resources and training for faculty not experienced in teaching large lecture classes? Is class size considered when determining departmental teaching loads?
6. Institution-specific mechanisms for growth or restriction
   a. What measures are available for restriction, growth, or restructuring of computing programs in response to enrollment pressures?
   b. What measures are available for managing course enrollment, declaration of major, or admission into the program?
   c. What options exist for building resources and capacity?
   d. What are the inherent limits or drawbacks of these measures? How will they affect quality of education, student satisfaction, the participation of students from underrepresented groups, and institutional balance?

These assessments will require the examination of institutional data. This could include application and admission rates and thresholds for entry into CS programs and courses, as well as student enrollment, performance, and attrition rates. Some of the necessary information should be available via the institution's administrative data systems; new data collection such as student surveys or discussions with faculty and staff may also be needed.

While there is no single, optimal strategy that is right for all, the committee believes that all institutions should be proactive and creative in responding to the challenge of large and increasing CS enrollments. Taking incremental actions to get through the next year or semester are unlikely to produce the best outcomes for the institution, and have in the past been associated with negative outcomes such as decreased participation of women undergraduates in computing. Accepting the overwhelmingly important role that computing will be playing in the future of society and the university, institutional leaders should view this as an important opportunity to be seized.

7

Recommendations

While enrollments in computing courses and degree programs vary among U.S. institutions of higher education, degree production has been surging on average since 2008, and many academic institutions are experiencing growth that has reached or exceeded the capacity of their departments. Furthermore, with the changing role of computing in society and the rapid evolution of computing fields and technologies, the committee sees both an urgent need and an opportunity to strategically evaluate the role of computing at academic institutions and to plan for a compelling future where student, departmental, institutional, and national needs can be met.

To this end, the committee makes the following recommendations:

RECOMMENDATION 1: The leaders of the institutions of higher education that have experienced rapid increases in computer science course enrollments should take deliberate actions to address this trend with a sense of urgency.

The increased interest and demand should be viewed as an opportunity for the institution to reassess the role of computing in general, now and in the future, for an inclusive student audience. With the institution's mission and values as context, leaders should develop plans that address the needs of non–computer science (CS) students as well as CS majors—both traditional and those in emerging programs—and opportunities for interdisciplinary collaboration.

RECOMMENDATION 2: A range of actions should be considered as part of a comprehensive institutional strategy, from targeted controls on enrollments or resource additions to meet demand, to more

extensive institutional changes that extend beyond the computer science department.

Chapter 6 provides a template that can help institutions take stock before considering potential actions, several of which are also discussed in that chapter. While responses should and will vary by institution, there are some common issues and elements that the committee calls out here. The committee also notes that there is no crisp delineation between short-term tactics and long-term strategies, or between local actions and broader institutional initiatives. Indeed, what may seem to be a short-term, local "fix" can have long-term consequences that affect the entire institution.

Universities should develop ways to manage fluctuations in enrollments, without following enrollment booms and busts too closely, as they may be unpredictable or unrelated to long-term trends. They should settle on reasonable targets for long-run growth in computer science faculty and computationally trained faculty, aim for those targets (which will vary among institutions), and remain open to adjustments over time. There is no single approach—a silver bullet—for responding to enrollment growth that will be optimal at all institutions. Every tactic has benefits and costs. Leaders will need to select strategies and make trade-offs that are appropriate to their circumstances and to their institution's mission and values, monitor the results over time, and update strategies as needed.

RECOMMENDATION 2.1: Institutions experiencing a computer science enrollment surge should seriously consider an increase in resources to address the rising workload on faculty and staff in computer science and related departments, and the limitations arising from inadequate facilities.

The key resources supporting and enabling a department's teaching mission—faculty, teaching staff, teaching assistants, facilities, and support staff—are all dependent on a department's budget. An institution's capacity to respond to increased student demand for computing courses is limited by constraints on any one of these resources, as discussed in Chapter 6. At the same time, institutions need to recognize the challenge computer science departments face in hiring qualified tenure and tenure-track faculty and teaching faculty, and the vast opportunities for such individuals in the private sector. When faculty hiring is not possible, resources would make a difference to enable hiring of undergraduate or graduate students or staff to increase instructional capacity and help manage large course and advising loads. Another strategy could be to provide additional compensation to those faculty taking on teaching loads that are significantly larger than those typical of other faculty across the institution.

RECOMMENDATION 2.2: Some institutions may view the imposition of limits on enrollment in computer science and related courses as desirable or unavoidable. However, before imposing limits on

course or major enrollments, the consequences of doing so should be considered comprehensively, and the benefits and costs weighed for the entire university community.

Limiting course enrollments may cut off students from their true passion. It may also introduce stress or an environment of real or perceived competition for students who desire to enter a CS program, which could discourage participation among underrepresented groups. At the same time, institutions should not accept students with the promise of entering a major when the constraints on resources make their admission into the program unlikely. Any measures to limit major admission or declaration can result in reduced demand for more advanced courses and can affect the overall climate in such courses, and could lead to unexpected declines in overall degree production. As discussed in Chapter 5, specific strategies for limiting enrollments could also have the effect of disproportionately limiting the opportunities of underrepresented minorities and thus decrease diversity in the field.

Limiting students' opportunities for taking CS courses may also affect the educational experiences of non-majors. Given the evidence of wide interest among non-CS majors, increasing requirements of CS courses for other majors, and increasing demand for computing skills across the workforce, institutions must understand and consider how limitations on CS enrollments will affect their entire student body, across all programs.

RECOMMENDATION 2.3: Institutional leadership should engage directly with computer science departments or programs to develop appropriate faculty hiring and faculty size targets, and develop strategies to improve faculty retention. Increasing the number and enhancing the role of academic-rank teaching faculty should be given serious consideration.

As institutions assess the role of computer science and the interests and needs of students, the reality of CS faculty hiring challenges and the opportunities available to new CS Ph.D.s need to be understood. As programs grow, the environment and workload for faculty needs to be taken into consideration. Institutions need to be proactive to help reduce the faculty retention challenges that departments face. Furthermore, the relatively small number of CS Ph.D.s pursuing an academic career, coupled with the broad opportunities for new Ph.D.s as well as CS faculty in the private sector, may impact faculty growth goals set by departments and institutions. While increases in today's CS bachelor's degree production will likely increase the number of Ph.D.s produced at some point in the future, this downstream growth of faculty potential will not provide a solution to the hiring problem in the near or mid-term. Furthermore, placing limits on CS major enrollments will likely prolong this challenge.

Larger departments have been increasingly hiring academic-rank teaching faculty to help deal with course enrollments and the increasing number of majors, but even this can be challenging. Departments need to implement effective strategies to mentor, evaluate, and promote this new type of faculty, including tenure practices. This includes providing professional development as well as integrating teaching faculty into departmental faculty activities, defining the expected scholarship and leadership activities, and defining best practices for their success.

RECOMMENDATION 2.4: Larger institutions—in particular, research universities—should reevaluate the organizational placement of the computer science department and other departmental units with a computational mission.

In particular, institutional leadership should consider whether a College of Computing could help to improve organizational efficiency and benefit its students. The organizational placement of the CS department can have significant impact on the computing education for all students. The organizational structure also impacts approval and reporting channels, and can have significant impact on how quickly and effectively a department can respond to important changes. The appropriate structure should reduce duplication in courses and programs; coordinated programs can lead to better graduation rates.

RECOMMENDATION 2.5: Institutions should pursue innovative strategies for using technology to deliver high-quality instruction at scale to large numbers of students. Institutions should also pursue additional, creative strategies for meeting demand for quality computer science courses and skills development among the entire student body.

In this era where the demand for computer science is high, CS is a natural discipline for such experimentation and innovation. While this is certainly under way at some institutions (and is the basis for the massive open online course phenomenon—though this approach has shown mixed results), there are further opportunities for using novel technologies to deliver high-quality instruction at scale. Computing researchers should make use of advances in their own fields and work with education researchers to better understand how students learn and how to improve the efficacy and quality of automated instruction, labs, examinations, and grading in undergraduate computing education. Institutions should support such collaborations by providing needed startup resources. Additional strategies could include using qualified faculty outside CS to cover CS classes, bringing back retired faculty, and offering more summer classes covered by teaching faculty.

RECOMMENDATION 3: Institutions should take deliberate actions to support diversity in computer science and related programs. In particular:

RECOMMENDATION 3.1: Institutions should assess how computer science enrollment growth, and any actions or strategies for responding to it, affects the diversity of their student bodies, and deliberately align their actions and the culture of their programs with best practices for diversity and retention.

As discussed in Chapter 5, there is research from which institutions can draw when considering their strategies. Actions understood to have a negative effect on the participation of women and underrepresented minorities in CS or science, technology, engineering, and mathematics (STEM) should be avoided. Methods for managing growth while actively increasing diversity should be sought.

RECOMMENDATION 3.2: Institutions should leverage the increasing interest in computer science and related fields, among both non-majors and intended majors, to engage, recruit, and retain more women and underrepresented minorities into the field and help address the diversity problem proactively.

While the current enrollment growth is a challenge for departmental resources, it comes with the opportunity to take advantage of the broad excitement around CS in order to help shape the future of the field, and who will be included.

RECOMMENDATION 4: The National Science Foundation (NSF) can be especially helpful in advancing undergraduate computer science education in the context of increasing enrollments, for both majors and non-majors. The following actions should receive serious consideration:

RECOMMENDATION 4.1: Use NSF's convening power to bring computer science faculty and institutional leaders together to identify best practices and innovation in computer science education in times of limited departmental resources. This should include assessment of the computer science skills and knowledge needed in non–computer science disciplines.

RECOMMENDATION 4.2: Support research on how best to use technology in teaching large classes. Such research should be multidisciplinary, spanning learning sciences, educational pedagogy for computer science, development and deployment of assessment instruments, and technology design.

RECOMMENDATION 4.3: Support research to advance the understanding of best practices for diversity in computing, including rigorous and longitudinal assessment of the efficacy of specific institutional practices, especially those taken or considered in times

of high enrollments. This research should be multidisciplinary, with experts in both micro- and macro-level social science research, statistics, computer science education, and diversity in STEM and computing.

RECOMMENDATION 4.4: Create an initiative to expand instructional resources in computer science, informed by an understanding of the constraints and dynamics of the supply and demand for computer science Ph.D.s. This might include research support and doctoral fellowships for domestic computer science undergraduates, and support for incorporating teaching into computer science doctoral programs and junior faculty research.

RECOMMENDATION 5: Computer science departments and the computing industry should develop new partnerships to help higher education meet workforce needs, continue to graduate well-prepared students, encourage industry to provide increased support for research funding, and allow a better exchange of Ph.D.-level researchers between academia and industry.

Academic institutions should pursue new partnerships with industry and to enable CS professionals in the private sector with academic experience to pursue an academic leave. This could open the door to teaching for individuals from industry, provide additional industry experience for CS courses, and provide industry an additional recruiting pipeline. Students would similarly benefit from the opportunity to network with professionals from the private sector.

RECOMMENDATION 6: Public institutions produce a significant fraction of each state's workforce and the nation's computer science undergraduate degrees. States should provide sufficient support to their public institutions to enable them to support fully their academic missions, including with respect to computer science education.

The widespread disinvestment by states in higher education has had a negative effect on all that these institutions do. Responding to high demand for CS education is extremely difficult when institutional budgets decline, as they have in most states over the last decade. Furthermore, strengthening CS programs can have positive benefits for regional economies.

RECOMMENDATION 7: To prepare students better for the expanding role of computing in academia, industry, and daily life underlying the increase in interest in computer science, government agencies and states should support local, state, and national programs for computing education for the purpose of increasing expo-

sure to computing, computational principles, information security, and data analytics throughout the K-12 pipeline.

Such initiatives should be informed by an understanding of which computer science principles and methods are most important in different academic disciplines and in daily life. They should also be linked to evidence about the CS and computing skills in demand in different industry sectors and occupational fields. These topics are important areas for future study.

RECOMMENDATION 8: Actions should be taken to facilitate an improved understanding of national undergraduate enrollment trends by improving the primary data available about them and facilitating the availability of that data in a timely fashion. In particular, the following actions should be considered:

RECOMMENDATION 8.1: Improved data sources about undergraduate enrollment should be pursued by federal and state governments in collaboration with academic institutions. To the extent possible, data should be made available in a time frame where the information can be useful for academic and government planning purposes.

This should include authoritative, longitudinal, and either comprehensive or representative data about course enrollments, declared majors, degree requirements, and the organizational unit responsible for administering degree programs. Data on enrollment trends should include details on the impact of pedagogical approaches and institutional environment on recruitment and retention of women and underrepresented minorities and the drivers of non-major enrollment in CS courses. Such data should be obtained at both the macro level, using rigorous sampling techniques to ensure representative data, and the micro level, by interviewing individual students and programs for a better understanding of individuals' interests.

Such timely information would make it easier to track trends in higher education and predict degree production and workforce trends. Larger institutions and those with institutional research offices may have appropriate resources and infrastructure to support this objective; state higher education systems could play a role in coordinating such efforts to minimize the burden on institutions that lack such resources.

RECOMMENDATION 8.2: The taxonomies and classifications for undergraduate computing degrees and jobs should be reexamined and updated, so that those used in national statistics are more easily brought into alignment, and map more directly to the current organization of computer science and related fields in higher education.

In particular, the Integrated Postsecondary Education Data System (IPEDS) Classification of Instructional Program (CIP) "Computer Science" classifier and the Standard Occupational Classifications (SOCs) used by the Bureau of Labor Statistics (BLS) should be brought into better alignment. This could be done by

- Revising the CIPs and SOCs to that they map to each other more directly, or
- Creating a clearer crosswalk, perhaps identifying in the SOC background information how the SOC relates to CIPs, preferably while maintaining a continuity of data that continues to enable analysis of long-term trends.

Identifying the preferred level of CS education associated with various CS occupations would also be helpful.

In addition, the computing-related CIPs should be reorganized, renamed, and regrouped to reflect the current organization of these fields in higher education. For example:

- The existing "detailed" CIP of "computer science" should be reexamined and potentially redefined to include fields such as computer engineering and software engineering, and to make "information technology" a distinct or more clearly grouped category.
- Guidance given to institutions about how to classify CS and related programs could be clarified to enable accurate data reporting and analysis.
- Efforts could be made, perhaps through interviews with individual institutions, to map the classification of historical data to current CIPs to enable continuous analysis of temporal trends in the evolution of CS and related fields.
- Information could be collected about the organizational placement of these degrees within an academic unit to enable analysis of the emergence and prevalence of different institutional models.

This would make it much easier to correlate undergraduate degree production with labor market trends, and to assess emerging trends in the landscape of computing.

RECOMMENDATION 8.3: In the absence of comprehensive national statistics, the computer science community, in collaboration with education, social sciences, and statistics researchers, should continue to pursue or refine effective strategies for tracking enrollment, retention, and graduation rates and measuring student diversity.

In particular, these strategies should be based on surveys that are either comprehensive or based on representative and statistically rigorous samplings across all institution types, with questionnaires crafted (and potentially administered) by (or with the guidance of) experts in survey design. The availability of such data in a timely fashion would be invaluable for informing academic institutions and federal agencies of current trends, and enabling these actors to make informed decisions in a reasonable time frame. Given the increasing requests for data made to institutions of higher education by state and federal agencies, accrediting groups, professional organizations, associations to which they belong, and organizations to which they subscribe, efforts to streamline such requests or use a common format would help to minimize the burden of such requests.

References

ACM (Association for Computing Machinery). 2017. ACM Richard Tapia Celebration of Diversity in Computing 2017 Tapia Conference. Online. Available at http://tapiaconference.org/.

ACM-W (Association for Computing Machinery Council on Women in Computing). 2017. Association for Computing Machinery Council on Women in Computing Home Page. ACM. Online. Available at https://womentest.acm.org/category/celebrations/.

Aguinis, H., S.A. Culpepper, and C.A. Pierce. 2016. Differential prediction generalization in college admissions testing. *Journal of Educational Psychology*. 108(7): 1045-1059.

Anita Borg Institute. 2017a. 2017 Grace Hopper Celebration of Women in Computing. Online. Available at https://anitaborg.org/event/2017-grace-hopper-celebration-women-computing/.

Anita Borg Institute. 2017b. BRAID: A Diversity Program. Online. Available at https://anitaborg.org/braid-building-recruiting-and-inclusion-for-diversity/.

ASEE (American Society for Engineering Education). 2015. Profiles of Engineering and Engineering Technology Colleges. Online. Available at https://www.asee.org/papers-and-publications/publications/college-profiles/2015-undergraduate-engineering-degrees.pdf.

BHEF (Business Higher Education Forum). 2014. BHEF Issue Brief: Data Science Emerges as Essential Tool for Decision Making and Innovation Across Industry Sectors. Online. Available at http://www.bhef.com/sites/default/files/BHEF_2014_data_science_0.pdf

BLS (Bureau of Labor Statistics). 2015. Employment Projections: 2014-2024: Table 11b. Online. Available at http://www.bls.gov/cps/cpsaat11b.htm.

Bound, J., B. Braga, J. Golden, and S. Turner. 2013. Pathways to adjustment: The case of information technology workers. *American Economic Review Papers and Proceedings*. 103(3): 203-207.

Bound, J., and N. Morales. 2016. Workforce Trends in Computer Science. Commissioned Study by the Committee on the Growth of Computer Science Undergraduate Enrollments, National Academies of Sciences, Engineering, and Medicine.

Breneman, D., and R. Freeman. 1974. *Forecasting the Ph.D. Labor Market: Pitfalls for Policy*. National Board of Graduate Education.

Brinkman, B., and A. Diekman. 2016. Applying the Communal Goal Congruity Perspective to Enhance Diversity and Inclusion in Undergraduate Computing Degrees. Paper presented at SIGCSE 2016. Memphis, TN. March 2-5.

Bryan, G.E. 1994. Not all programmers are created equal. *Proceedings of the Aerospace Applications Conference*, IEEE Computer Society. Los Alamitos, CA. Reprinted in Thayer, R. 1997. *Software Engineering Project Management*. 2nd ed. IEEE Computer Society.

Burning Glass Technologies. 2015a. Job Market Intelligence: Cybersecurity Jobs 2015. Online. Available at http://burning-glass.com/wp-content/uploads/Cybersecurity_Jobs_Report_2015.pdf.

Burning Glass Technologies. 2015b. Blurring Lines: How Business and Technology Skills Are Merging to Create High Opportunity Hybrid Jobs. Online. Available at http://burning-glass.com/wp-content/uploads/Blurring_Lines_Hybrid_Jobs_Report.pdf.

Burning Glass Technologies. 2016. Beyond Point and Click: The Expanding Demand for Coding Skills. Online. Available at http://burning-glass.com/research/coding-skills/.

CAHSI (Computing Alliance of Hispanic-Serving Institutions). 2016. Preview of Award 1042341—Annual Project Report. Online. Available at http://cahsi.cs.utep.edu/about?quicktabs_about=5#quicktabs-about.

CAHSI. 2017a. About CAHSI. Online. Available at http://cahsi.cs.utep.edu/about.

CAHSI. 2017b. CAHSI Summit. Online. Available at http://cahsi.cs.utep.edu/cahsisummit.

Camp, T. 2017. Booming Enrollments: Understanding the Surge. Presentation for Computing Research Association Conference at Snowbird, Utah, July 17-19.

Camp, T., W. Richards Adrion, B. Bizot, S. Davidson, M. Hall, S. Hambrusch, E. Walker, and S. Zweben. 2017a. Generation CS: The growth of computer science. *ACM Inroads*. 8(2): 44-50.

Camp, T., W. Richards Adrion, B. Bizot, S. Davidson, M. Hall, S. Hambrusch, E. Walker, and S. Zweben. 2017b. Generation CS: The mixed news on diversity and the enrollment surge. *ACM Inroads*. 8(3): 36-42.

Carlson, S. 2015. Colleges "unleashes the deans" with decentralized budgets. *Chronicle of Higher Education*. Online. Available at http://www.chronicle.com/article/Colleges-Unleash-the-Deans/151711/.

The Carnegie Classifications of Institutions of Higher Education. 2017. Basic Classification Description. Online. Available at http://carnegieclassifications.iu.edu/classification_descriptions/basic.php.

Cereijido, A., and A. Selyukh. 2016. Why aren't there more women in tech? A tour of Silicon Valley's leaky pipeline. *National Public Radio*. Online. Available at http://www.npr.org/sections/alltechconsidered/2016/12/21/505864391/why-arent-there-more-women-in-tech-a-tour-of-silicon-valleys-leaky-pipeline.

Chang, M.J., J. Sharkness, S. Hurtado, and C.B. Newman. 2014. What matters in college for retaining aspiring scientists and engineers from underrepresented racial groups. *Journal of Research in Science Teaching*. 51(5): 555-580.

Chapman, G. 2000. Gold rush mindset undermining programming field. *Los Angeles Times*. Online. Available at http://articles.latimes.com/2000/feb/14/business/fi-64176.

Chatlani, S. 2017. Number of minorities, women taking CS is skyrocketing thanks to STEM collaborations. *Education Dive*. Online. Available at https://www.educationdive.com/news/number-of-minorities-women-taking-cs-is-skyrocketing-thanks-to-stem-collab/448292/.

Cheryan, S., V.C. Plaut, P.G. Davies, and C.M. Steele. 2009. Ambient belonging: How stereotypical cues impact gender participation in computer science. *Journal of Personality and Social Psychology*. 97(6): 1045.

Code.org. 2017. Code.org Advocacy Coalition. Online. Available at https://code.org/advocacy.

Cohoon, J., and T. Luther. 2011. Analysis of a CS1 Approach for Attracting Diverse and Inexperienced Students to Computing Majors. Paper presented at SIGCSE 2011. Dallas, TX. March 9-12.

Cole, D., and A. Espinoza. 2008. Examining the academic success of Latino students in science, technology, engineering, and mathematics (STEM) majors. *Journal of College Student Development*. 49(4): 285-300.

College Board. 2017. Largest Course Launch in AP History. Online. Available at https://advancesinap.collegeboard.org/stem/computer-science-principles.

Conrad, S., S.S. Canetto, D. Macphee, and S. Farro. 2009. What attracts high-achieving, socio-economically disadvantaged students to the physical sciences and engineering? *College Student Journal*. 43(4): 1359-1369.

Cornell University. 2017. Information Science Major. Online. Available at https://admissions.cals.cornell.edu/academics/majors/information-science.

Cottam, J.A., S.S. Foley, and S. Menzel. 2010. Do Roadshows Work? Examining the Effectiveness of Just Be. Online. Available at https://pdfs.semanticscholar.org/3aec/ea9dc5cc853e091b37c90aaa12ad093cdd83.pdf.

CRA (Computing Research Association). 2015. The Taulbee Survey. Online. Available at http://cra.org/resources/taulbee-survey/.

CRA. 2017a. Generation CS: Computer Science Undergraduate Enrollments Surge Since 2006. Online. Available at http://cra.org/data/Generation-CS/.

CRA. 2017b. AP Computer Science Principles Course Increases High School Participation in CS. CRA Bulletin. Online. Available at http://cra.org/ap-computer-science-principles-course-exam-increases-high-school-student-participation-cs/.

CS Women UMass Amherst (Computer Science Women, University of Massachusetts, Amherst). 2017. CS Women UMass Amherst Home Page. Online. Available at http://cswomenumass.github.io/index.html.

CSWN (Computer Science Women's Network, Purdue University). 2017. Computer Science Women's Network Home Page. Online. Available at https://www.cs.purdue.edu/cswn/.

Cuny, J. 2015. Special Section on CS10K Community—Part 2: Computer Science Principles: Transforming K-12 computing education. *ACM Inroads*. 6(4).

CUSTEMS (Consortium for Undergraduate STEM Success). 2017. CUSTEMS Home Page. Online. Available at http://www.custems.org/.

Davis, C.G., and C.J. Finelli. 2007. Diversity and retention in engineering. *New Directions for Teaching and Learning*. 11: 63-71.

DHS (Department of Homeland Security). 2016. Cybersecurity Jobs Website. Online. Available at http://www.dhs.gov/topic/cybersecurity-jobs.

Dishman, L. 2016. Why Coding Is Still the Most Important Job Skill of the Future. Fast Company. Online. Available at https://www.fastcompany.com/3060883/why-coding-is-the-job-skill-of-the-future-for-everyone.

Donnelly, G. 2017. Tech employees overestimate how well their companies promote diversity. Fortune. Online. Available at http://fortune.com/2017/03/22/tech-employees-overestimate-how-well-their-companies-promote-diversity/.

Eagan, K., E.B. Sotelzenberg, J.J. Ramirez, M.C. Aragon, M. Ramirez Suchard, and C. Rios-Aguilar. 2016. The American Freshman: Fifty-Year Trends, 1966-2015. Higher Education Research Institute. Online. Available at https://www.heri.ucla.edu/monographs/50YearTrendsMonograph2016.pdf.

Eagan, Jr., M.K., S. Hurtado, and M.J. Chang. 2010. What Matters in STEM: Institutional Contexts That Influence STEM Bachelor's Degree Completion Rates. Presentation at the 2010 Annual Meeting of the Association for the Study of Higher Education. Indianapolis, IN. November 17-20.

Emanuel, E.J. 2013. Online education: MOOCs taken by educated few. *Nature*. 503(7476): 342.

Ensmenger, N.L. 2012. *The Computer Boys Take Over: Computers, Programmers, and the Politics of Technical Expertise*. MIT Press. Cambridge, MA.

Flores, A. 2017. Facts on U.S. Latinos, 2015: Statistical portrait of Hispanics in the U.S. Pew Research Center. Online. Available at http://www.pewhispanic.org/2015/04/19/statistical-portrait-of-hispanics-in-the-united-states-key-charts/#hispanic-pop.

Freeman, R. 2016. Workforce and Degree Trends Panel. Public Workshop of the National Academies Committee on the Growth of Computer Science Undergraduate Enrollments, National Academy of Sciences. Washington, DC. August 15.

Freeman, R.B. 1975. Supply and salary adjustments to the changing science manpower market: Physics, 1948-1973. *American Economic Review*. 65(1): 27-39.

Freeman, R.B. 1976. A cobweb model of the supply and starting salary of new engineers. *ILR Review*. 29: 236-248.

Gates, A.Q., S. Hug, H. Thiry, R. Alo, M. Beheshti, J. Fernandez, N. Rodriguez, and M. Adjouadi. 2011. The Computing Alliance of Hispanic-Serving Institutions: Supporting Hispanics at critical transition points. *Transactions on Computing Education*. 11(3): 16:1-16:21.

Gates, A.Q., H. Thiry, and S. Hug. 2016. Reflections: The Computing Alliance of Hispanic-Serving Institutions. *ACM Inroads*. 7(4): 69-73.

Geiser, S. 2015. The growing correlation between race and SAT scores: New findings from California. Center for Studies in Higher Education, Research and Occasional Paper Series. Online. Available at https://cshe.berkeley.edu/sites/default/files/publications/rops.cshe_.10.15.geiser.racesat.10.26.2015.pdf.

Google, Inc. and Gallup, Inc. 2016. Trends in the State of Computer Science in U.S. K-12 Schools. Online. Available at http://www.gallup.com/reports/196379/trends-state-computer-science-schools.aspx.

Heitin, L. 2015. Number of students taking AP science exams surges. *Education Week*. Online. Available at http://www.edweek.org/ew/articles/2015/09/09/number-of-students-taking-ap-science-exams.html.

Hug, S., M. McKay, and H. Thiry. 2017. CAHSI External Evaluation Report 2016-2017: Promoting Success for Hispanic Computing Students and Faculty. Online. Available at http://cahsi.cs.utep.edu/cahsifiles/Reports/evaluation/2016-2017_CAHSI_External_Evaluation_Report.pdf.

Hunt, J. 2016. White Paper: Does the Recent Increase in Computer Science Degrees Reflect Increased Demand? Commissioned Study by the Committee on the Growth of Computer Science Undergraduate Enrollments, National Academies of Sciences, Engineering, and Medicine.

Intel Corporation and Dalberg Global Development Advisors. 2016. Decoding Diversity: The Financial and Economic Returns in Tech. Online. Available at https://www.intel.com/content/www/us/en/diversity/decoding-diversity-report.html.

The Joint Task Force for Computing Curricula. 2005. Computing Curricula 2005: The Overview Report. ACM and IEEE. Online. Available at http://www.acm.org/education/education/curric_vols/CC2005-March06Final.pdf.

K-12 Computer Science. 2017. Defining Computer Science. Online. Available at https://k12cs.org/defining-computer-science/.

Kamenetz, A. 2017. Tens of Thousands More Women and Minorities Are Taking Computer Science. Online. Available at https://www.npr.org/sections/ed/2017/07/31/539853090/tens-of-thousands-more-women-and-minorities-are-taking-computer-science.

Katz, L.F., and A.B. Krueger. 2016. The Rise and Nature of Alternative Work Arrangements in the United States 1995-2015. No. w22667. National Bureau of Economic Research. Online. Available at http://www.nber.org/papers/w22667.

Kena, G., S. Aud, F. Johnson, X. Wang, J. Zhang, A. Rathbun, S. Wildinson-Fliker, and P. Kristapovich. 2014. The Condition of Education (NCES 2014-083). U.S. Department of Education, National Center for Education Statistics. Washington, DC.

Kizilcec, R.F., A.J. Saltarelli, J. Reich, and G.L. Cohen. 2017. Closing global achievement gaps in MOOCs. *Science*. 355(6322): 251-252.

Klawe, M. 2016. At Harvey Mudd College, the Ratio of Women in Computer Science Increased from 10 percent to 40% in 5 years. *Wired*. Online. Available at https://www.wired.com/2016/02/at-harvey-mudd-college-the-ratio-of-women-in-computer-science-increased-from-10-to-40-in-5-years/.

Leiner, B.M., V.G. Cerf, D.D. Clark, R.E. Kahn, L. Kleinrock, D.C. Lynch, J. Postel, L.G. Roberts, and S.S. Wolff. 1997. The past and future history of the Internet. *Communications of the ACM*. 40(2):102-108.

Leonhardt, D. 2017. America's Great Working-Class Colleges. *The New York Times*. Online. Available at https://www.nytimes.com/2017/01/18/opinion/sunday/americas-great-working-class-colleges.html.

MaGE (Megas and Gigas Educate Program). 2017. MaGE Training Course. Online. Available at https://sites.google.com/a/mtholyoke.edu/mage-training/.

Manning, W. 1989. Broadening the basis for admissions decisions. In *Key Issues in Minority Education: Research, Directions, and Practical Implications* (W. Ward and M. Cross, eds.). Center for Research on Minority Education, Norman, OK.

Margolis, J., and A. Fisher. 2002. *Unlocking the Clubhouse: Women in Computing*. MIT Press. Cambridge, MA.

Mattern, K.D., E.J. Shaw, and M. Ewing. 2011. *Advanced Placement® Exam Participation: Is AP® Exam Participation and Performance Related to Choice of College Major?*. College Board. Online. Available at http://professionals.collegeboard.com/profdownload/pdf/RR2011-6.pdf.

Misa, T.J., ed. 2011. *Gender Codes: Why Women Are Leaving Computing*. John Wiley & Sons, New York.

Mooney, G.M., and D.J. Foley. 2011. *Community Colleges: Playing an Important Role to the Education of Science, Engineering, and Health Graduates*. National Science Foundation. Arlington, VA.

Morrisett, G. 2016. The Role and Future of Computing in Universities Panel. Public Workshop of the National Academies Committee on the Growth of Computer Science Undergraduate Enrollments. Washington, DC. August 15.

NACE (National Association of Colleges and Employers). 2017a. Engineering Majors Top Class of 2017 Salary Projections. Online. Available at https://www.naceweb.org/job-market/compensation/engineering-majors-top-class-of-2017-salary-projections/.

NACE. 2017b. Computer Science Tabbed to Be Top Paid Across Regions. Online. Available at http://www.naceweb.org/job-market/compensation/computer-science-tabbed-to-be-top-paid-across-regions/.

NASEM (National Academies of Science, Engineering, and Medicine). 2017. *Information Technology and the U.S. Workforce: Where Are We and Where Do We Go from Here?* National Academies Press. Washington, DC. https://doi.org/10.17226/24649.

NCES (National Center for Education Statistics). 2010a. CIP 2010. Online. Available at https://nces.ed.gov/ipeds/cipcode/cipdetail.aspx?y=55&cipid=88073.

NCES. 2010b. ACT score averages and standard deviations, by sex and race/ethnicity, and percentage of ACT test takers, by selected composite score ranges and planned fields of study: Selected years, 1995 through 2010. Online. Available at https://nces.ed.gov/programs/digest/d10/tables/dt10_155.asp.

NCES. 2015. SAT mean scores of college-bound seniors, by race/ethnicity: Selected years, 1986-87 through 2014-2015. *Digest of Education Statistics*. Online. Available at https://nces.ed.gov/programs/digest/d15/tables/dt15_226.10.asp.

NCES. 2016. Integrated Postsecondary Education Data System (IPEDS). Online. Available at http://ncsesdata.nsf.gov/webcaspar/.

NCWIT (National Center for Women & Information Technology). 2014. What is the Impact of Gender Diversity on Technology Business Performance? Research Summary. Online. Available at https://www.ncwit.org/sites/default/files/resources/impactgenderdiversitytechbusinessperformance_print.pdf.

NCWIT. 2017. Aspirations in Computing. Online. Available at https://www.ncwit.org/programs-campaigns/aspirations-computing.

NSF (National Science Foundation). 2009. Broadening Participation in Computing. Online. Available at https://www.nsf.gov/publications/pub_summ.jsp?WT.z_pims_id=13510&ods_key=nsf09534.

NSF. 2012. Computing Education for the 21st Century. Online. Available at https://www.nsf.gov/publications/pub_summ.jsp?ods_key=nsf12527.

NSF. 2016a. Broadening Participation in Computing Alliance Program. Online. Available at https://www.nsf.gov/funding/pgm_summ.jsp?pims_id=503593.

NSF. 2016b. National Science Board Science & Engineering Indicators 2016. Online. Available at https://www.nsf.gov/statistics/2016/nsb20161/#/report/chapter-2/undergraduate-education-enrollment-and-degrees-in-the-united-states.

NSF. 2017. WebCASPAR: Integrated Science and Engineering Resources Data System. Online. Available at https://ncsesdata.nsf.gov/webcaspar/.

Newhall, T., L. Meeden, A. Danner, A. Soni, F. Ruiz, and R. Wicentowski. 2014. A Support Program for Introductory CS Courses That Improves Student Performance and Retains Students from Underrepresented Groups. Paper presented at SIGCSE 2014. Atlanta, GA. March 5-8.

Newman, K. 2016. The Role and Future of Computing in Universities Panel. Public Workshop of the National Academies Committee on the Growth of Computer Science Undergraduate Enrollments. Washington, DC. August 15.

Nobelprize.org. 2013. The Nobel Prize in Chemistry 2013. Online. Available at http://www.nobelprize.org/nobel_prizes/chemistry/laureates/2013/.

NRC (National Research Council). 2000. *Forecasting Demand and Supply of Doctoral Scientists and Engineers: Report of a Workshop on Methodology*. National Academies Press. Washington, DC. https://doi.org/10.17226/9865.

NRC. 2012. *Continuing Innovation in Information Technology*. National Academies Press. Washington, DC. https://doi.org/10.17226/13427.

Nunez, S. 2015. The use of academic data and demographic data from recently graduated high school students to predict academic success at Sauk Valley Community College, Ph.D. diss., Ferris State University.

Partovi, H. 2017. Girls set AP Computer Science record...skyrocketing growth outpaces boys. Online. Available at https://medium.com/@codeorg/girls-set-ap-computer-science-record-skyrocketing-growth-outpaces-boys-41b7c01373a5.

Peckham, J., L.L. Harlow, D.A. Stuart, B. Silver, H. Mederer, and P.D. Stephenson. 2007. Broadening Participation in Computing: Issues and Challenges. Paper presented at ITiCSE 2007. Dundee, Scotland, UK. June 23-27.

Pulimood, M., and U. Wolz. 2009. Problem Solving in Community: A Necessary Shift in CS Pedagogy. Paper presented at SIGCSE 2008. Portland, OR. March 12-15.

Purdue, M. 2017. AP computer science exam takers double; here's why. Online. Available at https://www.usatoday.com/story/tech/news/2017/07/18/code-org-helps-ap-computer-science-increase-diversity/486482001/ .

Purdue University. 2017. 2015-2016 (August 2015—December 2016—May 2016) Placement Results. Last updated April 21, 2017. Online. Available at https://www.cs.purdue.edu/corporate/placement/index.html.

PWiCS (Princeton Women in Computer Science). 2017. Princeton Women in Computer Science Home Page. Online. Available at https://princetonwics.wordpress.com/.

Rice, J.R., and S. Rosen. 1990. History of the Computer Sciences Department at Purdue University. Purdue University Computer Science Technical Reports Report Number 90-1003. Online. Available at https://pdfs.semanticscholar.org/8da3/8f7b5f21ae48747c19ccca5502058a5889de.pdf.

Sackman, H., W.J. Erikson, and E.E. Grant. 1968. Exploratory experimental studies comparing online and offline programming performance. *Communications of the ACM*. 11(1): 3-11. Online. Available at http://dx.doi.org/10.1145/362851.362858.

Santiago, D., E. Galdeano, and M. Taylor. 2015. The Condition of Latinos in Education: 2015 Factbook. Online. Available at http://www.edexcelencia.org/research/2015-factbook.

Sax, L.J., K.J. Lehman, J.A. Jacobs, M.A. Kanny, G. Lim, L. Monje-Paulson, and H.B. Zimmerman. 2017. Anatomy of an enduring gender gap: The evolution of women's participation in computer science. *Journal of Higher Education*. 88(2): 258-293.

Shackelford, R., A. McGettrick, R. Sloan, H. Topi, G. Davies, R. Kamali, J. Cross, J. Impagliazzo, R. LeBlanc, and B. Lunt. 2006. Computing Curricular 2005: The Overview Report. In *Proceedings of the 37th SIGCSE Technical Symposium on Computer Science Education (SIGCSE '06)*. ACM. New York, NY. 456-457. DOI=http://dx.doi.org/10.1145/1121341.1121482.

Simon, R.A., M.W. Aulls, H. Dedic, K. Hubbard, and N.C. Hall. 2015. Exploring student persistence in STEM programs: A motivational model. *Canadian Journal of Education*. 38(1): 1-27.

Soares, J.A. 2012. *SAT Wars: The Case for Test-Optional College Admission*. Teachers College Press. New York.

Starkman, R. 2017. Stanford Computer Science Launches New Masters of Education. Online. Available at https://www.huffingtonpost.com/ruth-starkman/stanford-computer-science_b_9713220.html.

Stock, W.G., and M. Stock. 2013. *Handbook of Information Science*. Walter de Gruyter, Berlin.

Tam, P.W., and K. Delaney. 2005. Google's growth helps ignite Silicon Valley hiring frenzy. *Wall Street Journal*. Online. Available at https://www.wsj.com/articles/SB113271436430704916.

Thiry, H., and S. Hug, 2016a. Recent Changes in Enrollment in CAHSI Departments. University of Texas at El Paso Computer Science Technical Report UTEP-CS0-16-84.

Thiry, H., and S. Hug. 2016b. CAHSI Annual Evaluation Report 2015-2016. Online. Available at http://cahsi.cs.utep.edu/cahsifiles/Reports/evaluation/2015-2016CAHSIAnnualEvaluationReport.pdf.

University of California at Berkeley. 2016. Class of 2016 Survey Results for Computer Science. Online. Available at https://career.berkeley.edu/sites/default/files/pdf/Survey/2016CompSci.pdf.

University of Illinois at Urbana-Champaign. 2017. Statistics. Online. Available at http://cs.illinois.edu/about-us/statistics.

Villa, E., A. Gates, K. Kephart, S. Hug, and H. Thiry. 2013. Affinity research groups in practice: Apprenticing students in research. *Journal of Engineering Education*. 102(3): 444-466, doi:10.1002/jee.20016.

Wiener, A. 2016. Why can't Silicon Valley solve its diversity problem. *New Yorker*. Online. Available at http://www.newyorker.com/business/currency/why-cant-silicon-valley-solve-its-diversity-problem.

Wills, C.E. 2016. Analysis of Current and Future Computer Science Needs via Advertised Faculty Searches for 2017. CRA Bulletin. Online. Available at https://cra.org/analysis-of-current-and-future-computer-science-needs-via-advertised-faculty-searches-for-2016/.

Wilson, Z.S., L. Holmes, M.R. Sylvain, L. Batiste, M. Johnson, S.Y. McGuire, S.S. Pang, and I.M. Warner. 2012. Hierarchical mentoring: A transformative strategy for improving diversity and retention in undergraduate STEM disciplines. *Journal of Science Education and Technology*. 21(1): 148-156.

Wing, J. 2016. Dimensions in Computing Panel. Public Workshop of the National Academies Committee on the Growth of Computer Science Undergraduate Enrollments, National Academy of Sciences. Washington, DC. August 15.

Women@CC (Women at the College of Computing, Georgia Tech). 2017. Women at the College of Computing. Online. Available at http://women.cc.gatech.edu/.

Women@SCS (Women at School of Computer Science, Carnegie Mellon University). 2017. Women@SCS. Online. Available at https://www.women.cs.cmu.edu/.

Zelkowitz, M.V. 2007. Maturation of Computer Science Research and Education at the University of Maryland. University of Maryland Computer Science Department and Institute for Advanced Study of Computer Science. Technical Report CS-TR-4882 and UMIACS-TR-2007-40, September 2007.

Zweben, S., and B. Bizot. 2017. 2016 Taulbee Survey, Generation CS Continues to Produce Record Undergrad Enrollment; Graduate Degree Production Rises at Both Master's and Doctoral Levels. *Computing Research News*. 29(5). Online. Available at http://cra.org/crn/wp-content/uploads/sites/7/2017/05/2016-Taulbee-Survey.pdf.

Appendixes

Appendix A

Statement of Task

An ad hoc committee will examine potential responses to the current large influx of undergraduate students enrolling in computing and computer science (CS) courses in 4-year institutions. This study will investigate the following:

- Current and projected patterns of enrollment in undergraduate courses in computer science, computer engineering (CE), and information (within undergraduate information schools), including an analysis of the factors that have driven recent growth and may drive future growth. Data will be disaggregated by type of 4-year institution (e.g., top 50, R-1). The study will include an analysis of enrollment patterns among CS/CE/information majors and minors and science, technology, engineering, and mathematics (STEM) and non-STEM majors taking service courses offered by CS/CE/information departments or enrolling in CS/CE/information courses on an elective basis. A primary goal of this effort is to determine whether the recent increases in enrollment are similar to other cyclic fluctuations that have occurred in the past or whether they are more likely to be sustained.
- Strategies that various institutions are using to respond most effectively to enrollment growth while maintaining or enhancing course access as well as the quality of instruction, considered by type of college or university. The study will examine the impacts those strategies are having on CS/CE/information departments in terms of, for example, faculty and graduate student hiring and workload (including non-CS faculty), student retention, and support for the needs of different categories of students (such as non-CS majors, CS minors, STEM majors, and non-STEM majors).

- The impact of enrollment growth on efforts to increase the enrollment of women and underrepresented minorities in CS/CE/information courses and degree programs, as well as on strategies for retaining those students in the CS/CE/information field and encouraging their pathways toward graduate degrees and careers in related fields.

The committee will produce a report with findings and recommendations, as well as questions for additional research.

Appendix B

Workshop Agenda

NAS Lecture Room, 2101 Constitution Avenue NW, Washington, DC
Monday, August 15, 2016

AGENDA

8:00 AM	Breakfast and Registration
9:00	**Welcome, Overview of Study, and Goals for Workshop** Jared Cohon and Susanne Hambrusch, Committee Co-Chairs
9:05	**Centrality and Dimensions of Computing** Moderator: Susanne Hambrusch, Purdue University Avi Rubin, Johns Hopkins University Alfred Spector, Two Sigma Investments Victoria Stodden, University of Illinois, Urbana-Champaign Jeannette Wing, Microsoft Research
10:30	Break
10:45	**Workforce Trends and Industry Needs** Moderator: Michael McPherson, Spencer Foundation Richard Freeman, Harvard University Susan Goldberger, Burning Glass Technologies Sarah Sampson, GE Digital Michael Wolf, Bureau of Labor Statistics

12:15 PM Lunch

1:30 **Impacts of Enrollment Management Strategies on Diversity in Computing**
Moderator: Valerie Taylor, Texas A&M University
Sarita Brown, *Excelencia* in Education
Joanna Goode, University of Oregon
Shirley Malcom, American Association for the Advancement of Science
Linda Sax, University of California, Los Angeles

3:00 Break

3:30 **The Role and Future of Computing in Universities**
Moderator: David Culler, University of California, Berkeley
Thomas Finholt, University of Michigan
Greg Morrisett, Cornell University
Katherine S. Newman, University of Massachusetts, Amherst
Rob Rutenbar, University of Illinois, Urbana Champaign

4:55 **Wrap-Up and Adjourn**

5:00 **Reception**

Appendix C

Commissioned Paper: Workforce Trends in Computer Science

John Bound and Nicolas Morales

August 2016

There has been a long-standing interest in understanding the nature of the educational pipeline for STEM careers. Classic research by economists (e.g., Arrow and Capron, 1959; Freeman, 1976; Ryoo and Rosen, 2004) has focused on how wages, employment, and educational decisions adjust to changes in demand for scientists and engineers. This work emphasized the notion that the supply of scientists and engineers is likely to be inelastic in the short run, as growth in supply requires expansion in postsecondary degree attainment in scientific fields, while supply is quite elastic over a longer time horizon. Of particular concern is that limits in the supply of science and engineering (S&E) workers during "boom" periods would limit productivity growth, while poor employment prospects for high-skill workers would follow in downturns.

Yet, entry to S&E fields from new college graduates is not the only pathway to adjustment. While early models of the scientific workforce focused exclusively on the enrollment response margin among U.S. students, such approaches do not account for either the flow of workers from other fields or the flow of foreign-trained S&E workers from abroad. Bound et al. (2013), focusing on the market for computer scientists and electrical engineers, argue that the availability of foreign skilled workers over the past few decades increased the responsiveness of the S&E labor market to shifts in the demand for these occupations. As shown in Figure C.1, they find that the wage response to the boom and bust for IT workers in the period surrounding the turn of the century was more muted than the boom and bust that occurred in the late 1970s and early 1980s. They argue that this was, in part, due to the increased availability of foreign skilled workers.

In a similar vein Bound et al. (2015) model how the labor market adjusted to the increase in the demand for computer scientists during the 1990s boom

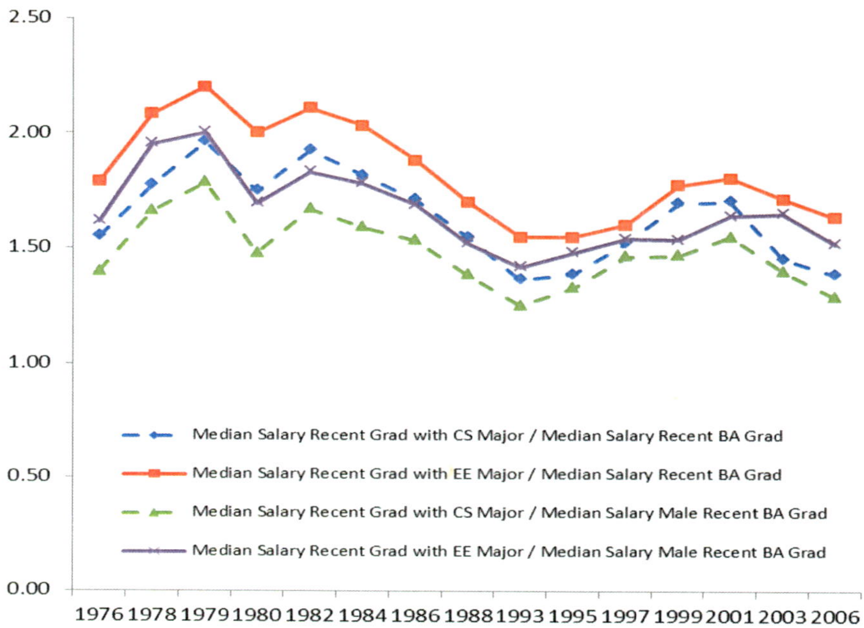

FIGURE C.1 Relative median earnings in IT occupations, 1976-2006. SOURCE: Bound et al. (2013).

not just by increases in enrollment in computer science majors and the flow of workers from other occupations but also by high-skilled foreign-born workers. In this report we update some of these earlier tabulations to show how the market for computer scientists is adjusting to recent increases in the demand for such individuals.

EMPLOYMENT

The share of college graduates working in computer science has been steadily increasing for the past 20 years, with the occupation share in computer science rising from 2.5 percent in 1994 to 5.5 percent in 2015, as shown in Figure C.2. The sharpest growth in employment occurred during the latter half of the 1990s after the introduction of the Internet for commercial purposes, which boosted productivity and increased demand for workers in computer science.[1]

[1] Throughout this paper we will refer to those working in computer science as those who show occupational codes of "Computer Systems Analysts and Computer Scientists" and "Computer Software Developers."

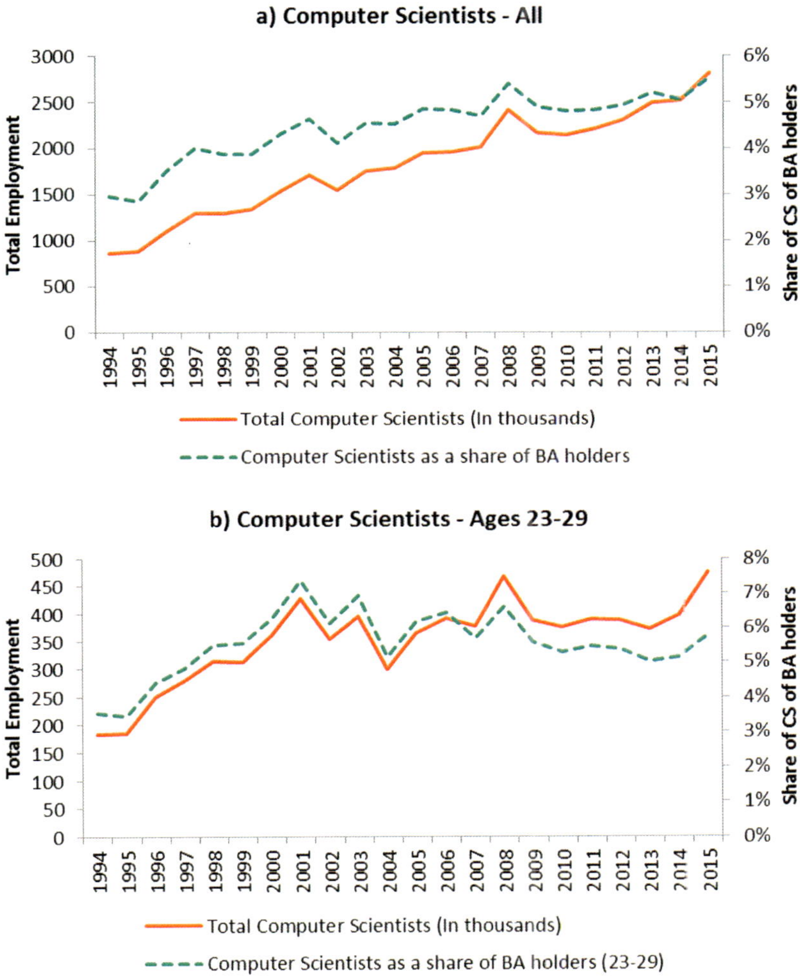

FIGURE C.2 Employment in computer science. SOURCE: Current Population Survey (CPS), March supplement.

Net employment in computer science increased by 650,000 positions during that period, and the share of college graduates working in computer science increased from 2.9 percent in 1995 to 4.3 percent in 2000. This IT boom was followed by the dot-com bust, which created significant job losses among computer scientists but did not stop the long-term growth of computer science among other college occupations. If we focus on younger workers age 23 to 29, there is employment growth over the 1990s, followed by a period of stagnation, with a spike just before the Great Recession, and then a rapid rise since 2013. The 23- to 29-year-old computer scientists seem to respond more to business cycle variations than the total number of computer scientists, as their labor supply fluctuates more throughout the period.

EARNINGS AND WAGES

Earnings followed a similar trend to employment during the late 1990s, as shown in Figure C.3. Median earnings for computer scientists increased by 12 to 15 percent between 1995 and 2000 when compared to wages of engineers (panel a)

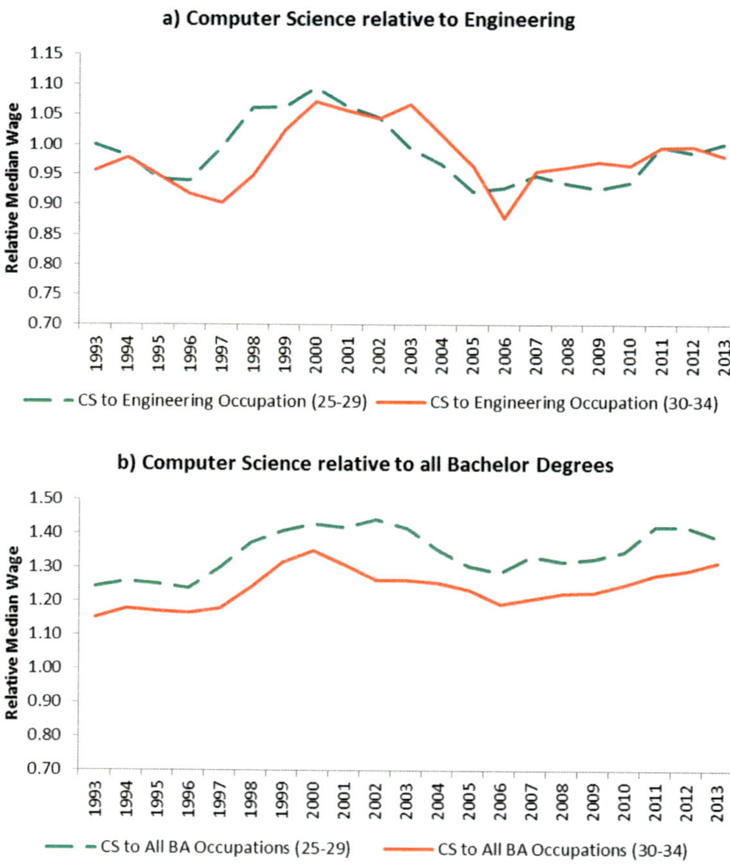

FIGURE C.3 Relative median annual wage by age group. SOURCE: CPS for median annual earnings by occupation (computer science, engineering, and college workers).

and almost 20 percent with respect to wages for all college graduates (panel b).[2] While employment as a share of college graduates kept increasing after the year 2000, relative earnings decreased up until 2006 before increasing again in the last decade, although at a much lower rate than observed during the IT boom in the 1990s. As noted by Bound et al. (2013), the decrease in earnings caused by the dot-com bust was less pronounced than the one observed after the hardware boom in the 1980s. The subsequent recovery also happened faster in the 2000s when compared to the bust in the 1980s, as relative earnings started increasing only 5 years after the bust. Overall, young workers (age 25-29) seem to have higher entry-level wages as computer scientists and engineers than in other occupations, as the series for young workers in Figure C.3, panel b, is consistently above the series for older workers (age 30-34).

SUPPLY-SIDE ADJUSTMENT

The increase of the computer science workforce as a share of total college graduates for the past 20 years can be attributed to three main sources: new graduates with degrees in computer science joining the labor market, workers from other fields who are drawn into computer science, and foreign workers who migrate to the United States to work as computer scientists. As shown in Figure C.4, the foreign source is particularly significant in computer science relative to other fields. Here and elsewhere we count as immigrants only those who report immigrating after they turned 22, treating those who immigrated as children (typically with their families) or as college students as U.S. residents. Historically, the share of foreign workers who work as computer scientists has been well above other fields such as engineering and other science, technology, engineering, and mathematics (STEM) occupations such as physics, mathematics, and biology.[3] While engineering had, on average, 15.6 percent of its workforce as foreign workers, computer science went from 10.6 percent in 1994 to 26.8 percent in 2015. Foreign workers who have college degrees, including those with advanced degrees, generally get to the United States through the H-1B visa program, which is targeted to high-skilled immigrants and has a yearly cap that limits the number of immigrants who can get into the country every year. H-1B visas expire after a period of 3 years (with the possibility of renewal for 3 more years), although a significant fraction of those on H-1Bs are able to become permanent residents. The immigrant share rose during IT booms and stagnated during the dot-com bust in the early part of the next decade. Indeed, while the H-1B visa cap has been reached for most years since the mid-1990s, this was not true in the years immediately following the dot-com bust.

[2] In the CPS, respondents are asked about earnings for the previous calendar year. We date the earnings by the year in which they were earned. Thus, the 2013 earnings number reflects responses in the 2014 survey.

[3] We define STEM fields as engineering, computer science, physical and life sciences, mathematics, and statistics. When we refer to "other STEM," we exclude engineering and computer science.

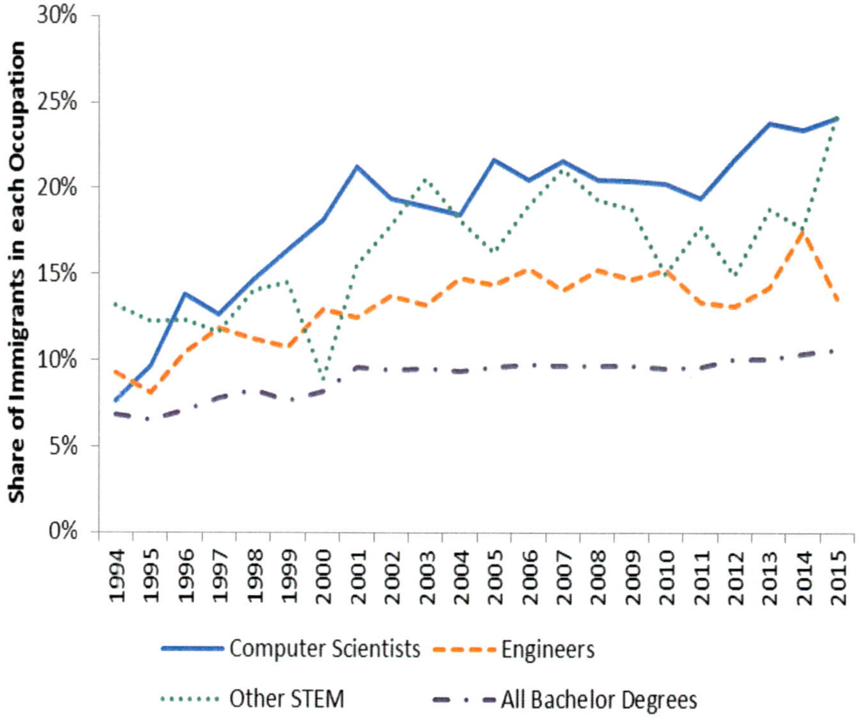

FIGURE C.4 Share of immigrants by occupation. SOURCE: Current Population Survey.

Degrees awarded in computer science respond to changes in wages but with a lag, which is understandable, considering students need time to adjust and change their college major choices. As shown in Figure C.5, panel b, bachelor's degrees in computer science as a share of total degrees had their biggest peaks during the early 1980s, after the hardware boom, and during the late 1990s, after the IT boom, and there is evidence of an increase since 2009 consistent with the relative wage recovery observed in Figure C.3.

Some simple calculations using earnings and degrees suggest that college degrees seem to be responding less to changes in earnings for young workers when compared to what they did during the IT boom of the 1990s. Between 1995 and 2000 median wages of computer scientists relative to all college graduates increased by 14.1 percent, while relative degree attainment in computer science in the same period increased by 44 percent. If instead we look at the period from 2008 to 2013, relative wages increased by 7.6 percent but relative degrees seem to have responded less than in the past, growing by just 12.5 percent during the period. It is hard to know how much to make of these differences. Such a lower

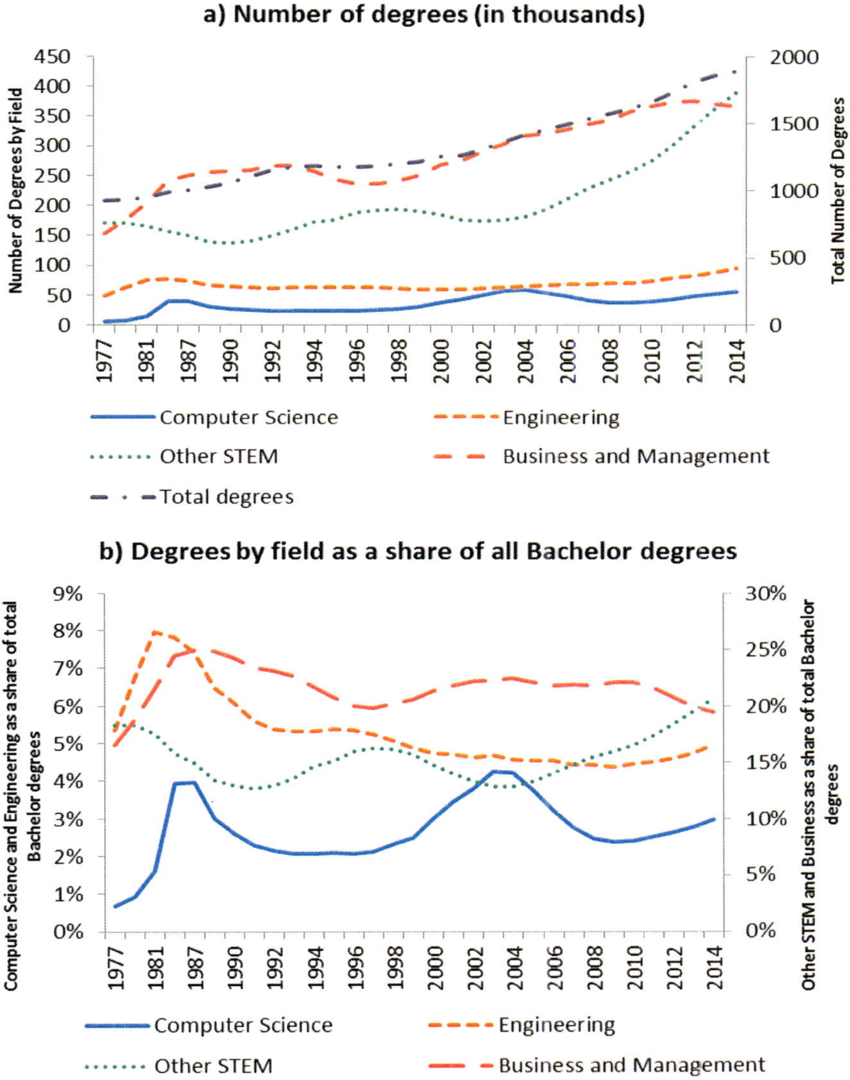

FIGURE C.5 Number of bachelor's degrees by field. SOURCE: Integrated Postsecondary Education Data System (IPEDS).

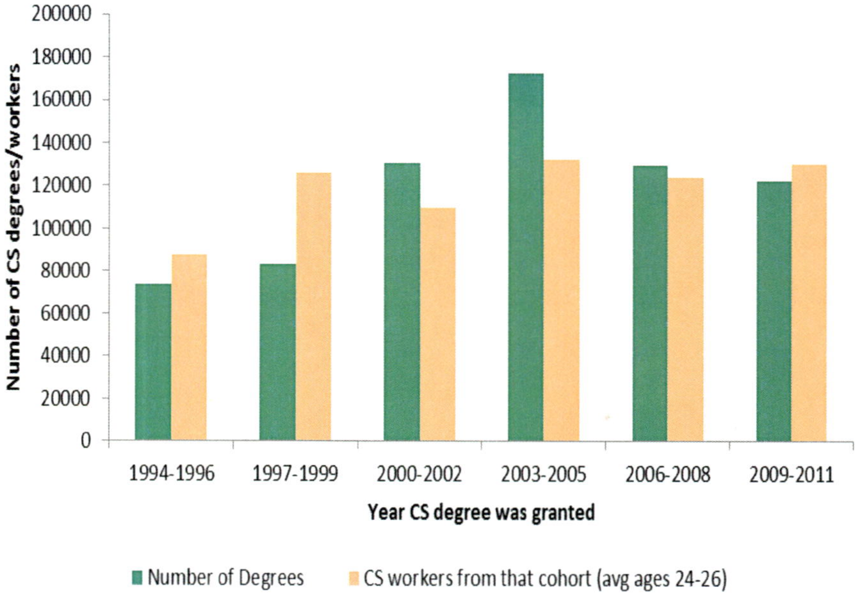

FIGURE C.6 Degrees in computer science versus workers in computer science by graduation year. SOURCE: Number of degrees from IPEDS and number of workers by cohort from the Current Population Survey. To calculate the number of workers from each cohort who work in computer science we assume students graduate at the age of 22 and count how many 24-year-olds are working as computer scientists 2 years later. We repeat the process for 25-year-olds 3 years later and 26-year-olds 4 years later and average across the three samples to get to the graduating cohort that ends up working as computer scientists in a given year.

response might be explained by different expectations of current students on how persistent the increase in earnings will be. If such a trend continues, we might see a larger response of degree attainment in computer science in subsequent years.

In Figure C.6 we compare the number of degrees that are produced in a given year with the employment in computer science for the cohort that graduated in that same year. During boom periods (e.g., 1994-1999 and 2009-2011), a larger number of college graduates end up working as computer scientists than those who obtained undergraduate degrees in computer science.[4] This trend was re-

[4] We emphasize that here we compare degrees awarded to the number of individuals working in the field. Even when these numbers line up, this does not imply that all of those with computer science degrees work as computer scientists or that all those working as computer scientists have undergraduate degrees in the field.

versed during the decade after the dot-com boom, with the number of individuals who obtained degrees exceeding the number who ended up working as computer scientists. This pattern reinforces the idea that enrollment and graduation decisions respond to a lag in changes in earnings, such that workers who are not computer scientists move into the field when demand is high and workers with computer science degrees move out of the field when demand is low. It is also a signal of recovery that between 2009 and 2011, we see higher employment levels in computer science than those graduating in the field, which is consistent with the recent increase in demand for computer scientists.

Figure C.6 also highlights the importance of distinguishing between two groups: those who work as computer scientists and those who get college degrees in computer science but do not necessarily work as computer scientists once they join the labor market. As shown in Table C.1, those who work as computer scientists majored in a variety of fields other than computer science and information degrees. Some of these are closely related fields such as engineering or mathematics, but a nontrivial fraction come from other backgrounds such as business management, economics, and finance.

When looking at those who get their degrees in computer science, these degree recipients are more concentrated in computer science occupations, although more than 40 percent of them go to work in diverse fields other than computer science.[5] Tables C.1 and C.2 use data from the period between 2009 and 2014, which was a period of high demand where people were being pulled into computer science from other occupations. It makes sense then that a majority of degree holders in computer science work as computer scientists, while the computer science occupation reflects inflow from a number of fields.

There is significant heterogeneity in earnings that depends on undergraduate degree field of study. Table C.3 shows estimates of a simple linear regression where we regressed the natural logarithm of annual earnings for those who work as computer scientists on indicators for the bachelor's degree field these workers obtained. The coefficients in Table C.3 can be interpreted as the average extra percent earnings that a worker in computer science with a given degree gets when compared to a computer scientist with a non-STEM degree. Among those who work as computer scientists, those who have a computer science degree earn 17 percent more than non-STEM degree holders. Those drawn into computer science who have engineering or other STEM degrees earn on average 19 and 12 percent higher respectively than those who have non-STEM degrees and work as computer scientists. Foreigners who immigrated after turning 22 and who, presumably, obtained their college degree outside the United States also earn a premium, though most of this premium can be explained by the fields in which

[5] We define those who earn a bachelor's degree (B.A.+B.S.) in computer science as those who state the following degree fields in the ACS: "Computer and Information Systems," "Computer Programming and Data Processing," "Computer Science," "Information Sciences," "Computer Information Management," and "Computer Networking and Telecommunications."

TABLE C.1 Main Bachelor's Degree for Those Working as Computer Scientists (2009-2014)

Main Bachelor's Degree	Age 23-29	Age 30-39	Foreign 23-39
Computer science	23.9%	22.2%	25.0%
Computer engineering	6.9%	5.0%	11.7%
Computer and information	6.7%	7.5%	5.9%
Electrical engineering	4.4%	4.5%	15.2%
Business management and administration	4.3%	5.6%	1.3%
Management information	3.1%	4.4%	0.5%
Economics	2.6%	1.8%	0.9%
Information sciences	2.4%	2.3%	0.7%
Finance	2.4%	1.7%	0.5%
General business	2.4%	2.9%	2.1%
Mathematics	2.3%	2.3%	3.0%
Other	38.5%	39.7%	33.3%
Number of observations	15,008	26,674	13,167

SOURCE: American Community Survey (ACS).

TABLE C.2 Occupation for Those Who Obtained a Computer Science Bachelor's Degree (2009-2014)

	Age 23-29	Age 30-39
Computer software developers	37.7%	30.7%
Computer systems analysts	22.5%	21.1%
Managers and administrators	5.3%	11.8%
Subject instructors (high school/college)	1.6%	1.0%
Management analysts	1.6%	2.0%
Repairers of data processing equipment	1.4%	0.9%
Supervisors and proprietors of sales jobs	1.2%	1.5%
Other	28.7%	31.1%
Number of observations	10,781	23,835

SOURCE: American Community Survey (ACS).

TABLE C.3 Degree Wage Premium for Those Working as Computer Scientists (2009-2014)

	Log (Annual Wage)	Log (Annual Wage)	Log (Annual Wage)	Log (Annual Wage)
Computer and information systems degree	0.001 [0.007]	0.0574[c] [0.0157]	–0.00156 [0.011]	–0.0139 [0.0101]
Computer programming and data processing degree	–0.015 [0.021]	0.0414 [0.0522]	–0.0491 [0.0413]	0.000708 [0.028]
Computer science degree	0.167[c] [0.004]	0.241[c] [0.01]	0.162[c] [0.00732]	0.149[c] [0.00583]
Information sciences degree	0.059 [c] [0.011]	0.0611[a] [0.0251]	0.0393[a] [0.0186]	0.0804[c] [0.0166]
Computer information management degree	–0.069[c] [0.016]	0.0266 [0.0311]	-0.0717[b] [0.0273]	-0.0935[c] [0.0268]
Computer networking and telecommunications degree	–0.049[a] [0.021]	0.0472 [0.0424]	-0.0371 [0.0324]	-0.0889[a] [0.0355]
Engineering degree	0.193[c] [0.005]	0.253[c] [0.0113	0.195[c] [0.0084	0.174[c] [0.00612
Other STEM degree	0.124[c] [0.005]	0.112[c] [0.0163]	0.102[c] [0.011]	0.128[c] [0.00672
Foreign CS worker	0.144[c] [0.00397]	0.221[c] [0.0114]	0.168[c] [0.00657]	0.104[c] [0.00553]
N	108,226	15,582	34,439	57,888
Adjusted R-squared	0.182	0.105	0.091	0.089
Sample	All CS workers	Age 23-29	Age 30-39	Age 40+

NOTE: Standard errors in brackets; [a] $p < 0.05$, [b] $p < 0.01$, [c] $p < 0.001$. The dependent variable is log annual wage, and we include covariates such as gender, indicators for Hispanic and black non-Hispanic, age group indicators (22-29, 30-39, 40+), indicators for highest degree attained (master's, professional degree, and Ph.D.), and year-fixed effects for 2010-2014. We also include a foreign worker indicator and set degree indicators to zero when the individual is foreign. Sample includes all workers in computer science between 2009 and 2014 who attained a bachelor's degree or higher, who are not self-employed, and who have been working full time for at least one year. The omitted degree category is non-STEM degrees. SOURCE: American Community Survey.

these individuals obtained their undergraduate degrees. The natural interpretation of the premium such individuals earn is that they are more productive either because of the skills they possess or because of the jobs they are in. While a computer science or information sciences degree does earn a premium with respect to non-STEM degrees, other degree holders such as computer information management earn somewhat less, on average, than non-STEM degree holders who work as computer scientists.

In columns 3 through 5 in Table C.3 we split the sample by age. The large earnings premium observed for those with degrees in engineering or computer science declines perceptibly but does not disappear.

We carry out a similar analysis by looking at the earnings of those who have degrees in computer science and look at the average returns of working in a given occupation compared to non-STEM occupations. Table C.4 shows that those with degrees in computer science who work as software developers or engineers earn substantial premiums over those working in other occupations. Excluding immigrants does not significantly change these results.

To conclude our analysis we look into the characteristics of those working in computer science as well as computer science bachelor's degree holders in Table C.5. Women are underrepresented when compared to all bachelor's degree holders, since only 25.1 percent of those working in CS and 25.7 percent of those who get degrees in computer science are women, compared to 49.6 percent among all bachelor's degrees in our sample. Despite this underrepresentation the share of women in computer science is higher than in engineering, where only 13.3 percent of their workers and 13.7 percent of their degree holders are women.

Blacks and Hispanics do not seem underrepresented in computer science when looking at degrees, since they are at or above the all bachelor's degrees

TABLE C.4 Occupation Wage Premium for Those Who Have a Computer Science-Related Degree (2009-2014)

	Log (Annual Wage)	Log (Annual Wage)
Computer systems analysts and computer scientists	0.022^{a} [0.006]	0.011 [0.006]
Computer software developers	0.181^{a} [0.005]	0.180^{a} [0.006]
Engineering occupation	0.159^{a} [0.012]	0.157^{a} [0.014]
Other STEM occupation	0.002 [0.018]	0.0212 [0.021]
N	65,681	54,443
Adjusted R-squared	0.172	0.176
Sample	All CS graduates	CS graduates excluding foreign workers

NOTE: Standard errors in brackets; ^{a} $p < 0.001$. The dependent variable is log annual wage, and we include covariates such as gender, indicators for Hispanic and black non-Hispanic, age group indicators (22-29, 30-39, 40-49, +50), indicators for highest degree attained (master's, professional degree, and Ph.D.), and year-fixed effects for 2010-2014. Sample includes all workers who attained a bachelor's degree in computer science, who are not self-employed, and who have been working full time for at least one year. The years of the sample are between 2009 and 2014. The omitted occupation category is non-STEM occupations. SOURCE: American Community Survey.

TABLE C.5 Diversity Measures by Occupation and Bachelor's Degree (2009-2014)

	Occupations			Bachelor's Degrees			All Bachelor's Degrees
	Computer Science	Engineering	Other STEM	Computer Science	Engineering	Other STEM	
% Female	25.1%	13.3%	40.8%	25.7%	13.7%	41.4%	49.6%
% Black, non-Hispanic	5.9%	4.0%	5.1%	9.2%	4.5%	5.9%	7.6%
% Hispanic	4.6%	5.6%	4.9%	6.9%	7.7%	5.5%	7.0%
Number of observations	132,144	84,312	49,677	83,330	241,519	265,571	2,788,574

NOTE: Sample includes employed workers who obtained a bachelor's degree from a 4-year institution or higher. SOURCE: American Community Survey, years 2009-2014.

average. They do seem to migrate out of the computer science occupation toward other jobs, since the percentage of blacks and Hispanics working as computer scientists is lower than the all bachelor's degrees average.

In this paper we look into the labor market for computer scientists and find that, since 2006, workers in this occupation experienced a recovery both in employment and earnings that keeps going until today, although at a slower pace than the increase in demand observed in the late 1990s due to the IT boom. When demand for computer scientists increases, supply can adjust through three different margins: a larger inflow of immigrants who work as computer scientists, a larger rate of enrollment in computer science undergraduate majors, and drawing workers that majored in other fields to work as computer scientists. We find evidence of an increase in all three sources of computer scientists at a lower rate than the one observed during the 1990s boom, consistent with the slower recovery of relative earnings.

REFERENCES

Arrow, Kenneth J., and William M. Capron. 1959. Dynamic shortages and price rises: The engineer-scientist case. *Quarterly Journal of Economics* 73(2): 292-308.

Bound, John, Breno Braga, Joseph M. Golden, and Sarah Turner. 2013. Pathways to adjustment: The case of information technology workers. *American Economic Review Papers and Proceedings* 103(3): 203-207.

Bound, John, Breno Braga, Joseph M. Golden, and Gaurav Khanna. 2015. Recruitment of foreigners in the market for computer scientists in the United States. *Journal of Labor Economics* 33(S1): S187-S223.

Freeman, Richard B. 1976. A cobweb model of the supply and starting salary of new engineers. *Industrial and Labor Relations Review* 29(2): 236-248.

Ryoo, Jaewoo, and Sherwin Rosen. 2004. The engineering labor market. *Journal of Political Economy* 112(1): SI 10-40.

Appendix D

White Paper: Does the Recent Increase in Computer Science Degrees Reflect Increased Demand?

Jennifer Hunt
Rutgers University and NBER[1]

October 6, 2016

ABSTRACT

Since 2009 there has been an increase in the number of computer and information science bachelor's degrees similar in speed and magnitude to the increase induced by the 1990s dot-com and Y2K-related demand. However, both speed and magnitude are more modest than earlier booms when measured as a share of bachelor's degrees awarded. Furthermore, there has been an equal increase in the share of engineering bachelor's degrees, suggesting that common forces may be affecting the two fields. Data on employment and wages suggest the increase in computer science and engineering bachelor's degrees is caused by the combination of a moderate shift out (increase) in labor demand and a moderate shift out (increase) in labor supply—that is, some of the increase in enrollment is responding to something other than wages. The shift out in demand may be caused by higher demand for quantitative skills, or new developments in the joint use of digital and mechanical technology, such as robotics. The shift out in supply may reflect a move toward recession-proof majors.

In this paper I assess possible reasons for the large increase since 2009 in bachelor's degrees conferred in computer science (CS). I begin by documenting the rise in degrees awarded in computer science and related fields. I then examine employment and wages in computer science as well as engineering and natural science to examine whether the increased choice of computer science as a major appears to be responding to increased demand. I close by speculating what forces

[1] Prepared for the National Academy of Sciences Committee on the Growth of Computer Science Undergraduate Enrollments. E-mail: jennifer.hunt@rutgers.edu.

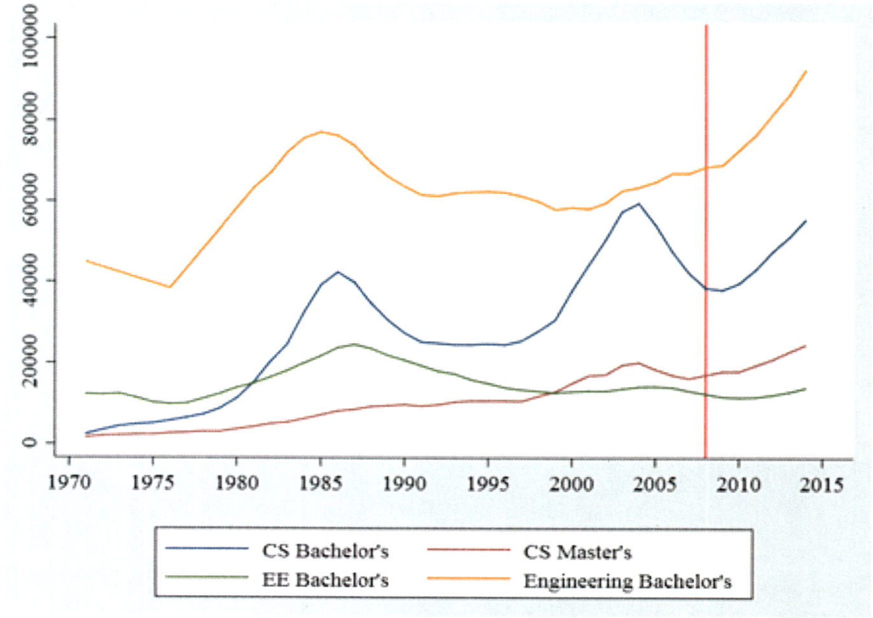

FIGURE D.1 Degrees awarded by field. CS denotes computer and information science; EE denotes electrical engineering. SOURCE: National Center for Education Statistics.

could be affecting demand for and supply of college-educated computer workers. I do not study increased enrollment in computer science by non-majors.

GROWTH IN COMPUTER SCIENCE DEGREES

In Figure D.1, the number of computer and information science (henceforth computer science) bachelor's degrees awarded (blue line) shows the well-known cyclical pattern of boom and bust around an upward trend. Degrees awarded have risen sharply since 2009.[2] Computer science masters's degrees (red line) have trended upward but are almost acyclical, unlike computer science bachelor's degrees, though they experienced a small echo of the early 2000s boom and bust; the trend pace of expansion has quickened since 2010. By comparison electrical engineering bachelor's degrees (green line) shared in the boom and bust of the 1980s, but did not share the cycle of the 2000s and do not exhibit an upward trend, nor any unusual increase since 2009. Bachelor's degrees in engineering as a whole (yellow line) differ from those in electrical engineering in experiencing strong growth in majors since 2000 and especially since 2009,

[2] Data are available only through academic year 2013-2014.

driven by growth in most subfields other than electrical engineering, particularly mechanical engineering.

It is well known that there has been a large increase both in the number of students on temporary visas and in the number of foreign-born workers on temporary visas in the information technology industry, but Figure D.2 shows that recent trends in CS and engineering degrees awarded are not driven by students on temporary visas.

The sizes of the computer science booms and busts look different if one views them as a share of all bachelor's degrees conferred. Figure D.3 shows that the pace at which computer science bachelor's degrees have been expanding recently is much slower than in the two previous booms. If the trend continued at the same pace in 2015 and 2016, the cumulative magnitude of the recent boom would be about half the size of the 1990s boom.

Figure D.3 also shows that it is only since 2009 that engineering bachelor's degrees have increased as a share of all bachelor's degrees. In fact, Figure D.4 shows that the share of engineering degrees has evolved identically to the share

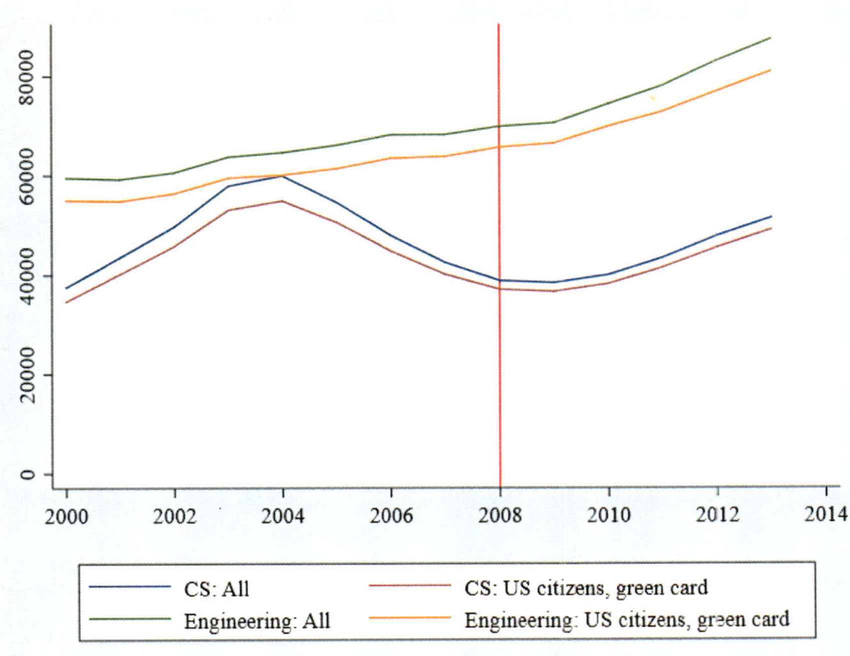

FIGURE D.2 Bachelor's degrees awarded by field and citizenship. CS denotes computer and information science; green card denotes lawful permanent residents. SOURCE: National Science Board—Science and Engineering Indicators 2016.

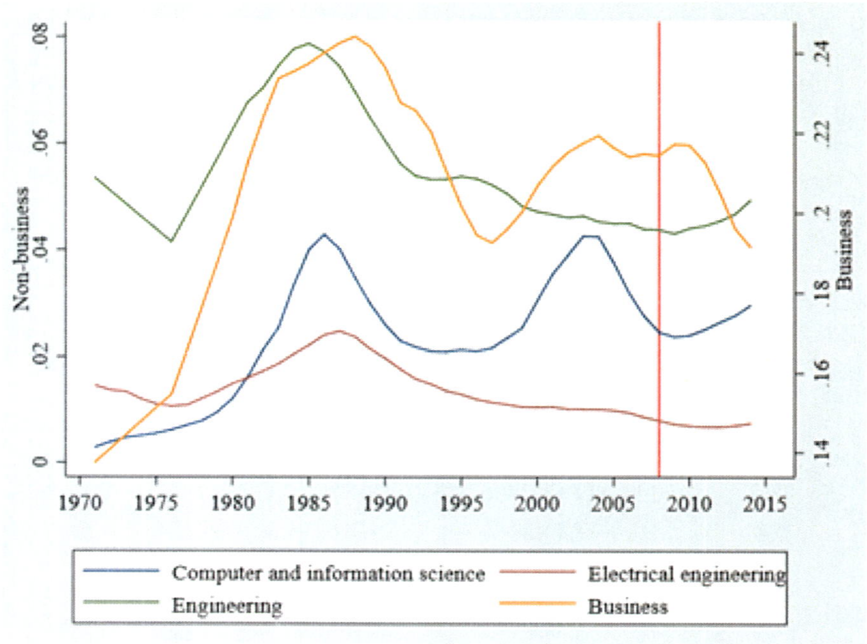

FIGURE D.3 Bachelor's degrees awarded by field as a share of all bachelor's degrees. Shares of computer and information science, electrical engineering, and engineering plotted using the left axis; shares of business plotted using the right axis. SOURCE: National Center for Education Statistics.

of computer science degrees since 2008. The two booms are therefore likely to have a common cause.

EXPLANATIONS FOR PAST BOOMS AND BUSTS IN COMPUTER SCIENCE DEGREES

The principle of boom and bust in degrees awarded in a particular field was established by Freeman (1975). He explained the theory that a sharp increase in labor demand for a type of college worker initially causes their wages to spike, since in the short run their numbers do not increase much. The wage spike causes enrollment in the field to rise, and with a 4-year lag, the new workers enter the market, depressing the wage. Because students do not realize that the initial spike in the wage is higher than the long-run equilibrium wage, too many students move into the field, and when they graduate, they depress the wage below the equilibrium wage. This then leads to a reduction in the number of students in the field, which raises the wage with a 4-year lag. With these cycles, the wage

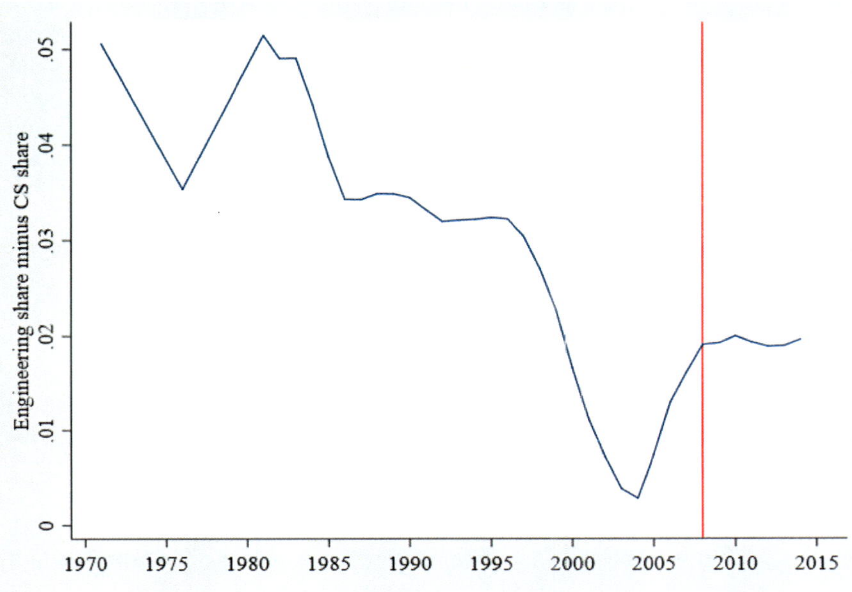

FIGURE D.4 Difference between shares of bachelor's degrees awarded in engineering and computer science. CS denotes computer and information science. SOURCE: NCES and author's calculations.

converges to the long-run equilibrium. Freeman showed that the market for physicists worked in this way in response to the founding of NASA and the associated sudden increase in demand for physicists in the 1960s.

Similarly, the late 1970s and early 1980s was a period with a sudden jump in the demand for computer scientists (and electrical engineers) following breakthroughs in semiconductors and microprocessors, while the 1990s was a period with a sudden jump in the demand for computer scientists and programmers (but not electrical engineers) due to the establishment of the World Wide Web and the need to reprogram computers ahead of the turn of the millennium (Y2K). Wages rose, students flocked to majors associated with the booming fields, the response turned out to be greater than that required, and wages and enrollments fell (see, for example, Bound et al., 2013).

ARE COMPUTER SCIENCE DEGREES RISING CURRENTLY BECAUSE DEMAND IS RISING?

The current boom in enrollment and degrees awarded in computer science has not yet received the same attention as the earlier cycles. There has not been any single technological breakthrough that is obviously on the scale of the breakthroughs that caused the two earlier booms, but it is conceivable that several smaller increases in demand, such as in response to the availability of Big Data, have combined to have a more gradual effect. I turn to labor market data from the Current Population Surveys 1979-2014 to assess whether demand for computer scientists appears to have jumped. These individual-level data do not include information on the field of the bachelor's (or any other) degree, but permit a long time series.

I begin by examining employment by occupation, to see whether the increased enrollment in computer science (and information technology) bachelor's programs, reported elsewhere, is reflected in increased employment in computer occupations. Panel A of Figure D.5 shows that the share of workers in computer occupations (blue line) has increased steadily, except for in the early 2000s, overtaking the share in engineering occupations (red line), and increasing fastest in the 1990s.[3] Panel B shows the 1990s acceleration is more marked in a sample of college graduates, and that the increase of the recent years contrasts more sharply with the plateau of the early 2000s.

In panel C, I limit the sample to college graduates 22 to 26 years of age, to see more clearly whether the recent increase in employment in panel B is linked to recent graduates. The graph confirms an increase in the share of workers in computer occupations since 2010. This graph also shows clearly earlier boom and bust cycles: employment in computer occupations rose sharply in the early 1980s, before falling for 10 years, then rose the fastest of any period in the second half of the 1990s, before falling rapidly for 5 years.

A 1980s boom and bust in employment in engineering occupations is also clearly visible, though occurring slightly earlier than the computer occupations cycle; there is no 1995-2005 cycle. In contrast to computer science, there is no increase in employment in engineering occupations corresponding to the post-2009 increase in engineering degrees. This apparent puzzle can be explained by the fact that engineering bachelor's degree holders (graduates) enter a wider variety of jobs than computer science graduates (see also Altonji et al., 2013; Hunt, 2015). American Community Survey data from 2014 show that 51 percent of employed computer science graduates age 22 to 26 worked in computer science occupations, compared to 36 percent of employed engineering graduates who worked in engineering occupations. These data also show that from 2009 to 2014, the share of engineering graduates working in engineering occupations declined 4.7 percentage points, offset by a rise in the share working as managers including engineering managers (up 1.6 percentage points), as professionals in business operations (up 0.8 percentage points—e.g., management analysts), and finance, insurance, and real estate (up 0.4 percentage points).[4]

---

[3] Mathematics occupations are included with computer occupations, as the combined group is easier to define consistently over time in the face of changes in occupational codes.

[4] Field of bachelor's degrees is available only in the American Community Survey from 2009.

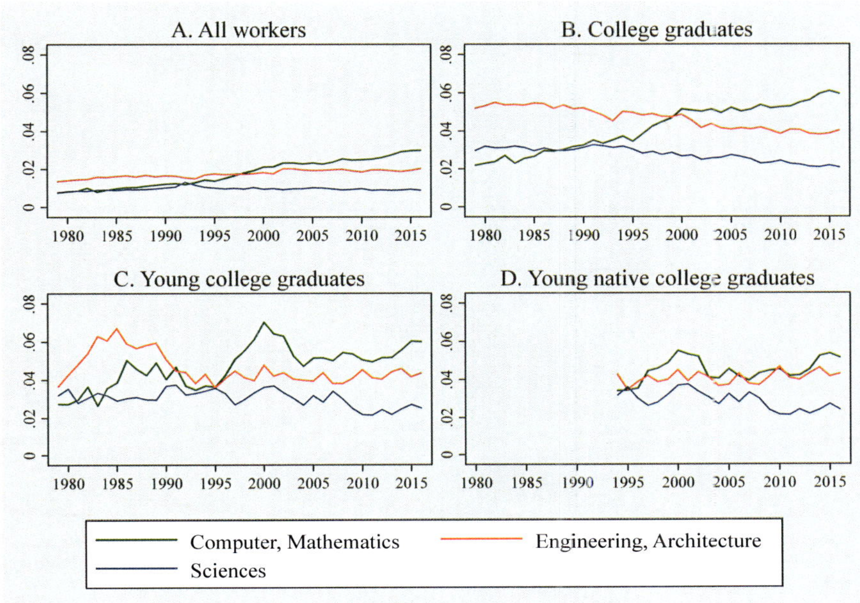

FIGURE D.5 Share of workers in computer and related occupations. All workers are age 18-64; young workers are age 22-26. Computer occupations include computer programming. SOURCE: Current Population Survey Merged Outgoing Rotation Groups, 1979-2015.

Panel D shows that the recent increase in employment in computer occupations and the 1995-2005 cycle are still visible when I limit the sample to workers born in the United States (data on birthplace are available only from 1994). A comparison of panels C and D shows, however, that foreign-born workers contributed more to the 1990s boom than to the current boom: while for all young college graduates in panel C the 1990s boom dwarfs the current boom, for the native-born in panel D the booms are similar in size, albeit smaller. The important role of an increased number of foreign-born workers in the 1990s boom is well known (e.g., Bound et al., 2015). The H-1B visa cap is now lower (at least for for-profit firms) than it was in that period, so this contrast alone does not rule out a similar jump in labor demand across the two periods.

In Figure D.6, I display real median wages (in 2014 dollars) for the same samples as in Figure D.5. In none of the panels are computer occupation wages (blue line) trending up in recent years, though young workers' wages fell during the Great Recession and have since recovered. Wages in computer occupations caught up with those of engineering occupations between 1979 and 2000, with spurts corresponding to the employment booms (panel A), and have been on a

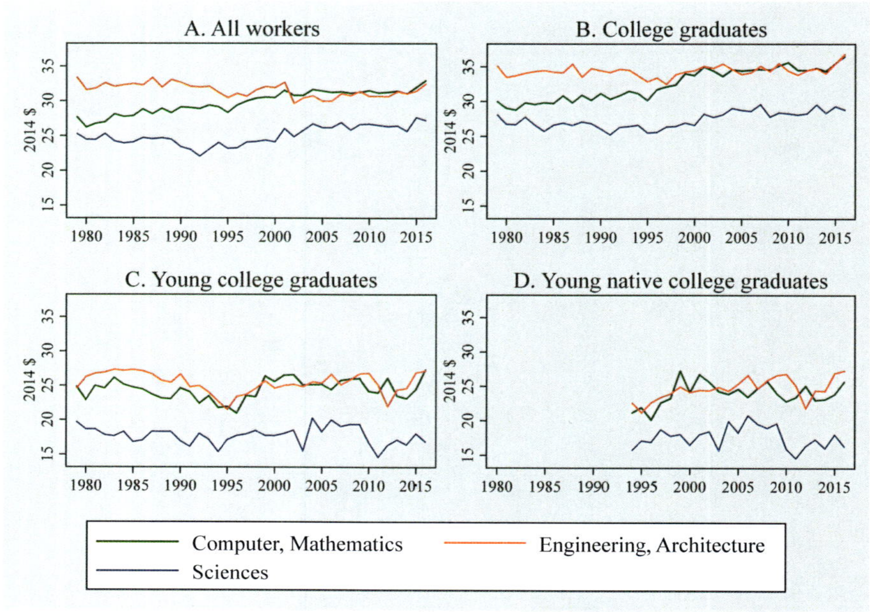

FIGURE D.6 Median hourly wages of workers in computer and related occupations. All workers are age 18-64; young workers are age 22-26. Computer occupations include computer programming. SOURCE: Current Population Survey Merged Outgoing Rotation Groups, 1979-2015.

plateau since then. The pattern is similar for college graduates in panel B. Similarly to employment patterns, wage patterns are more cyclical for young college graduates in computer occupations than for all college graduates (panel C). After wage increases in 1980-1985, the period of the employment increase, wages decline sharply for 3 years in the employment bust period. Wages rise to a new peak in 1996-2000, plateau, then decline equally sharply to a plateau that has lasted to the present. Patterns for the native-born in panel D are similar.

The wages of engineering occupations (red line) do not show any increase in the period of the employment expansion in the 1980s in any of the panels (possibly the wage increased before 1979 when the data begin) but do show a decline as employment in those occupations declined. The fact that engineering occupation wages grew in the late 1990s despite an obvious cause or an increase in employment suggests that some of the (greater) wage gain in computer occupations may reflect the generally booming economy and rising wages in the late 1990s.[5]

[5] Patterns are similar to Figure D.6 if we use weekly wages, or the 75th percentile of hourly wages.

Looking at patterns of employment and wages is not enough to determine whether supply or demand or both are shifting, but nevertheless, the contrast between the current increase in computer science degrees and employment with no change in wages and earlier booms, which were accompanied or preceded by rise in wages, is very suggestive, ruling out a recent sudden increase in demand for computer science graduates as the sole explanation. The most likely explanation is that demand has indeed shifted somewhat, but that a concurrent shift in supply has kept wages constant even several years after the demand increase, dampening the Freeman-style cycle that the shift in demand would normally have stimulated. In other words, the increase in enrollment, degrees, and employment is in part spurred by something other than wages. A similar conclusion can be reached about supply and demand for engineering graduates.

WHAT COULD HAVE CAUSED THE DEMAND FOR COMPUTER SCIENCE MAJORS TO SHIFT OUT?

There is a common view that there is currently unprecedented progress in computer science that is likely to have increased demand for computer science majors. This view must be reconciled with the similar patterns in number of majors and wages for engineering majors. While it is possible that the two groups are subject to different supply and demand forces that happen to be the same size, a simpler explanation is that the two groups are subject to the same forces. A possible common force on the demand side would be an increase in demand for college graduates with quantitative skills. Another would be technological breakthroughs in the joint use of digital and mechanical technology, such as robotics: the rise of mechatronics as a vocational degree is consistent with this. The fact that the increased number of engineering graduates is not translating into increased employment in engineering or computer occupations seems supportive of the first theory.

WHAT COULD HAVE CAUSED THE SUPPLY OF COMPUTER SCIENCE MAJORS TO SHIFT OUT?

One possible explanation for the increased attraction of computer science and engineering degrees could be the Great Recession: students shifted to majors that weather recessions better. Altonji et al. (2013) show that prior to the Great Recession (though less so during the Great Recession), science, technology, engineering, and mathematics majors graduating in a recession suffered less deterioration of their employment and wage outcomes than other majors. The timing of the increased computer science and engineering degrees is fairly consistent with this (see Figure D.3, where the red vertical line indicates 2008). The shift in preferences over majors cannot have been simply toward practical majors, as Figure D.3 shows a large fall in bachelor's degrees in business since the recession (note the use of the right-hand scale).[6] Another possibility is that computer science jobs or careers have become more attractive because the nature of the tasks performed in the jobs or the objects of inquiry have become more interesting, or because they have become interesting to a wider group, such as women. The percent increase in computer science degrees awarded to women since 2009 has been the same as for men, and women receive a small minority of computer science degrees (22 percent in 2014). Increased appeal to women therefore does not seem to be an explanation.

CONCLUSION

Since 2009 there has been an increase in the number of computer and information science bachelor's degrees similar in speed and magnitude to the increase induced by the 1990s dot-com and Y2K-related demand. However, both speed and magnitude are more modest than earlier booms when measured as a share of bachelor's degrees awarded. Furthermore, there has been an equal increase in the share of engineering bachelor's degrees, suggesting that common forces may be affecting the two fields. Data on employment and wages suggest the increase in computer science and engineering bachelor's degrees is caused by the combination of a moderate shift out (increase) in labor demand and a moderate shift out (increase) in labor supply—that is, some of the increase in enrollment is responding to something other than wages. The shift out in demand may be caused by higher demand for quantitative skills, or new developments in the joint use of digital and mechanical technology, such as robotics. The shift out in supply may reflect a move toward recession-proof majors.

REFERENCES

Altonji, Joseph G., Lisa B. Kahn, and Jamin D. Speer. 2013. Cashier or Consultant? Entry Labor Market Conditions, Field of Study, and Career Success. Yale University working paper.

Bound, John, Breno Braga, Joseph M. Golden, and Sarah Turner. 2013. Pathways to adjustment: The case of information technology workers. *American Economic Review* 103(3): 203-207.

Bound, John, Breno Braga, Joseph M. Golden, and Gaurav Khanna. 2015. Recruitment of foreigners in the market for computer scientists in the United States. *Journal of Labor Economics* 33(3): S187-S223.

Freeman, Richard B. 1975. Supply and salary adjustments to the changing science manpower market: Physics, 1948-1973. *American Economic Review* 65(1): 27-39.

Hunt, Jennifer. 2015. Are immigrants the most skilled US computer and engineering workers? *Journal of Labor Economics* 33(3): S39-S77.

[6] The juxtaposition of these lines begs the question of whether some degrees previously called business degrees might have been renamed as information science degrees.

Appendix E

Summary of Data from the Consortium for Undergraduate STEM Success

Allan Moser and Lynne Molter
Department of Engineering
Swarthmore College

October 3, 2016

The data used in this analysis come from the Consortium for Undergraduate STEM Success (CUSTEMS). As described on the CUSTEMS website (custems.org),

> The Consortium for Undergraduate STEM Success (CUSTEMS) is a collaboration of post secondary institutions interested in addressing issues relating to undergraduate degree completion in STEM (Science, Technology, Engineering, and Mathematics) fields, with particular focus on under-represented students. CUSTEMS combines student academic data from participating institutions with survey responses from those same students to inform institutions about patterns of student migration into and out of STEM fields.

Twenty-four institutions participated in this consortium: 16 HBCUs, 5 private liberal arts colleges, and 3 public research universities. Participants in the consortium provided Admissions, Academic, and Grade files containing information for their students covering a time span from 2008 to 2014. The coverage of data from institutions varied, with some providing information across all years and all types of records, and other providing only partial data for one or two years.

Admissions records include demographic information such as sex, race, home zip codes, guardian education level, SAT or ACT scores, and anticipated major for the entering student. Academic records were submitted for each student at the end of the academic year. Ideally, there should be one academic record for each year of an individual student's attendance. These records include the academic year, class (e.g., freshman, sophomore), PELL eligibility, GPA, and anticipated (or declared) major indicated by Classification of Instructional

Program (CIP) codes. Records for grades were also submitted at the end of each academic year. For each student, there is a record for each course the student took that year including the course abbreviation (e.g., CS, Phys), course number, course level, course credits, and course grade. Importantly, each type of record includes the institution Integrated Postsecondary Education Data System (IPEDS) code and student ID, enabling linkage of the records for individual students.

Data for this study were obtained from the last CUSTEMS release in May 2016. They contain 95,518 admissions, 115,303 academic, and 293,800 grade records. Record types were linked by forming a unique identifier for each student consisting of the concatenated institution IPEDS code and student ID. Not all records could be linked, since some institutions provided only partial data. In addition some records could not be used because necessary data elements, such as anticipated major, were missing. Linkage between valid admissions and academic records provided 54,981 unique student cases. Requiring linked grade records reduced this number to 19,788 cases.

DISCUSSION OF STUDENTS ENROLLED IN COMPUTER SCIENCE CLASSES

The Grade file contains information for each course taken by a student. Out of the 24 institutions participating in CUSTEMS, 16 contributed to the Grade File. Course abbreviations and numbers may be the same for different institutions, so individual courses were identified by combining the institution IPEDS code with the course abbreviation and course number. Doing so, we found 4,079 unique courses.

Identifying which of these courses are computer science (CS) was not straightforward. Courses with abbreviations such as CompSci or CS could be safely assumed to be computer science related. Courses with names such as "EEGR 409" (C Programming Apps) and "GEEN 101" (Software Design and Modeling) were not obvious from the abbreviation, however. Considerable effort, including searching school websites and course catalogues, was required to identify which of the 4,079 courses were, indeed, associated with computer science. Even with carefully reading course descriptions, it was not always clear, since there is considerable overlap between some science and engineering courses and computer science courses. For example, courses from the same school with the same abbreviation, "ECE," had titles that were clearly computer science related, such as "Data Mining and Machine Learning" (ECE 321), and courses that were not, such as "Electrical Circuits" (ECE 225). Additionally, it is possible that the same course may be cross-listed at a given school under a different course abbreviation and number. In many cases a judgment call was required. There will be valid differences in opinion about whether a given course should or not be listed in the computer science category.

A total of 387 unique courses associated with a student record in both the Admissions and Academic files were identified as computer science related. We categorized the computer science courses as being (1) introductory, (2) intermediate, or (3) advanced. Although the course level should have been provided in the Grade file record, this entry was often omitted. Where possible, school course numbering systems were used to estimate course level (e.g., 100 for introductory, 200 for intermediate, 300/400 for advanced), though numbering systems were not always this straightforward. In some cases best guesses were made based on course titles, or by looking up the courses online. One task that we were not able to accomplish was determining specific individual successor courses, since this again would require an understanding of individual school's degree requirements.

SUMMARY OF ANALYSIS

The analysis using Grade files for individual students provided the data for all students, of any major, taking computer science classes. This provides fine-grained detail for each computer science course. While there is much detail in the individual course statistics, the clearest trends emerge from aggregating course information by level (introductory, intermediate, or advanced). The aggregated data show a disparity between the percentage of men and women taking computer science courses, even at the introductory level, with 63 percent of the enrollment male and 37 percent female. This disparity increases significantly moving from introductory to intermediate levels: 76 percent male, 24 percent female. The asymmetry continues to slightly increase for advanced courses: 77 percent male, 23 percent female. A similar disparity exists for racial categories. Enrollment in introductory courses is comprised of 71 percent non-underrepresented-minority (non-URM) and 29 percent URM students. As in the case of gender this disparity grows for intermediate-level courses: 88 percent non-URM, 12 percent URM. There is a slight decrease in the disparity moving from intermediate to advanced courses, but it is probably not statistically significant.

The migration analysis presents the data in terms of major field of study. This analysis shows a net increase in computer science majors from entering major to last reported major. Again, there is a disparity between the percentage of male and female computer science majors: 5.5 percent of male students enter a major in computer, while the percentage for women is 1.4 percent. The percentage increase due to migration into the field is substantially higher for women (~30 percent) than men (~10 percent); however, this change does not bring the post-migration ratio to parity, with 6.0 percent of males and 1.8 percent of females reporting CS as a major. The percentages of men and women in computer science both increase, but with the larger number of incoming men, a small percentage increase still results in a larger overall gain in numbers: an increase of 161 men and 124 women. Comparing URM to non-URM, 4.5 percent of URM students enter as computer science majors, while a smaller percentage, 2.9 percent, of non-URM students start with this major. There is a net in-migration into the field for each category; however, the percent increase in non-URM is substantially higher, with a growth of 6 percent, compared to only 2 percent for URM.

There are several avenues for additional research using these data. Results for this analysis were primarily descriptive. More sophisticated statistical methods could be employed to better determine the significance of differences. Additionally, different and perhaps finer (when the numbers permit) categorizations could be made, such as female URM, male URM, female non-URM, and male non-URM. We could also use additional attributes in the data set. For example, we considered only SAT scores, which left a large percentage of cases classified as unknown. ACT scores are available for many students. We could bring the SAT and ACT scores into concordance, significantly reducing the unknowns for this category. In addition to the admissions, grade, and academic files, there is also an entering student survey (ESS) file that we did not use. The ESS provides additional information on student preparation and attitudes.

Appendix F

List of WebCASPAR/IPEDS Database Query Parameters Used to Obtain Data in Report Plots

Many of the plots in this report were generated by staff of the National Academies of Sciences, Engineering, and Medicine using publicly available data from the National Center for Education Statistics (NCES) Integrated Postsecondary Education Data System (IPEDS) to examine historical degree completions trends. These data were accessed via the online Web-based Computer-Assisted Science Policy Analysis and Research (WebCASPAR) System, managed by the National Science Foundation (NSF), https://ncsesdata.nsf.gov/webcaspar/. Minimal computation was applied (for example, adding, multiplying, or dividing one data set by another) to retrieved data prior to plotting. In general, lines connecting the data points were plotted without symbols representing each point to make the plots easier to read. This appendix describes details of what data were used in each of these plots—including Data Source, Survey, and Classifications Variables—for the interested reader who might want to reproduce these data sets. The descriptions are organized by figure number in the following.

FIGURE 2.1

Caption:
Historical year-to-year U.S. production of bachelor's degrees in computer and information science and support services (CIS, black line), core CS (dark gray line), and computer engineering (CE, light gray line), in absolute number (top row) and as a percentage (bottom row) of all bachelor's degrees at all institutions (left column) and at not-for-profit institutions (right column). The total number of bachelor's degrees produced in the United States each year in all fields is included in the top row for all institutions (left panel) and for not-for-profit institutions

(right panel) as a dashed line for reference, with the vertical scale indicated on the right-hand axis.

IPEDS Data:

Number of Degrees, All Institutions

CIS degree completions by year

Data Source: IPEDS Completions Survey
IPEDS Completions Survey: Degrees/Awards Conferred (NCES Population of Institutions)
Year: All values
Academic Discipline, Detailed (standardized): Computer Science
Level of Degree or Other Award: Bachelor's Degrees

Core CS degree completions by year

Data Source: IPEDS Completions Survey
IPEDS Completions Survey: Degrees/Awards Conferred (NCES Population of Institutions)
Year: All values
Academic Discipline, 6-Digit CIP: 11.0101, "Computer and Information Sciences, General"; 11.0701, "Computer Science"
Level of Degree or Other Award: Bachelor's Degrees

CE degree completions by year

Data Source: IPEDS Completions Survey
IPEDS Completions Survey: Degrees/Awards Conferred (NCES Population of Institutions)
Year: All values
Academic Discipline, 4-Digit CIP: 14.09 (Computer Engineering)
Level of Degree or Other Award: Bachelor's Degrees

Total degree completions by year

Data Source: IPEDS Completions Survey
IPEDS Completions Survey: Degrees/Awards Conferred (NCES Population of Institutions)
Year: All values
Level of Degree or Other Award: Bachelor's Degrees

Number of Degrees, Not-for-Profit Institutions
Plot includes data for only 1987 on, as for-profits were not directly identified prior to 1987.

CIS degree completions by year

Data Source: IPEDS Completions Survey
IPEDS Completions Survey: Degrees/Awards Conferred (NCES Population of Institutions)
Year: All values
Academic Discipline, Detailed (standardized): Computer Science
Level of Degree or Other Award: Bachelor's Degrees
Institutional Control (survey-specific): Public Institutions, Private Institutions: Nonprofit

Core CS degree completions by year

Data Source: IPEDS Completions Survey
IPEDS Completions Survey: Degrees/Awards Conferred (NCES Population of Institutions)
Year: All values
Academic Discipline, 6-Digit CIP: 11.0101, "Computer and Information Sciences, General"; 11.0701, "Computer Science"
Level of Degree or Other Award: Bachelor's Degrees
Institutional Control (survey-specific): Public Institutions, Private Institutions: Nonprofit

CE degree completions by year

Data Source: IPEDS Completions Survey
IPEDS Completions Survey: Degrees/ Awards Conferred (NCES Population of Institutions)
Year: All values
Academic Discipline, 4-Digit CIP: 14.09 (Computer Engineering)
Level of Degree or Other Award: Bachelor's Degrees
Institutional Control (survey-specific): Public Institutions, Private Institutions: Nonprofit

Total degree completions by year

Data Source: IPEDS Completions Survey
IPEDS Completions Survey: Degrees/ Awards Conferred (NCES Population of Institutions)
Year: All values
Level of Degree or Other Award: Bachelor's Degrees
Institutional Control (survey-specific): Public Institutions, Private Institutions: Nonprofit
Share: Percentages determined by dividing CS and CE bachelor's degree completions by year (described earlier), respectively, each by the total number of bachelor's degrees produced in each year (left-hand plot) and the total number of degrees produced at not-for-profit institutions (right-hand plot) in the corresponding year.

FIGURE 2.2

Caption:
Number and share of U.S. degrees in CIS awarded to students designated as temporary residents of the United States (foreign students).

IPEDS Data:

Number of CIS Degrees Awarded to Temporary Residents over Time
Data Source: IPEDS Completions Survey by Race
IPEDS Completions Survey by Race: Degrees/Awards Conferred by Race (NCES Population of Institutions)
Year: All values
Academic Discipline, Detailed (standardized): Computer Science
Race & Ethnicity (survey-specific): Temporary Resident
Level of Degree or Other Award: Bachelor's Degrees, Master's Degrees, Doctorate Degrees (including Doctorate Degrees, Doctorate Degree-Research/Scholarship, Doctorate Degree-Professional Practice, Doctorate Degree-Other)

Plot includes data for only 1977 on. Data for all category of "Doctorate" degree in a given year was added together to yield the total.

Percentage of CIS Degrees Awarded to Temporary Residents over Time
Absolute numbers of each level of CS degree completed by temporary residents produced in a given year were divided by the total number of the corresponding type of CS degree produced in the corresponding year to yield

the data plotted. Total numbers of each level of CS degree were obtained via the following query:

Data Source: IPEDS Completions Survey by Race
IPEDS Completions Survey by Race: Degrees/ Awards Conferred by Race(NCES Population of Institutions)
Year: All values
Academic Discipline, Detailed (standardized): Computer Science
Level of Degree or Other Award: Bachelor's Degrees, Master's Degrees, Doctorate Degrees (including Doctorate Degrees, Doctorate Degree-Research/Scholarship, Doctorate Degree-Professional Practice, Doctorate Degree-Other)

FIGURE 2.3

Caption:
Bachelor's degree production from 1987 to 2015 in CIS and CE at public, private, and for-profit institutions reporting to IPEDS.

IPEDS Data:

CIS Degree completions by year and for-profit status

Data Source: IPEDS Completions Survey
IPEDS Completions Survey: Degrees/Awards Conferred (NCES Population of Institutions)
Year: All values
Academic Discipline, Detailed (standardized): Computer Science
Level of Degree or Other Award: Bachelor's Degrees
Institutional Control (survey-specific): Public Institutions, Private Institutions: Nonprofit, Private Institutions: For-Profit

Computer Engineering Degree completions by year and for-profit status

Data Source: IPEDS Completions Survey
Year: All values
Academic Discipline, 4-Digit CIP: 14.09 (Computer Engineering)
Level of Degree or Other Award: Bachelor's Degrees
Institutional Control (standardized): Public Institutions, Private Institutions: Nonprofit, Private Institutions: For-Profit

FIGURE 2.4

Caption:
Total annual bachelor's degree production over time for public, private, and for-profit institutions (all academic fields). Private not-for-profit and private for-profit institutions were not distinguished prior to 1987.

IPEDS Data:

Bachelor's degree completions by year and institution type

Data Source: IPEDS Completions Survey
IPEDS Completions Survey: Degrees/Awards Conferred (NCES Population of Institutions)
Year: All values
Level of Degree or Other Award: Bachelor's Degrees
Institutional Control (survey-specific): Public Institutions, Private Institutions: Nonprofit, Private Institutions: For-Profit

Prior to 1987, IPEDS did not distinguish between private for-profit and private not-for-profit institutions; the total number of degrees completed at all private institutions is plotted as a dashed line prior to 1987. Degrees awarded at institutions without a designated Institutional Control (of which there are relatively few) are not plotted.

FIGURE 2.5

Caption:
CIS bachelor's degree production by category of institution. Categories include only not-for-profit institutions, unless otherwise indicated.

IPEDS Data:

Bachelor's degree completions by year and institution type

Data Source: IPEDS Completions Survey
IPEDS Completions Survey: Degrees/Awards Conferred (NCES Population of Institutions)
Year: All values
Academic Discipline, Detailed (standardized): Computer Science
Level of Degree or Other Award: Bachelor's Degrees
Carnegie Classification 2010, Basic (survey-specific): Research Universities-Very High Research Activity, Research Universities-High Re-

search Activity, Doctoral/Research Universities, Master's Colleges and Universities, Baccalaureate Colleges, Associate's Colleges
Institutional Control (survey-specific): Public Institutions, Private Institutions: Nonprofit, Private Institutions: For-Profit

Data retrieved were added together to create the categories plotted as indicated in the text.

FIGURE 2.6

Caption:
Historical CIS bachelor's degree production at not-for-profit doctoral (Ph.D.-granting) institutions, including very-high-research-activity institutions, high-research-activity institutions, and other doctoral institutions, 1987-2017.

IPEDS Data:

CIS bachelor's degree completions by year and institution type

Data Source: IPEDS Completions Survey
IPEDS Completions Survey: Degrees/Awards Conferred (NCES Population of Institutions)
Year: All values
Academic Discipline, Detailed (standardized): Computer Science
Level of Degree or Other Award: Bachelor's Degrees
Carnegie Classification 2010, Basic (survey-specific): Research Universities-Very High Research Activity, Research Universities-High Research Activity, Doctoral/Research Universities
Institutional Control (survey-specific): Public Institutions, Private Institutions: Nonprofit

Data series for public institutions and private non-profit institutions were combined to provide total number of degrees produced in each category at known nonprofit institutions. Institutions for which for-profit status was unknown were not included.

FIGURE 2.7

Caption:
Historical annual degree production in CIS by level of degree. All institutions are illustrated in the left-hand panel, and not-for-profits only in the right-hand panel. Data are for all institutions that reported to IPEDS.

IPEDS Data:

Data Source: IPEDS Completions Survey
IPEDS Completions Survey: Degrees/Awards Conferred (NCES population of Institutions)
Year: All values
Academic Discipline, Detailed (standardized): Computer Science
Level of Degree or Other Award: All
Institutional Control (survey-specific): All

Data series for public institutions and private non-profit institutions were combined to provide total number of degrees produced in each category at known non-profit institutions. Institutions for which for-profit status was unknown were not included. Data for all types of doctorate degree and for all types or certificate, respectively, were combined.

FIGURE 3.2

Caption:
Share of undergraduates participating in CS bachelor's degree programs at the beginning and end of the undergraduate career. The dotted line indicates the fraction of freshmen at U.S. not-for-profit institutions intending to major in CS from 1971 to 2015, according to the HERI CIRP survey results. The fraction of bachelor's degree recipients from 1966 to 2015 whose degrees were in CIS and core CS, according to the IPEDS NCES completions data, is included for all institutions prior to 1987 (dashed line), and not-for-profit institutions from 1987 to 2015 (solid line).

IPEDS Data:

CS bachelor's degree completions at not-for profit institutions were divided by the total number of bachelor's degree completions at nonprofit institutions for each year.

CIS bachelor's degree completions

Data Source: IPEDS Completions Survey
IPEDS Completions Survey: Degrees/Awards Conferred (NCES Population of Institutions)
Year: All values
Academic Discipline, Detailed (standardized): Computer Science
Level of Degree or Other Award: Bachelor's Degrees
Institutional Control: Public Institutions, Private Institutions: Nonprofit

Core CS bachelor's degree completions

Data Source: IPEDS Completions Survey
IPEDS Completions Survey: Degrees/Awards Conferred (NCES Population of Institutions)
Year: All values
Academic Discipline, 6-Digit CIP: 11.0101, "Computer and Information Sciences, General"; 11.0701, "Computer Science"
Level of Degree or Other Award: Bachelor's Degrees
Institutional Control: Public Institutions, Private Institutions: Nonprofit

Total degree completions by year

Data Source: IPEDS Completions Survey
IPEDS Completions Survey: Degrees/Awards Conferred (NCES Population of Institutions)
Year: All values
Level of Degree or Other Award: Bachelor's Degrees
Institutional Control: Public Institutions, Private Institutions: Nonprofit

FIGURE 3.13

Caption:
U.S. degree production for 2015 in several STEM fields, defined using the "detailed" CIPs from IPEDS (here, "Computer Science" corresponds to the entire 11 series of CIPs). The left-hand panel displays total number of degrees for each field, broken down by level of degree. The right-hand panel displays the percentage of the total accounted for by each level of degree for each field. Includes degrees and certificates awarded at all institutions; excluding the for-profits does not have a major impact on the distribution of degree types for a given field.

IPEDS Data:

Total numbers of each degree type in each discipline were divided by the total number of bachelor's degrees in a given year in that discipline to yield their corresponding share of the total for the discipline.

Degree completions by year and field

Data Source: IPEDS Completions Survey
IPEDS Completions Survey: Degrees/Awards Conferred (NCES Population of Institutions)
Year: 2015

Academic Discipline, Detailed (standardized): Electrical Engineering, Physics, Mathematics and Statistics, Computer Science, Biological Sciences, Psychology, Economics
Level of Degree or Other Award: All

CE degree completions by year

Data Source: IPEDS Completions Survey
IPEDS Completions Survey: Degrees/Awards Conferred (NCES Population of Institutions)
Year: 2015
Academic Discipline, 4-Digit CIP: 14.09 (Computer Engineering)
Level of Degree or Other Award: All

Total degree completions by year

Data Source: IPEDS Completions Survey
IPEDS Completions Survey: Degrees/Awards Conferred (NCES Population of Institutions)
Year: 2015
Level of Degree or Other Award: All

FIGURE 3.15

Caption:
Ph.D. production in CS and related fields; for-profit Ph.D.s have been excluded. Top panel shows the number of Ph.D.s conferred in a given year in CIS (CIP 11.x series, solid black line), core CS (CIPs 11.0101 and 11.0701, short-dashed black line), and IS (CIP 11.0401, long-dashed black line). Bottom panel illustrates the share of these degrees going to temporary U.S. residents (international students).

IPEDS Data:

CIS degree completions by year

Data Source: IPEDS Completions Survey
IPEDS Completions Survey: Degrees/Awards Conferred (NCES Population of Institutions)
Year: All values
Academic Discipline, Detailed (standardized): Computer Science
Level of Degree or Other Award: Doctorate Degrees
Institutional Control: Public Institutions, Private Institutions: Nonprofit

Core CS degree completions by year

> **Data Source:** IPEDS Completions Survey
> **IPEDS Completions Survey:** Degrees/Awards Conferred (NCES Population of Institutions)
> **Year:** All values
> **Academic Discipline, 6-Digit CIP:** 11.0101, "Computer and Information Sciences, General"; 11.0701, "Computer Science"
> **Level of Degree or Other Award:** Doctorate Degrees
> **Institutional Control:** Public Institutions, Private Institutions: Nonprofit

IS degree completions by year

> **Data Source:** IPEDS Completions Survey
> **IPEDS Completions Survey:** Degrees/Awards Conferred (NCES Population of Institutions)
> **Year:** All values
> **Academic Discipline, 6-Digit CIP:** 11.0401, "Information Science/Studies"
> **Level of Degree or Other Award:** Doctorate Degrees
> **Institutional Control:** Public Institutions, Private Institutions: Nonprofit

FIGURE 4.1

Caption:
The number of computer workers (defined as "Computer Systems Analysts," "Computer Scientists," and "Computer Software Developers") holding bachelor's degrees (in any field) over time compared to the cumulative number of CIS bachelor's degrees awarded over time (1994-2015), in millions.

IPEDS Data:

> **Data Source:** IPEDS Completions Survey
> **IPEDS Completions Survey:** Degrees/Awards Conferred (NCES Population of Institutions)
> **Year:** All values
> **Academic Discipline, Detailed (standardized):** Computer Science
> **Level of Degree or Other Award:** Bachelor's Degrees

The number of CIS bachelor's degrees were added cumulatively over time to obtain the plotted data.

FIGURE 4.2

Caption:
Share of computer workers who hold bachelor's degrees (in any field) between 23 and 29 years of age (solid line), and share of all bachelor's degrees awarded in CIS (dashed line) each year from 1994 to 2015.

IPEDS Data:

CIS degree completions by year

Data Source: IPEDS Completions Survey
IPEDS Completions Survey: Degrees/Awards Conferred (NCES Population of Institutions)
Year: All values
Academic Discipline, Detailed (standardized): Computer Science
Level of Degree or Other Award: Bachelor's Degrees

Total degree completions by year

Data Source: IPEDS Completions Survey
IPEDS Completions Survey: Degrees/Awards Conferred (NCES Population of Institutions)
Year: All values
Level of Degree or Other Award: Bachelor's Degrees

FIGURE 5.2

Caption:
Percentage of reported CIS bachelor's degrees conferred to women at for-profit (dotted gray line), not-for-profit (dotted black line), and all (solid black line) institutions.

IPEDS Data:

The number of women completing CIS bachelor's degrees at not-for-profit institutions (public plus private) and for-profit institutions was divided by the total number of CIS bachelor's degrees completed for the same institutional control to yield the plotted data.

CIS bachelor's degree completions by year for women

Data Source: IPEDS Completions Survey
IPEDS Completions Survey: Degrees/ Awards Conferred (NCES Population of Institutions)
Year: All values
Academic Discipline, Detailed (standardized): Computer Science
Level of Degree or Other Award: Bachelor's Degrees
Gender: All
Institutional Control: All

FIGURE 5.3

Caption:
Share of all reported CIS bachelor's degrees conferred, by race/ethnicity for all institutions (top panel) and not-for-profit institutions (bottom panel). The curve labeled "URM" is the combined share of the following underrepresented minority groups: black, non-Hispanic; Hispanic or Latino; and American Indian or Alaska Native. "Other/unknown race/ethnicity" includes students of two or more races and students for whom race/ethnicity is unknown. "Temporary resident" corresponds to foreign students, and is exclusive of the other categories, as defined by NCES. Categories displayed add to 100 percent at any point in time.

IPEDS Data:

The number of students identified by race/ethnicity completing CIS bachelor's degrees at all institutions (left panel), and not-for-profit institutions (public plus private, right-hand panel) was divided by the total number of CIS bachelor's degrees completed each year to yield the plotted data.

CS bachelor's degree completions by year

Data Source: IPEDS Completions Survey by Race
IPEDS Completions Survey by Race: Degrees/Awards Conferred by Race (NCES Population of Institutions)
Year: All values
Academic Discipline, Detailed (standardized): Computer Science
Level of Degree or Other Award: Bachelor's Degrees
Race & Ethnicity (Historical): All
Institutional Control (survey-specific): All

FIGURE 5.4

Caption:
Share of reported CIS bachelor's degrees conferred to underrepresented minority groups at all (top panel) and not-for-profit (bottom panel) institutions.

IPEDS Data:

The data plotted were obtained as were those in Figure 5.3; each underrepresented minority group is plotted separately.

FIGURE 5.5

Caption:
Number of CIS bachelor's degrees reported (solid lines, left vertical axis) from 1990 to 2015 to Hispanic or Latino, non-Hispanic black, American Indian or Alaska Native, and non-Hispanic white students, by "institutional control," including for-profit status of institution. The total number of CIS bachelor's degrees produced over time for all races/ethnicities is plotted as a reference (dashed line, right vertical axis).

IPEDS Data:

CS bachelor's degree completions by year

Data Source: IPEDS Completions Survey by Race
IPEDS Completions Survey: Degrees/Awards Conferred (NCES Population of Institutions)
Year: All values
Academic Discipline, Detailed (standardized): Computer Science
Level of Degree or Other Award: Bachelor's Degrees
Race & Ethnicity (Historical): All
Institutional Control: All

FIGURE 5.6

Caption:
Number of CIS bachelor's degrees reported (1990-2015) to female (left panel) and underrepresented minority female (right panel) students, by for-profit status of institution. The total number of degrees produced over time for all races/ethnicities is plotted as a reference (dashed line, right vertical axis).

IPEDS Data:

CS bachelor's degree completions by year

Data Source: IPEDS Completions Survey
IPEDS Completions Survey: Degrees/Awards Conferred (NCES Population of Institutions)
Year: All values
Academic Discipline, Detailed (standardized): Computer Science
Level of Degree or Other Award: Bachelor's Degrees
Gender: All
Institutional Control: All

FIGURE 5.8

Caption:
Reported share of bachelor's degrees in core CS, CE, and IS at not-for-profit institutions conferred to women between 2009 and 2015.

IPEDS Data:

Bachelor's degree completions by year

Core CS bachelor's degree completions by year

Data Source: IPEDS Completions Survey
IPEDS Completions Survey: Degrees/Awards Conferred (NCES Population of Institutions)
Year: 2009-2015
Academic Discipline, 6-Digit CIP: 11.0101, "Computer and Information Sciences, General"; 11.0701, "Computer Science"
Level of Degree or Other Award: Bachelor's Degrees
Gender: All
Institutional Control(survey-specific): Public Institutions, Private Institutions: Nonprofit

IS bachelor's degree completions by year

Data Source: IPEDS Completions Survey
IPEDS Completions Survey: Degrees/Awards Conferred (NCES Population of Institutions)
Year: 2009-2015

Academic Discipline, 6-Digit CIP: 11.0401, "Information Science/ Studies"
Level of Degree or Other Award: Bachelor's Degrees
Gender: All
Institutional Control(survey-specific): Public Institutions, Private Institutions: Nonprofit

CE bachelor's degree completions by year

Data Source: IPEDS Completions Survey
IPEDS Completions Survey: Degrees/Awards Conferred (NCES Population of Institutions)
Year: 2009-2015
Academic Discipline, 4-Digit CIP: 14.09, "Computer Engineering"
Level of Degree or Other Award: Bachelor's Degrees
Gender: All
Institutional Control (survey-specific): Public Institutions, Private Institutions: Nonprofit

The number of degrees for women was divided by the total number of degrees in each year to obtain the plotted data.

FIGURES 5.9–5.11

Caption (FIGURE 5.9):
Share of bachelor's degrees in core CS, CE, and IS at not-for-profit institutions reported for black, non-Hispanic students between 2009 and 2015.

Caption (FIGURE 5.10):
Share of bachelor's degrees in core CS, CE, and IS at not-for-profit institutions reported for American Indian or Alaska Native (non-Hispanic) students between 2009 and 2015.

Caption (FIGURE 5.11):
Share of bachelor's degrees in core CS, CE, and IS at not-for-profit institutions reported for Hispanic or Latino students between 2009 and 2015.

IPEDS Data for Figures 5.9-5.11:

Core CS bachelor's degree completions by year

Data Source: IPEDS Completions Survey by Race

IPEDS Completions Survey: Degrees/Awards Conferred (NCES Population of Institutions)
Year: 2009-2015
Academic Discipline, 6-Digit CIP: 11.0101, "Computer and Information Sciences, General"; 11.0701, "Computer Science"
Level of Degree or Other Award: Bachelor's Degrees
Race & Ethnicity (Historical): All
Institutional Control (survey-specific): Public Institutions, Private Institutions: Nonprofit

<u>IS bachelor's degree completions by year</u>

Data Source: IPEDS Completions Survey by Race
IPEDS Completions Survey: Degrees/Awards Conferred (NCES Population of Institutions)
Year: 2009-2015
Academic Discipline, 6-Digit CIP: 11.0401, "Information Science/Studies"
Level of Degree or Other Award: Bachelor's Degrees
Race & Ethnicity (Historical): All
Institutional Control (survey-specific): Public Institutions, Private Institutions: Nonprofit

<u>CE bachelor's degree completions by year</u>

Data Source: IPEDS Completions Survey by Race
IPEDS Completions Survey: Degrees/Awards Conferred (NCES Population of Institutions)
Year: 2009-2015
Academic Discipline, 4-Digit CIP: 14.09, "Computer Engineering"
Level of Degree or Other Award: Bachelor's Degrees
Race & Ethnicity (Historical): All
Institutional Control (survey-specific): Public Institutions, Private Institutions: Nonprofit

FIGURE 5.12

Caption:
Share of female (left panel) and male (right panel) undergraduates at U.S. not-for-profit institutions participating in CS bachelor's degree programs at the beginning and end of the undergraduate career. The dotted lines indicate the fraction of female (left panel) and male (right panel) freshmen intending to major in CS from

1970 to 2015, according to the HERI CIRP survey. The solid line indicates the fraction of female (left panel) and male (right panel) bachelor's degree recipients from 1966 to 2015 whose degree was in CIS, according to the IPEDS NCES completions data for all not-for-profit institutions.

IPEDS Data:

The number of students of each gender completing CS bachelor's degrees at not-for-profit institutions was divided by the total number of students of the same gender completing bachelor's degrees in any field at not-for-profit institutions in a given year to yield the plotted data.

<u>CS bachelor's degree completions by year</u>

Data Source: IPEDS Completions Survey
IPEDS Completions Survey: Degrees/Awards Conferred (NCES Population of Institutions)
Year: All values
Academic Discipline, Detailed (standardized): Computer Science
Level of Degree or Other Award: Bachelor's Degrees
Gender: All
Institutional Control (survey-specific): Public Institutions, Private Institutions: Nonprofit

<u>Bachelor's degree completions by year</u>

Data Source: IPEDS Completions Survey
IPEDS Completions Survey: Degrees/Awards Conferred (NCES Population of Institutions)
Year: All values
Level of Degree or Other Award: Bachelor's Degrees
Gender: All
Institutional Control (survey-specific): Public Institutions, Private Institutions: Nonprofit

FIGURE 5.13

Caption:
Percentage of students in underrepresented groups at U.S. not-for-profit institutions participating in CS bachelor's degree programs at the beginning and end of the undergraduate career. The dotted lines indicate the fraction of freshmen of the corresponding group intending to major in CS from 1970 to 2015, according to

the HERI CIRP survey. The solid line indicates the fraction completing a bachelor's degree in CIS in the year indicated, according to IPEDS completions data.

IPEDS Data:

The number of students in each underrepresented minority group completing CIS bachelor's degrees at not-for-profit institutions was divided by the total number of students in the same underrepresented minority group completing bachelor's degrees in any field at not-for-profit institutions in a given year to yield the plotted data series.

<u>CIS bachelor's degree completions by year (underrepresented minority)</u>

Data Source: IPEDS Completions Survey data by Race
IPEDS Completions Survey by Race: Degrees/Awards Conferred by Race (NCES Population of Institutions)
Year: All values
Academic Discipline, Detailed (standardized): Computer Science
Level of Degree or Other Award: Bachelor's Degrees
Race & Ethnicity (Historical): All

<u>Bachelor's degree completions by year (underrepresented minority)</u>

Data Source: IPEDS Completions Survey by Race
IPEDS Completions Survey by Race: Degrees/Awards Conferred by Race (NCES Population of Institutions)
Year: All values
Level of Degree or Other Award: Bachelor's Degrees
Race & Ethnicity (Historical): All

FIGURE 5.18

Caption:
Share of all U.S. CIS associate's degrees conferred by race/ethnicity. The curve labeled "URM" is the combined share of the following underrepresented minority groups: black, non-Hispanic; Hispanic or Latino; and American Indian or Alaska Native. "Other or unknown race or ethnicity" includes students of two or more races and students for whom race/ethnicity is unknown. "Temporary resident" corresponds to foreign students, and is exclusive of the other categories, as defined by NCES. The sum of all curves is 100 percent in any given year.

IPEDS Data:

Total numbers of CIS associate's degrees for each race/ethnic group were divided by the total number of CIS associate's degrees in a given year to yield the corresponding share of all CS associate's degrees.

<u>CIS associate's degree completions by year (race)</u>

Data Source: IPEDS Completions Survey by Race
IPEDS Completions Survey by Race: Degrees/Awards Conferred by Race (NCES Population of Institutions)
Year: All values
Academic Discipline, Detailed (standardized): Computer Science
Level of Degree or Other Award: Associate's Degrees
Race & Ethnicity (Historical): All

FIGURE 5.19

Caption:
Share of all U.S. CIS associate's degrees conferred to women and to underrepresented minority groups.
IPEDS Data:

Total numbers of CS associate's degrees for women were divided by the total number of associate's degrees in a given year to yield the corresponding share of all CS associate's degrees.

<u>CIS associate's degree completions by year (gender)</u>

Data Source: IPEDS Completions Survey
IPEDS Completions Survey: Degrees/Awards Conferred (NCES Population of Institutions)
Year: All values
Academic Discipline, Detailed (standardized): Computer Science
Level of Degree or Other Award: Associate's Degrees
Gender: Female

Appendix G

Biographical Information

STUDY COMMITTEE

JARED LEIGH COHON (NAE), *Co-Chair*, served as the eighth president of Carnegie Mellon University in Pittsburgh, Pennsylvania. He is currently a university professor in the Carnegie Mellon College of Engineering. He holds a B.S. in civil engineering from the University of Pennsylvania and M.S. and Ph.D. degrees in civil and environmental engineering from Massachusetts Institute of Technology, earned in 1972 and 1973, respectively. Prior to Carnegie Mellon, Cohon was the dean of the School of Forestry and Environmental Studies and professor of environmental systems analysis at Yale University from 1992 to 1997 and was a faculty member in the Department of Geography and Environmental Engineering and assistant and associate dean of engineering and vice provost for research at Johns Hopkins University from 1973 to 1992. Cohon stepped down from his position as president of Carnegie Mellon in 2013 and returned to the faculty as a university professor in the Departments of Civil and Environmental Engineering and Engineering and Public Policy and director of the Wilton E. Scott Institute for Energy Innovation. In 2014 Carnegie Mellon announced that the University Center would be renamed in honor of President Cohon and will be called the Cohon University Center.

SUSANNE E. HAMBRUSCH, *Co-Chair*, is professor of computer sciences at Purdue University. She received the Diplom Ingenieur in computer science from the Technical University of Vienna, Austria, in 1977, and a Ph.D. in computer science from Penn State in 1982. In 1982 she joined the faculty at Purdue University. She served as the department head of the Computer Science Department from 2002 to 2007. She has held visiting appointments at the Technical University of

Graz, Austria, and the International Computer Science Institute at the University of California, Berkeley. From 2010 to 2013 she served as the director of the Computing and Communication Foundations Division in the CISE Directorate at National Science Foundation (NSF), where she successfully led the development of several new crosscutting programs including Cyber-Enabled Sustainability Science and Engineering and Exploiting Parallelism and Scalability, and the U.S.-Israel Collaboration in Computer Science.

M. BRIAN BLAKE Ph.D. is executive vice president for academic affairs and provost at Drexel University. As the highest ranking academic officer, he oversees all academic programs across the 15 schools and colleges and over 26,000 students. Blake came to Drexel from the University of Miami, where he set research and teaching priorities and led faculty enhancement efforts as vice provost for academic affairs, and oversaw 155 graduate programs serving more than 5,700 students as dean of the Graduate School. Previously, he was associate dean for research and graduate studies at the University of Notre Dame College of Engineering, and chaired the Georgetown University Department of Computer Science as it launched its first graduate program. Blake has directed computer science labs funded by more than $10 million in sponsored research awards; authored 170-plus publications and chaired six conferences; edited major journals including his current service as editor-in-chief of *IEEE Internet Computing*; and advised dozens of students at every level from post-doctoral fellowships through doctoral, master's, and undergraduate studies. Blake is a senior member of the Institute of Electrical and Electronic Engineers (IEEE) and an Association for Computing Machinery (ACM) distinguished scientist. Blake's industry experience includes 6 years as a software engineer and architect at Lockheed Martin, General Dynamics, and the MITRE Corporation before entering academia full time. Blake also holds appointments in the College of Engineering (as professor in the Department of Electrical and Computer Engineering) and in the College of Medicine (as professor of neuroengineering).

TRACY CAMP is department head and professor in the Department of Computer Science at the Colorado School of Mines. Her current research interests include the credibility of ad hoc network simulation studies and the use of wireless sensor networks in geosystems. Dr. Camp is an ACM fellow, an ACM distinguished lecturer, and an IEEE senior member. She has enjoyed being a Fulbright scholar in New Zealand (in 2006) and a distinguished visitor at the University of Bonn, Germany (in 2010). In 2007 Dr. Camp received the Board of Trustees Outstanding Faculty Award at the Colorado School of Mines; this award was given only five times between 1998 and 2007. Dr. Camp is currently chairing a Computing Research Association (CRA) committee addressing the booming enrollments in undergraduate computer science courses, and is currently co-chair of the Computing Research Association's Committee on the Status of Women in Computing

Research (CRA-W). She received her Ph.D. in computer science from the College of William & Mary.

DAVID E. CULLER (NAE) received his B.A. from the University of California, Berkeley, in 1980, and an M.S. and a Ph.D. from MIT in 1985 and 1989, respectively. He joined the EECS faculty in 1989 and is the founding director of Intel Research, UC Berkeley, and was associate chair of the EECS Department from 2010 to 2012 and chair from 2012 to 2014. He won the Okawa Prize in 2013. He is a member of the NAE, an ACM fellow, and an IEEE fellow. He has been named one of *Scientific American*'s Top 50 researchers and the creator of one of MIT's *Technology Review*'s 10 Technologies That Will Change the World. He was awarded the NSF Presidential Young Investigator and the Presidential Faculty Fellowship. His research addresses networks of small, embedded wireless devices; planetary-scale Internet services; parallel computer architecture; parallel programming languages; and high-performance communication. This includes TinyOS, Berkeley Motes, PlanetLab, Networks of Workstations (NOW), Internet services, Active Messages, Split-C, and the Threaded Abstract Machine (TAM).

SUSAN B. DAVIDSON is a computer scientist known for her work in databases and bioinformatics. She is currently Weiss Professor of Computer and Information Science at the University of Pennsylvania. Her dissertation work on distributed databases included results on statistical and mathematical techniques for data resolution as well as mechanisms to avoid database conflicts. Davidson has also done research in bioinformatics, where her work (with collaborators) on data integration was commercialized by GeneticXChange. She is also currently serving on the board of the Computing Research Association. She received her Ph.D. in computer science from Princeton University.

BRIAN K. FITZGERALD serves as the CEO of the Business-Higher Education Forum (BHEF), developing long-term strategy for the membership organization. Under Dr. Fitzgerald's leadership, BHEF's National Higher Education and Workforce Initiative (HEWI) has emerged as the organization's strategic enterprise. Through BHEF member collaboration HEWI includes regional projects focused on business–higher education partnerships in selected states, as well as national networks that disseminate insights and scale effective practices. HEWI deploys a model of strategic business engagement in higher education to address members' high-skill, high-priority workforce needs. The *Wall Street Journal* featured BHEF and its work in a front-page article, and the NSF recognized HEWI's success with a 5-year, $4.5 million grant to increase persistence and diversity in undergraduate STEM education. Dr. Fitzgerald earned his master's and doctoral degrees from the Harvard Graduate School of Education, where he also served on the alumni council for 4 years and as its chair. He currently serves on the Dean's Leadership Council. He received his bachelor's degree from the Massachusetts College of Liberal Arts, which named him distinguished alumnus and awarded him an honorary doctorate in public service.

ANN Q. GATES is professor and chair of the Computer Science Department at the University of Texas, El Paso. Her areas of research are in software engineering and cyberinfrastructure, with an emphasis on workflows, ontologies, and formal software specification. Gates directs the NSF-funded Cyber-ShARE Center, which focuses on developing and sharing resources through cyberinfrastructure to advance research and education in science. She was a founding member of the NSF Advisory Committee for Cyber-infrastructure. Gates served on the IEEE-Computer Society (IEEE-CS) Board of Governors from 2004 to 2009. In addition she chairs the IEEE-CS Educational Activity Board's Committee of Diversity and External Activities and has established a model for specialized student chapters focused on leadership, entrepreneurship, and professional development. She is a member of the Computer Science Accreditation Board (2011-2013). Gates leads the Computing Alliance for Hispanic-Serving Institutions and is a founding member of the National Center for Women in Information Technology. In 2010 Gates received the Anita Borg Institute Social Impact Award and the 2009 Richard A. Tapia Achievement Award for Scientific Scholarship, Civic Science, and Diversifying Computing, and was named to *Hispanic Business* magazine's 100 Influential Hispanics in 2006 for her work on the Affinity Research Group model.

CHARLES ISBELL has been a leader in education efforts both at Georgia Tech's College of Computing, where he is senior associate dean for academic affairs, and nationally, where he co-chairs the Computing Research Association's Subcommittee on Education. At Georgia Tech Dr. Isbell was one of the co-leaders of the Threads reform of the undergraduate computing curriculum. Threads was a successful, comprehensive restructuring of the computing curriculum that provided a cohesive, coordinated set of contexts—or threads—for teaching and learning computing skills, with a goal of making computing more inclusive, relevant, and exciting for a much broader student audience. Dr. Isbell has won numerous teaching awards. Dr. Isbell received his Ph.D. from MIT's AI Lab (now CSAIL). His research focuses on artificial intelligence and machine learning.

CLAS A. JACOBSON is chief scientist, controls, for United Technologies Corporation (UTC). In this role he works with the UTC business units to provide advice on controls technology in both products as well as development processes to enhance product quality, functionality, and engineering effectiveness. Prior to his role as chief scientist he has worked at United Technologies Research Center (UTRC) in management and scientific positions since 1995. He was director of the Carrier Program Office. He also was director of the Systems Department at UTRC, responsible for 140 staff working in the systems engineering areas emphasizing mathematical modeling and analysis. Dr. Jacobson received his Ph.D.

in electrical engineering in 1986 from Rensselaer Polytechnic Institute. He was an associate professor at Northeastern University in Boston from 1986 to 1995 and conducted research in control systems.

MICHAEL S. McPHERSON is president emeritus of the Spencer Foundation, a private foundation that grants funds to support research that will contribute to the understanding of education and the improvement of its practice. Prior to joining the foundation in 2003 he served as president of Macalester College in St. Paul, Minnesota, for 7 years. A nationally known economist whose expertise focuses on the interplay between education and economics, McPherson spent the 22 years prior to his Macalester presidency as professor of economics, chairman of the Economics Department, and dean of faculty at Williams College in Williamstown, Massachusetts. He holds a B.A. in mathematics, an M.A. in economics, and a Ph.D. in economics, all from the University of Chicago. He has served as a trustee of the College Board, the American Council on Education, and Wesleyan University. He was a fellow of the Institute for Advanced Study and a senior fellow at the Brookings Institution.

ERIC ROBERTS received his Ph.D. in applied mathematics from Harvard University in 1980 and went on to teach at Wellesley College from 1980 to 1985, where he chaired the Computer Science Department. From 1985 to 1990, he was a member of the research staff at Digital Equipment Corporation's Systems Research Center in Palo Alto, California, where his research focused on programming tools for multiprocessor architectures. In 1990 Roberts joined the Stanford faculty, where he is now a professor of computer science and a Bass University fellow in undergraduate education. From 1990 to 2002 Professor Roberts was associate chair and director of Undergraduate Studies for Computer Science. In that capacity he was the principal architect of Stanford's introductory programming sequence. He has written six computer science textbooks that are used at many colleges and universities throughout the world. His current research focuses on computer science education, particularly for underserved communities. From 1998 to 2005 Roberts directed the Bermuda Project, which developed the computer science curriculum for Bermuda's public secondary schools.

VALERIE TAYLOR is the director of the Mathematics and Computer Science Division at Argonne National Laboratory. Prior to joining Argonne, she held multiple leadership roles as a faculty at Texas A&M University. Most recently, she served as the senior associate dean of academic affairs in the College of Engineering, a Regents Professor, and the Royce E. Wisenbaker Professor in the Department of Computer Science and Engineering. Prior to that, she served as head of Computer Science and Engineering from 2003 until 2011. Before joining Texas A&M, Dr. Taylor was a faculty member in Northwestern University's Electrical Engineering and Computer Science Department for 11 years. Dr. Taylor has authored or coauthored over 100 papers on high performance computing. She has developed and used models to analyze and improve the performance of many parallel, scientific applications, including finite element applications, molecular dynamics, cosmology, earthquake simulations, ocean modeling, and magnetic fusion. Dr. Taylor is a fellow of the IEEE and of the ACM. She has received numerous awards for distinguished research and leadership, including the 2001 IEEE Harriet B. Rigas Award for significant contributions in engineering education; the 2002 Outstanding Young Engineering Alumni Award from the University of California at Berkeley; the 2002 A. Nico Habermann Award for increasing diversity in computing; and the 2005 Tapia Achievement Award for Scientific Scholarship, Civic Science, and Diversifying Computing. She is also the Executive Director of the Center for Minorities and People with Disabilities in Information Technology (CMD-IT). Dr. Taylor earned her bachelor's degree in electrical and computer engineering and master's degree in computer engineering from Purdue University in 1985 and 1986, respectively. She received her Ph.D. in electrical engineering and computer science from the University of California at Berkeley in 1991.

JODI TIMS is a professor of computer science at Baldwin Wallace University in Berea, Ohio, a liberal arts-based college with approximately 3000 undergraduate students and a student-faculty ratio of approximately 13:1. She is currently serving as chair of the Department of Mathematics and Computer Science. She began teaching at the university level in 1982 at the University of Pittsburgh at Johnstown (UPJ) as an instructor of mathematics. Upon completing her M.S. in computer science at the University of Pittsburgh in 1988, Dr. Tims became an assistant professor of computer science at UPJ. In 1992 she received the Edward A. Vizzini Natural Science Division Award for Excellence in Teaching and in 1994 was tenured and promoted to associate professor. After earning her Ph.D. in computer science from the University of Pittsburgh, with an emphasis on programming languages and compilation for distributed memory parallel systems, she accepted a position as associate professor and coordinator of computer science at Saint Francis University, Loretto, Pennsylvania. She accepted her current position at Baldwin Wallace in 2002 and was promoted to full professor in 2004. In addition to her teaching and administrative responsibilities, she serves on numerous college-wide committees, is a member of the Regional Information Technology Engagement board of Northeast Ohio, and is a member of the ACM-W executive council, leading the Regional Celebrations of Women in Computing project. She served as program chair for the Ohio Celebration of Women in Computing (OCWiC) held in 2009 and 2011 and general chair of that event for OCWiC 2013, and is now serving as chair of the newly formed OCWiC executive board.

SARAH E. TURNER is the chair of the Department of Economics at the University of Virginia. Dr. Turner specializes in research on the economics of education in the United States. She has written extensively on the economics of higher education, including the behavioral effects of financial aid policies and the entry of new providers. She has served as a visiting scholar at the Russell Sage Foundation, and received the Milken Institute Award for Distinguished Economic Research, "Trade in University Training." Some of her recent research has addressed the labor market for IT workers and college enrollment during the Great Recession. She received her Ph.D. in economics from the University of Michigan.

STAFF

EMILY GRUMBLING is a program officer with the Computer Science and Telecommunications Board of the National Academies of Sciences, Engineering, and Medicine. She previously served as an AAAS Science and Technology Policy fellow in the Directorate for Computer and Information Science and Engineering at the National Science Foundation (2012-2014), and as an American Chemical Society (ACS) congressional fellow in the U.S. House of Representatives (2011-2012). Dr. Grumbling currently serves as a volunteer associate of the ACS Committee on Environmental Improvement. She received her Ph.D. in physical chemistry from the University of Arizona in 2010 and her B.A. with a double major in chemistry and film/electronic media arts from Bard College in 2004.

JON EISENBERG is director of the Computer Science and Telecommunications Board of the National Academies. He has also been study director for a diverse body of work, including a series of studies exploring Internet and broadband policy and networking and communications technologies. From 1995 to 1997 he was an AAAS Science, Engineering, and Diplomacy fellow at the U.S. Agency for International Development, where he worked on technology transfer and information and telecommunications policy issues. Dr. Eisenberg received his Ph.D. in physics from the University of Washington in 1996 and B.S. in physics with honors from the University of Massachusetts at Amherst in 1988.

KATIRIA ORTIZ is a research associate with the Computer Science and Telecommunications Board of the National Academies of Sciences, Engineering, and Medicine. She previously served as an intern for the Federal Bureau of Investigation and as an undergraduate research assistant at the Cybersecurity Quantification Laboratory at the University of Maryland, College Park. She received her M.A. in international science and technology policy from The George Washington University and her B.S. in cell biology and molecular genetics and B.A. in criminology and criminal justice from the University of Maryland, College Park.

TOM RUDIN is the Director of the Board on Higher Education and Workforce at the National Academies of Sciences, Engineering, and Medicine—a position he assumed in mid-August 2014. Prior to joining the Academies, Mr. Rudin served as senior vice president for career readiness and senior vice president for advocacy, government relations and development at the College Board from 2006-2014. He was also vice president for government relations from 2004-2006 and executive director of grants planning and management from 1996-2004 at the College Board. Before joining the College Board, Mr. Rudin was a policy analyst at the National Institutes of Health in Bethesda, Maryland.

In 1991, Mr. Rudin taught courses in U.S. public policy, human rights, and organizational management as a visiting instructor at the Middle East Technical University in Ankara, Turkey. In the early 1980s, he directed the work of the Governor's Task Force on Science and Technology for North Carolina Governor James B. Hunt, Jr., where he was involved in several new state initiatives, such as the North Carolina Biotechnology Center and the North Carolina School of Science and Mathematics. He received a B.A. degree from Purdue University, and he holds master's degrees in public administration and in social work from the University of North Carolina at Chapel Hill.

Appendix H

Acronyms and Abbreviations

ACM	Association for Computing Machinery
ACM-W	Association for Computing Machinery's Council on Women in Computing
ACS	American Community Survey
AP	Advanced Placement
BHEW	Board on Higher Education and Workforce
BLS	Bureau of Labor Statistics
BRAID	Building, Recruiting, and Inclusion for Diversity
CAHSI	Computing Alliance for Hispanic-Serving Institutions
CCF	Computing and Communication Foundations
CE	computer engineering
CIP	Classification of Instructional Program
CIRP	Cooperative Institutional Research Program
CIS	computer and information science and support services
CISSP	Certified Information Systems Security Professional
CMD-IT	Center for Minorities and People with Disabilities in IT
CPS	Current Population Survey
CRA	Computing Research Association
CRA-W	Computing Research Association's Committee on the Status of Women in Computing Research
CS	computer science
CSP	Computer Science Principles
CSTA	Computer Science Teachers Association

CSTB	Computer Science and Telecommunications Board
CUSTEMS	Consortium for Undergraduate STEM Success
CyberSEES	Cyber-Enabled Sustainability Science and Engineering
EE	electrical engineering
HBCUs	historically black colleges and universities
HERI	Higher Education Research Institute
HEWI	Higher Education and Workforce Initiative
IPEDS	Integrated Postsecondary Education Data System
IS	information science
LAC	liberal arts college
MOOC	massive open online course
MSI	minority-serving institution
NACE	National Association of Colleges and Employers
NAE	National Academy of Engineering
NAM	National Academy of Medicine
NAS	National Academy of Sciences
NCES	National Center for Education Statistics
NCWIT	National Center for Women & Information Technology
NDC	non-doctoral college; refers to institutions with CS units that do not have Ph.D. programs
NSF	National Science Foundation
PEDS	Performance Evaluation of Distributed Systems
PLTL	peer-led team learning
RCM	Responsibility Center Management
S&E	science and engineering
SaTC	Secure and Trustworthy Cyberspace
SOC	Standard Occupational Classification
STEM	science, technology, engineering, and mathematics
TA	teaching assistant
URM	underrepresented minority
UTA	undergraduate teaching assistant

WebCASPAR	Web-based Computer-Assisted Science Policy Analysis and Research System
XPS	Exploiting Parallelism and Scalability